# *Black Detroit and the Rise of the UAW*

# Other books by August Meier and Elliott Rudwick

**BY AUGUST MEIER**

*Negro Thought in America, 1880–1915* (1963)

*Negro Protest Thought in the Twentieth Century* (1965)

(Co-edited with Francis L. Broderick)

**BY ELLIOTT RUDWICK**

*W.E.B. Du Bois: A Study in Minority Group Leadership* (1960)

*Race Riot at East St. Louis, July 2, 1917* (1964)

**BY AUGUST MEIER AND ELLIOTT RUDWICK**

*From Plantation to Ghetto* (1966; third edition, 1976)

*CORE: A Study in the Civil Rights Movement, 1942–1968* (1973)

*Along the Color Line* (1976)

*Black Nationalism in America* (1970)

(Co-edited with John H. Bracey, Jr.)

*Black Protest Thought in the Twentieth Century* (1971)

(Co-edited with Francis L. Broderick)

# Black Detroit
# and
# the Rise of the UAW

AUGUST MEIER AND ELLIOTT RUDWICK

OXFORD UNIVERSITY PRESS
Oxford   New York   Toronto   Melbourne

Oxford University Press
Oxford   London   Glasgow
New York   Toronto   Melbourne   Wellington
Nairobi   Dar es Salaam   Cape Town
Kuala Lumpur   Singapore   Jakarta   Hong Kong   Tokyo
Delhi   Bombay   Calcutta   Madras   Karachi

First published by Oxford University Press, New York, 1979
First issued as an Oxford University Press paperback, 1981

Library of Congress Cataloging in Publication Data
Meier, August, 1923–
    Black Detroit and the rise of the UAW.
    Bibliography: p.
    Includes index.
    1. Afro-Americans—Employment—Michigan—Detroit.
2. Trade-unions—Michigan—Detroit—Afro-American
participation.   3. Detroit—Economic conditions.
4. International Union, United Automobile, Aerospace,
and Agricultural Implement Workers of America.
I. Rudwick, Elliott M., joint author.   II. Title.
F574.D49N46   331.88′12′920977434   78-26809
ISBN 0-19-502561-X
ISBN 0-19-502895-3 pbk.


Printed in the United States of America

For
Paul and Louise
and
Es and Sey

# Preface

This book developed out of the research for our long-range study of the history of the NAACP. Although the Association's principal emphasis was on securing enforcement of the black man's constitutional rights under the 14th and 15th Amendments, during the Depression and the New Deal it developed a significant concern for the economic problems of the black masses. Partly because the organization was subjected over the years to criticism for having ignored this issue and partly because the New Deal era witnessed a major reorientation in the relationship between blacks and the American labor movement, we became interested in examining in depth the development of the NAACP's concern with economic problems in general and with discrimination by organized labor in particular. Others have given a fair amount of attention to the modifications of the NAACP's program during the 1930s.[1] Nevertheless, as yet there has been no comprehensive analysis of the fairly voluminous materials in the NAACP's Archives dealing with

1. Raymond Wolters, *Negroes and the Great Depression: The Problem of Economic Recovery* (Westport, Conn., 1970), Part III; B. Joyce Ross, *J. E. Spingarn and the Rise of the NAACP 1911–1939* (New York, 1972), chapters 6–8.

the Association's fight since its founding in 1909 against discrimination in the American Federation of Labor craft unions and the new relationships that developed with the Congress of Industrial Organizations in the mass production industries during the 1930's.

Our volume began as a brief case study to illuminate the Association's changing relationship with organized labor during the New Deal period, and originally we had intended to do simply a detailed investigation of the NAACP's role in the 1941 strike of the United Auto Workers against the Ford Motor Company. According to NAACP traditions, this event, when Secretary Walter White personally flew to Detroit to help the UAW persuade black strikebreakers to leave the factory, was considered pivotal in leading to a historic alliance between the NAACP and the new industrial unions. White, in fact, devoted a chapter in his autobiography to the UAW strike at Ford, which he entitled, "Turn to the Left at Detroit."[2]

Our research, however, revealed that the incident was far less important than NAACP traditions suggest. The Association had actually endorsed industrial unions considerably earlier, and White's involvement in Detroit neither had visible impact upon the outcome of the strike nor much effect on the UAW's actions toward black workers. Yet as our research proceeded, there unfolded a far more important story—an incredibly rich and complex account of the transformation in the relations between a black community and organized labor in a major industrial city. Given the fact that the UAW is generally conceded to have been among the most racially equalitarian of the CIO unions, Detroit is a particularly useful locale for such a study. In tracing the shift of black sentiment from pro-industry to pro-union, we first focused on a detailed analysis of the Detroit black community, its leadership and its cleavages, trying to pinpoint exactly how and when the change occurred. This in turn led us to study the particular nature of the Negroes' role in the auto industry, especially their important position at Ford, and the relationship of black community leaders to that company. At

2. Walter White, *A Man Called White* (New York, 1948), chapter 27.

the same time we found that UAW policies toward blacks were far from static and so we sought to understand the course of their development and their circular interaction with the changes and attitudes among black workers and spokesmen.

With the Ford strike seeming to mark a decisive shift in the thinking of Detroit blacks and in their relationship with the UAW, we tried next to explore how much, over the following couple of years, the union actually lived up to its promise of fighting industrial discrimination and remedying the grievances of the black workers. Here again a highly complex picture emerged, and we found that the UAW was characterized by marked cleavages, ambivalences, and inconsistencies. In the end only partial solution of the blacks' grievances was attained, and indeed it became clear that the important job advances that blacks made in the auto industry during World War II were the product of a complicated interaction involving not only blacks and union leaders but the crucial intervention of the federal bureaucracies as well. Simultaneously we traced the friendship that was growing between black Detroit and the UAW stemming from efforts to remedy the city's racial problems outside the job market. We found that the union's stance at critical junctures on issues ranging from job bias, through housing discrimination, to police brutality during the 1943 riot created an image for the UAW that culminated in a close civic and political alliance with black Detroit.

What began as a relatively simple narrative thus grew into a far more complicated project with ramifications for several broader topics: for labor history, for the black urban experience, and for the way in which federal bureaucracies can create social change. Accordingly, in this volume we have sought to place our findings in the larger context of developments at the national level in the labor movement, in the wartime manpower policies of Roosevelt's Administration, and in the stance of major race advancement organizations. Yet throughout we have consciously focused our attention on Detroit as a local history case study that illuminates much about the larger American society as well.

We are indebted to many individuals for assistance in the course of our research and writing. First we want to acknowledge a special kind of debt to Lloyd H. Bailer for the important contribution made by his unpublished 1943 dissertation at the University of Michigan, "Negro Labor in the Automobile Industry." This manuscript, along with his earlier unpublished chapter in Paul H. Norgren, "Negro Labor and Its Problems," a research memorandum prepared for the Carnegie-Myrdal Study of the Negro in America, 1940, formed in themselves an invaluable primary resource on blacks in the automobile industry.

We appreciate the generosity of a number of people who consented to interviews. Many were gracious enough to talk with us on several occasions. A complete list of the persons interviewed is given in our Bibliographical Essay; but among those who played prominent roles in the events we describe, we wish to express particular appreciation for the extraordinary richness and the usefulness of the information shared with us by Christopher Columbus Alston, Gloster Current, J. Lawrence Duncan, Frank Evans, Louis E. Martin, Oscar Noble, and Shelton Tappes.

It is a singular pleasure to acknowledge the assistance of scholars in the field of labor history who critically read the entire manuscript: Walter Galenson and David Brody; and two younger men, Ray Boryczka and Peter Friedlander, who shared with us their specialized knowledge of the details of UAW history. Raymond Wolters, a specialist on blacks in the New Deal period, also carefully read the manuscript. We found the comments of these five scholars enormously provocative and insightful, even where we did not fully agree with them or were unable to adopt their specific suggestions.

We are appreciative of the help provided by a number of libraries: The Walter P. Reuther Library of Labor and Urban Affairs at Wayne State University; the Manuscript Division of the Library of Congress; the Burton Historical Collection of Detroit Public Library; the Ford Archives at Dearborn, Michigan; the Schomburg Collection of the New York Public Library; the National Archives and the Regional Federal Records Center in Chicago; the Chicago Historical Society; the libraries of Catholic University and Kent State University and the Bentley Library of the University of Michigan. In particular we want to thank for their unfailing helpfulness Sally Osgood, Linda Burroughs, and Helen Peoples of the Kent State University Library; Joseph B. Howerton of the National Archives; Dione Miles of the Reuther Library; and Joe Sullivan of the Library of Congress.

We are also indebted to the Michigan State Library and to the State Historical Society of Wisconsin for the use, on interlibrary loan, of microfilm copies of newspapers and their collections. And we want to thank the following officials of the AFL-CIO for arranging access to portions of the AFL Archives at their headquarters in Washington: Tom Kahn, William Pollard, and Lane Kirkland.

Gloster Current not only sent us a copy of the minutes of the Detroit NAACP Branch during the early 1940's, but kindly supplied detailed annotations and explanations of them for our benefit. David Moulton generously gave us a copy of his paper on "George Addes and the UAW: An Investigative Look at the Forgotten Man of Autoworker History." Nelson Lichtenstein supplied us with copies of relevant materials from the War Labor Board Archives and the Richard Deverall Papers that we had not personally seen. Leon Litwack called our attention to the blues song about blacks and the Ford Company quoted in Chapter I. Dominick D'Ambrosio, president of the Allied Industrial Workers of America AFL-CIO, formerly the United Automobile Workers-AFL, very generously let us have a copy of the relevant sections of the minutes of the Homer Martin faction's 1939 UAW Convention.

We wish to thank Marge Evans, Marvella Pierce, and Norman Farrell for their conscientious and expeditious typing of the final manuscript.

Most of the research for this book was done under grants from the John Simon Guggenheim Memorial Foundation and the National Endowment for the Humanities, and some of the research and most of the writing was accomplished during our year at the

Center for Advanced Study in the Behavioral Sciences at Stanford, California. Throughout, we have had the support of the Kent State University Office of Research and Sponsored Programs and we particularly wish to express our appreciation to its head, Dean Eugene P. Wenninger, for his unstinting encouragement through the years. Needless to say, none of these agencies is in any way responsible for the interpretations or point of view expressed in this book.

And finally we express our appreciation to Sheldon Meyer, vice-president of Oxford University Press, for his warm support as our plans evolved and this volume took shape.

*Kent, Ohio*                                                           A.M.
*January* 1979                                                        E.R.

# Contents

*Black Detroit and the Rise of the UAW*

# I

# *Black Detroit and the Automobile Industry,*
# *1917–1937*

As contemporaries recognized, the New Deal era marked a watershed in relations between blacks and organized labor. Since the
turn of the century the mainstream of the labor movement—the
AFL unions and the Railway Brotherhoods—had with few excep-
tions excluded blacks or restricted them to jim crow units. Although there were occasional labor organizations like the United
Mine Workers that exhibited egalitarian racial practices and considerable interracial solidarity, both rank-and-file black workers
and Negro leaders and advancement organizations were typically
suspicious of trade unionism. Indeed they often demonstrated
marked loyalty to employers who hired significant numbers of
Negroes, regarding them as benefactors, even though they rarely
placed blacks on an equal footing with whites. Then during the late
1930's and early 1940's, the rise of the CIO industrial unions, with
their egalitarian policy of organizing workers regardless of race,
markedly changed the relationship between the black community
and organized labor. Supported in spirit by a growing band of
Negro radicals and liberal New Dealers, black workers in the mass
industries became members and officers in the new unions, while

the NAACP and the Urban League endorsed collective bargaining and also the CIO. As the prominent black journalist George S. Schuyler observed in 1937: "Here at long last were color prejudice and discrimination being effectively attacked through labor association. . . . Of course the labor movement is far from perfection on the race question. But not in fifty years has America witnessed such interracial solidarity."[1]

Yet as Schuyler suggested, the transition was not a smooth one. Given both the patterns of union discrimination, and the petit bourgeois outlook of most black leaders, Negro skepticism about labor organizations was not easily effaced. In fact there was vigorous debate over the sincerity of the CIO, and serious cleavages developed within the leading race advancement organizations about the appropriateness of supporting the new industrial unions and their organizing drives. Moreover, the CIO unions themselves, though embracing a racially egalitarian ideology, were inconsistent when it came to battling discrimination against black workers and, constrained by the prejudices of the white rank and file, often failed to live up to their official principles. Much progress was indeed made by black workers in the mass industries during the CIO's early years, but ironically this came about largely through the intervention of wartime federal manpower agencies, most of which—except for the Fair Employment Practices Committee (FEPC)—were concerned with effective mobilization of scarce labor resources, and not with racial justice.

Detroit presents in microcosm an unusually vivid and illuminating case study of the evolving relationships between blacks and the new industrial unions during the Great Depression and World War II. It possessed in the Ford Motor Company one of the largest and least discriminatory employers of black labor in America, and in the United Automobile Workers (UAW) one of the most racially egalitarian leaderships among the CIO unions. The city also had a substantial and articulate black middle class, and its Urban League and NAACP affiliates were among the most influential local black advancement organizations in the country.

Moreover as a major center of war industry, Detroit received considerable attention from the FEPC and the war manpower agencies. Accordingly, developments in the Motor City during the UAW's formative years epitomized the complex interplay among all these elements—management practices, black and white workers' attitudes, the racial policies of the new industrial unions, the actions of wartime federal bureaucracies, and the gradual shift in opinion among black elites—that ultimately led to a close working alliance between blacks and the CIO.

## 1

> I'm goin' to Detroit, get myself a good job,
> Tried to stay around here with the starvation mob.
>
> I'm goin' to get me a job, up there in Mr. Ford's place,
> Stop these eatless days from starin' me in the face.
> *Blues song of the 1920's* [2]

In 1934, with the depression crisis beginning to make economic problems a salient concern for the NAACP, and with a collective bargaining agreement in the auto industry apparently imminent, the Association's Secretary, Walter White, noted that the black worker had found unusual opportunities in the Detroit factories, where "he has encountered many forms of discrimination . . . yet . . . has attained skilled and better-paid jobs to a greater degree" than anywhere else.[3] Essentially this unusual position of black labor was due to the Ford Motor Company, which in its Detroit area plants employed about one-half of the blacks in the entire auto industry,[4] and which enjoyed the virtually unanimous admiration of the city's black community.

It was during the labor shortage of World War I and the resulting migration from the South to northern industrial centers like Detroit that Negroes had first gained a foothold in auto manufacturing. Several firms turned to this untapped reservoir, and Packard, which in May 1917 had 1100 blacks on its payroll, was actually the first significant employer of Negroes in the industry. A high company official explained, "We have found in the Packard plant that the Negro . . . is a good worker, considerably better than the average European immigrant."[5] Dodge was another leading manufacturer which began to hire a substantial number of blacks at that time, working closely with the Detroit Urban League in the recruitment and supervision of its black labor force.[6] But by 1919 Ford, rapidly expanding its recruitment among the migrants,* was emerging as the city's leading employer of blacks, the number in the company's work force rising from a mere 50 in January 1916 to 2,500 four years later (out of a total of 57,000). As Ford enlarged its operations in the 1920's and developed the gigantic River Rouge plant, its workers included more and more blacks—5,000 by 1923 (out of a total Detroit area work force of 110,000) and 10,000 by 1926. No other company came near that figure; at that time Dodge Brothers, the second highest, employed only 850. In the latter part of the decade, between ten and twelve thousand blacks worked among the 100,000 employees at the Rouge, while even during the wide fluctuations in employment that accompanied the depression of the 1930's blacks held their own in this vast plant where they were concentrated. (Thus in 1937 they numbered 9,825, nearly 12 percent of all workers there.)[7]

Ford was not entirely unique; elsewhere at certain small companies blacks formed an even higher proportion of the work force (about 25 percent at Bohn Aluminum and 30 percent at Midland Steel, a maker of steel body frames for Chrysler and Ford), and at Briggs, a body manufacturing company that was the fourth largest employer of blacks in the industry, the approximately 1300 Negroes constituted nearly 10 percent of the work force. Yet in terms of sheer numbers Ford was without peer. Between 1937 and 1941 the company, averaging 11,000 Negroes, employed perhaps two-

---

* Ford had actually employed some blacks even earlier. Thus the *Crisis* in 1914 reported that "The Ford Automobile Shop began to discriminate against colored people in some lines of work, but this has been stopped and three colored electricians are now employed in the plant at a wage of nine dollars a day. One of them works side by side with Mr. Ford." (*Crisis* 8 [July 1914], 141.)

thirds of the blacks working in the city's automobile factories—
over five times as many as any other car manufacturer in Detroit.
Chrysler, which had absorbed the Dodge Company, ranked second with about two thousand. At General Motors, which in absolute numbers rivaled, and state-wide even exceeded, Chrysler in
its total employment of blacks, the 2800 Negro employees in 1941
formed a minuscule 3 percent of its Michigan work force, and most
of these were actually employed in the outlying cities of Pontiac,
Saginaw, and Flint, rather than in Detroit itself.[8]

These differences among the manufacturers indicated a highly
uneven distribution of blacks within the industry which, when
analyzed, reveal discriminatory practices even among companies
most inclined to hire them. Although the proportion of blacks in
the industry nationwide stabilized at around 4 percent, few were
to be found outside of Michigan.[9] Even Ford virtually refused to
utilize blacks except as menials at its plants outside of metropolitan
Detroit,[10] and in the Motor City, as noted earlier, confined them
almost entirely to the massive River Rouge complex. Similarly at
Chrysler, blacks worked almost entirely in the Dodge Division,
especially at Dodge Main in Hamtramck, while at General Motors
the small concentrations of blacks in production were to be found
at Buick in Flint, at Chevrolet Grey Iron foundry in Saginaw, at
Pontiac, and at Chevrolet Forge Spring and Bumper in Detroit.[11]

It is true that as a group, black workers in the automobile factories earned more money than those employed in other industries,
and, indeed, the wage differential between blacks and whites in
the auto plants was relatively small. Yet this situation arose from
the concentration of blacks in the fairly well-paid but disagreeable
and dangerous foundry jobs that whites tried to avoid.[12] An observer in the late 1920's noted, for example, that at Chrysler and
Chevrolet blacks were employed as paint-sprayers; at another firm
"certain dangerous emery steel grinding jobs were given only to
Negroes." At Briggs, which had a particularly high proportion of
heavy, unpleasant jobs, blacks were assigned principally to the
dirtiest and most disagreeable ones, notably in the Mack Avenue

plant's paint-spray and wet-sanding department, where they constituted three-fourths of the workers.[13] Pre-eminently, however,
blacks labored at the hot and heavy work in the foundries. At both
Packard and Chrysler's Dodge Main plant on the eve of World
War II, most of the blacks were foundry workers, while many of
the others were sprayers and sanders. In General Motors, the
Buick, Pontiac, and Chevrolet plants also concentrated blacks in
the foundries; while GM's Fisher Body was lily-white except for
the custodians. Even at Ford, black employees disproportionately
held down the disagreeable jobs. Nearly half of them were in the
foundry, and in two of the toughest jobs—the shakeout and the
reels—they formed over 50 percent of the labor force. Substantial
numbers were also found in the onerous heat treatment and paint-
spraying departments and in the rolling mill.[14]

Yet Henry Ford was unique in the wide range of opportunities
he offered Negro blue-collar workers. Since the early 1920's they
were in all manufacturing departments and in some supervisory
positions. Only a handful of other firms utilized blacks on assembly
lines or in production jobs outside the foundries: Midland Steel,
where some blacks did the particularly heavy jobs on the assembly
lines,[15] and Briggs, where a few were to be found in assembly
work, in semi-skilled jobs, and as straw bosses.[16] At Ford, however, not only were many blacks on assembly lines, but others
were employed in laboratories and drafting rooms; as bricklayers,
crane operators, and mechanics; and in such highly skilled trades
as electricians and tool-and-die makers (of which there were about
seventy-five each in 1939). Only at Ford were blacks admitted to
apprentice schools; black and white Ford employees operated machinery and worked together on assembly lines in mixed pairs; and
occasional individuals held such positions as time-keeper in department 87, head in the dynometer room, and personal dietician of
Henry Ford. James C. Price, who in 1924 had become the company's first black salaried employee, had responsibility for purchas-
ing abrasives and industrial diamonds; he was regarded as one of
the industry's outstanding men in this specialty. Finally the com-

pany had more black foremen than the rest of the industry combined, and in contrast to the rare cases where such individuals were to be found elsewhere, these men often supervised mixed crews. For example, one black foreman headed an all-Polish group of thirty-five men during the 1920's and 1930's. The most outstanding was Eugene J. Collins, put in charge of a unit in the die-casting department in 1924, and fifteen years later named the first Negro general foreman, supervising a mixed force of 6 foremen and 400 workers.[17] Accordingly, even though blacks were disproportionately concentrated in the foundry, were underrepresented in the white-collar, supervisory, and skilled jobs, and found promotions difficult to get, nevertheless, as the labor economist Herbert Northrup observed, before World War II blacks at Ford "came closer to job equality . . . than they did at any large enterprise . . . recorded in the literature."[18]

Complementing this unusual employment pattern, Ford had developed during the 1920's an equally unusual personnel policy that strengthened the loyalty of his black workers and tied the company closely to the Negro community. Unlike other employers who recruited their black workers through the Detroit Employers Association, the local Urban League, and (during the 1930's) the Michigan Unemployment Commission,[19] Ford established his own contacts among key black leaders, especially among the clergy. And in a further marked departure from the practice of other companies, Ford employed a couple of black personnel workers. Placed under Harry Bennett in the Service Department that later became so notorious for its regimentation and intimidation of Ford workers, these two men were given considerable authority over hiring and internal factory discipline.

The roots of this system went back to 1919 when top executive Charles Sorensen invited Rev. Robert L. Bradby, pastor of Detroit's oldest and largest black religious institution, the Second Baptist Church, to a luncheon meeting with Henry Ford and other key executives. Concerned about the inefficiency of some workers, and the frequency of bloody fights within the plant between black and white workers, and among the blacks themselves, Ford personally outlined to Bradby his desire to recruit carefully selected Negro workmen. The preacher agreed both to recommend "very high type fellows" for jobs at Ford and to help the company resolve its internal personnel problems, promising "to acquaint the colored workers with the responsibilities of employment . . . telling them that they should be 'steady workers' so as to prove the worthiness of colored industrial workers." For the next half-dozen years he roamed the Highland Park and Rouge plants at will, resolving interracial conflicts and tensions, and instilling among the Negro workers behavior patterns conforming to the model desired by Henry Ford.[20]

By 1923, as Ford stepped up recruitment of blacks, Sorensen obtained the help of Father Everard W. Daniel, the newly named pastor of black Detroit's third oldest congregation, St. Matthew's Protestant Episcopal Church. About the same time Donald J. Marshall, a policeman who worshipped at St. Matthew's, was hired by the Ford Service Department, and within a few months he had achieved supervisory and hiring authority over black personnel, reporting directly to Sorensen and Bennett. Subsequently in 1935 he was joined on the personnel staff by the University of Michigan black football star Willis Ward. Assigned responsibility for settling disputes involving black workers, the two men could dismiss whites who mistreated blacks, and were able to establish a reputation for helping blacks get fair treatment when problems arose. Henry Ford, an Episcopalian, became especially interested in Father Daniel, donating funds for the parish house and from 1929 onward, attending services at St. Matthew's at least once a year. Daniel in fact became more influential than Bradby, and overt rivalry actually developed between the Baptist preacher on one side and the Episcopalian clergyman and his parishioner, Marshall, on the other. Although Marshall and Ward took over internal personnel matters entirely, both preachers remained prominently involved in the recruitment of workers. In addition Marshall, who supervised the hiring of Negroes, honored recommendations from other ministers, and from businessmen, politicians, lawyers, and physicians as well.[21] It became virtually impossible to obtain a job at Ford's without the recommendation of a minister or other influential member of the black community.[22]

The Ford Motor Company's racial practices developed in a national context of intense Negrophobia and labor unrest that followed the First World War. The UAW would later charge that the roots of Ford's employment policy lay in a calculated attempt to discourage unionism by exploiting racial hostility in his work force. Certainly in 1941 Ford had no scruples about using blacks as strikebreakers to preserve the open shop. Yet the empirical evidence extant does not demonstrate that his actions originated with that purpose in mind. Ford was clearly influenced by a fear of collective bargaining and labor radicalism on the one hand, and on the other by the popular racist theories of the day—best represented by Madison Grant and Lothrop Stoddard. But his own position was a highly individualistic one, seemingly rooted in a very personal brand of paternalistic philanthropy. Ford's paternalism toward his workers has been widely recognized, and in part his hiring of black workers reflected the same philanthropic concern that led him to include in his labor force cripples, ex-convicts, and the blind.[23] In Ford's view Negroes, like these other disadvantaged groups, were social outcasts who needed and would appreciate his help.

Actually, Ford displayed considerable ambivalence in his racial attitudes. No supporter of the virulent anti-black sentiments so salient at the time, he believed that Negroes were entitled to constitutional rights and economic opportunity. Yet sharing the widespread idea that race was an inescapable distinction governing human history, he also believed in innate black-white differences and in the desirability of racial segregation. Thus his newspaper, the Dearborn *Independent*, excoriated "flabby-minded sophists" who "preach how terrible it is to recognize this determining fact—this natural fact of race." Subscribing to the notion that "Anglo-Saxon–Celtic peoples," were alone capable of sustaining democratic institutions, he was suspicious of the new immigration from Southern and Eastern Europe, and regarded Jews as a particularly alien and pernicious "race." His views about blacks, on the other hand, were more ambiguous: "Race lines are fixed. Nature punishes transgression with destruction. These are facts. And [yet] Race Rights are also facts." Indeed the Negro "is a human being" and an American citizen.[24] Blacks should have decent neighborhoods, but residential segregation and social separation must prevail. "Racial differentiation . . . makes the assimilation involved in social 'equality' as impossible for the Africans as for the Asiatic elements of the population of this republic." Indeed, blacks as much as whites were opposed to "mixing the races": "The Negro does not want to crowd in among the whites; what he does want is the air, sunlight, space and sanitation which are to be had in white residential sections. He should have all these things in his own quarter."[25]*

For Ford, the "superior" race was duty-bound to give philanthropic service to subordinate races. "Dominance is an obligation. The whole solution of the race question as of every other, lies in the stronger serving the weaker, the abler serving the less developed. . . . The superior racial stream was equipped for the service of the other, not for exploitation and suppression." To the whites Ford declared, "The race that calls itself superior can only prove its superiority by superior ability to help the others, and can only retain its superiority by actually fulfilling its racial destiny as helper of the others." Thus securing justice for Negroes was the

---

* Dearborn, where Ford himself lived, barred blacks, and its citizens used to brag that "the sun never set on a Negro in Dearborn." (See Lester Velie, "Housing: Detroit's Time Bomb," *Colliers*, Nov. 23, 1946, pp. 75–76). Characteristically, in the aftermath of the celebrated Ossian Sweet case, in which blacks were charged with the murder of a white man during a mob attack on a black family who had just moved into a white neighborhood, Ford was interested not in furthering black rights to live where they chose, but in improving the housing in black areas. (See Nahum D. Brascher to Claude A. Barnett, Sept. 13, 1925, and Brascher, undated letter [1925], to Barnett, in Associated Negro Press Archives. For recent account of the Sweet case, see David A. Levine, *Internal Combustion: The Races in Detroit, 1915–1926* [Westport, Conn., 1976], 158–65).

responsibility of well-intentioned whites, who realized that basically the race question was an economic problem amenable to intelligent solution: "When there are enough jobs to go around in this country, when every man shall have opportunity to go forth in the morning to perform the work he is best fitted to do, and to receive a wage which means a secure family life, there will be no race question." Ford concluded that whenever blacks had received a fair chance their labor made them an asset to the community: "The Negro needs a job, he needs a sense of industrially 'belonging,' and this it ought to be the desire of our industrial engineers to supply."[26]

Although organized labor was scarcely a serious threat during the early years of the auto industry,[27] Ford was nevertheless exceedingly apprehensive about unions. One of the reasons that the Ford Company had introduced the five dollar-a-day wage in 1914 had been to stave off what was perceived as the dangerous organizing efforts of the Industrial Workers of the World (IWW),[28] and while the post–World War I unrest and radicalism created no immediate problem for his company, he worried about the wave of industrial strikes and the aggressive, revolutionary radicalism of both the IWW and the newborn Communist party. Bolshevism, which the *Dearborn Independent* identified with both Jews and IWW-syndicalism, was seen as making serious inroads inside the AFL and endangering the capitalist system. Ford was clearly concerned: "Strikes grow more numerous and threatening every year, not because labor grows more threatening or less American, but because each succeeding strike has a deeper alien fringe around it and is a signal for the activity of Bolshevik and anarchist groups that are not related to the strike at all." Yet the AFL's moderate leaders did not have Ford's trust: "Industrial justice" would come not through unions or strikes which unscrupulous labor officials always fomented, but through the enlightened self-interest of intelligent employers, whose "friendliness and common sense" would win their employees' loyalty."[29]

While no explicit connections have been uncovered between

Henry Ford's concern about radicalism and industrial strife on the one hand and his philanthropy toward blacks on the other, he did see in black America an eager reservoir of workers committed to the American system. The auto magnate pictured blacks as a quiet, compliant people, loyal to employers and the nation. "The Negro," he said, "is a human being, capable of integrity, loyalty and domestic peace and prosperity." The Dearborn *Independent* was startled by the "strange unrests and convulsions" among post-war blacks, detecting in the heightened militance "a spirit wholly unlike the Negro at his normal self." Charging that Jews were using the black man "as a tool," Ford's paper complained that the Negro "is being tampered with by influences cleverer than anything he could devise." Indeed, the radical socialist propaganda of A. Philip Randolph's *Messenger* magazine was attributed to a Jewish conspiracy "to Bolshevize the Negro" masses with "the spirit of syndicalist rebellion." Ford, assuming that militant agitation was alien to blacks and only stirred up by malevolent Jews, declared, "Let the man of color distrust those false friends who mingle with him to get his money, who seek an alliance with him on the alleged common ground of 'oppression,' and who expose their whole hand when they urge him to that kind of Bolshevism found only in Moscow and on the East Side of New York." Later the Dearborn *Independent* would triumphantly assert that the good sense of black Americans would prevent them from being ensnared, because "the destiny of the white race and the black race in this continent is to live together in the same economic system, and together they will resist all attempts to destroy the white man's civilization which is the black man's best security."[30]

Yet the very uniqueness among American industrialists of Ford's policy toward blacks suggests that beyond self-interest and the imperatives of successful industrial management lay a genuine philanthropic impulse. Actually Ford had taken a personal interest in certain individual Negroes, placing them in responsible positions even before instituting the large-scale recruitment of blacks late in the war. Over the years he encouraged the research of George

Washington Carver and displayed a warm interest in Tuskegee Institute,[31] while Mrs. Henry Ford entertained black women's groups and church clubs at their estate.[32] Ford's major black philanthropy was the rehabilitation of the poverty-stricken black community at Inkster, Michigan, during the 1930's, providing employment and underwriting a public school, medical facilities, and a food commissary for its residents.[33] Of course Dearborn, which was adjacent to Inkster, rigorously excluded blacks, but this did not trouble the auto magnate who believed in social segregation while insisting on offering blacks economic opportunity at the River Rouge plant in the face of the kind of white worker resentment[34] that helped impede their employment elsewhere. Yet, whatever the complex web of motivations that led Ford to display a considerable, albeit paternalistic, concern for blacks, clearly he viewed the race as a docile and grateful people constituting a valuable component in his labor force.

Ford's employment practices had a profound effect upon Detroit's blacks. It is true that the company's Negro employees suffered from the same grievances as the white employees (the lack of seniority, the speed-up, the spying on workers' outside activities, and the personnel office's arbitrary policies).* It was also true, as we have seen, that discrimination existed even at the Rouge—not to mention the virtual exclusion of blacks from Ford's other plants. Yet what really mattered in the thinking of Detroit's Negroes was the unparalleled range of jobs open to them in Ford's largest factory. As a reporter for the Associated Negro Press recalled on the occasion of Henry Ford's death in 1947, "Back in those days [1920's and early 1930's] Negro Ford workers almost established class distinctions here. . . . the men began to feel themselves a little superior to workers in other plants. They wore their badges

---

* By the 1930's Marshall had become a cynical individual given to exercising arbitrary power over black workers at the Rouge. He was even accused of selling jobs there. (David L. Lewis, "History of Negro Employment in Detroit Area Plants of Ford Motor Company 1914–1941" [paper submitted in partial fulfillment of the requirements of History 334, University of Michigan, 1954], Reuther Library, p. 25).

as a mark of distinction on the lapels of their coats on Sunday.
Then, 'I work for Henry Ford,' was a boastful expression." In
short, in the minds of most blacks at Rouge, the company "represented a haven in an otherwise unfriendly industrial world."[35]

## 2

In addition to thus securing the faithfulness of his black labor
force, Ford had fashioned a close alliance with the leadership of
the black community. His actions both directly and indirectly accentuated their bourgeois outlook and their skepticism of trade
unions. For some leaders, particularly ministers, his policies provided very concrete material rewards. As Ralph Bunche observed:
"The fact is that the possibility of getting a job at the Ford Motor
Company has been the incentive in many instances for Negroes'
joining church. Naturally a minister encounters least difficulty in
running his church when the bulk of his congregation is gainfully
employed. It follows that the minister will cater to the positions
taken by the company which employs large numbers of his flock."
For some preachers, who accepted donations of coal from the company or insisted that individuals whom they recommended for jobs
make cash contributions to the church, the financial benefits were
even more direct.[36]

Not only did the firm's methods of labor recruitment establish
close and immediate ties to the preachers and other key elements
in the city's black elite, but the fact that Ford employed ten to
twelve thousand blacks, who together with their families comprised about one-fourth of the local black community, obviously by
and of itself carried considerable weight. A careful student of the
situation in the late 1930's observed: "There is hardly a Negro
church, fraternal body, or other organization in which Ford workers are not represented. Scarcely a Negro professional or business
man is completely independent of income derived from Ford employees. When those seeking Ford jobs are added to this group, it
is readily seen that the Ford entourage was able to exercise a dom-

inating influence in the community." The income of Ford's black workers was the cornerstone for the prosperity of the black community's business and professional people. The latter, acutely aware of how much black Detroit's economic well-being and their own livelihood depended on the company, believed that what was best for Ford was best for the race.[37] Black Detroiters genuinely appreciated Ford's philanthropy. For some Ford was the greatest businessman in the world, but beyond that he was "the Negro's friend" who "could do no wrong." His racial ambivalences were apparently unknown to them, and a man like Father Daniel would almost surely have been amazed to learn that upon one of the auto magnate's annual visits to St. Matthew's he could write in his notebook, "We are going out in society . . . to a nigger church."[38]

Ford and Sorensen, in establishing close ties with Bradby and Daniel, had chosen well among Detroit's black leaders. They were the city's two most important Negro ministers, each representing a different segment in the community. Bradby, raised in poverty in Canada, headed Detroit's largest black church, an institution that drew its strength from the stream of poor southern migrants that began with World War I. Daniel, a native of the Virgin Islands, whose diplomas from New York University and Union Theological Seminary made him the city's best-educated black clergyman, presided over a smaller congregation, but one that included many influential members of the black upper class.[39] Their influence in other black community institutions was substantial. Both men—particularly Bradby—were on good terms with the local Urban League head, were active in the affairs of the local NAACP branch, and maintained warm contacts with the Booker T. Washington Trade Association, composed of the very businessmen whose prosperity so depended on the Ford workers. This organization, affiliated with the National Negro Business League, had been founded in 1930 by the pastor of Detroit's second oldest and second largest black church, Rev. William H. Peck of Bethel A.M.E. Church. A graduate of Wilberforce University, and personally close to the other two leading ministers, Peck was also involved to some extent in the Ford Company's worker recruitment. The members of the Trade Association, which he headed for a decade, not only espoused a black capitalist ideology, but during the 1930's were frankly open shop in their sympathies. Another close associate of Peck was one of Bethel's stewards, Wilbur C. Woodson, a graduate of Ohio State University and secretary since 1931 of the black St. Antoine YMCA, who was similarly known for his conservative views and his reservations about labor unions.[40]

Epitomizing the views of Detroit's Negro elite on labor questions in general and unions in particular was the stand taken by the city's two principal race advancement organizations—the Urban League affiliate and the NAACP branch. Both were pro-management, greatly admired the Ford Motor Company and the Ford family, endorsed the open shop, and, even after their national organizations openly favored the interracial industrial unionism of the CIO, remained hostile to the UAW.

The Detroit Urban League, founded in 1916, was financed by the Community Chest and the aggressively anti-union Employers Association of Detroit. Since 1918 it had been headed by J. C. Dancy, Jr., a conservative spokesman allied with Detroit business interests, whose father, the Recorder of Deeds for the District of Columbia at the turn of the century, had been Booker T. Washington's close friend. The Detroit League quickly became so important a supplier of blacks for white employers that during the 1920's half of the city's black wage earners reportedly obtained work through the organization.[41] These included many jobs at companies like Chrysler, Dodge, Studebaker, Briggs, and Cadillac.[42] Especially significant was the relationship between the League affiliate and Dodge, the second largest employer of blacks in the auto industry, both before and after its merger with Chrysler in 1928. The presence of blacks at Dodge stemmed directly from an appeal personally made by Dancy to John Dodge back during the First World War, and was sustained through the years by the interest of C. T. Winegar, the company's personnel director who ultimately joined the Detroit Urban League's board of trustees in 1937.[43]

The Ford Motor Company of course recruited its black workers through other channels, but Dancy and his associates held the Ford enterprise in very high esteem,[44] and from the beginning the relations between Rev. Robert Bradby and the Urban League, both on the national and local levels, were intimate and close.[45] For their part, officials at the League's New York headquarters regarded Dancy as having considerable influence with the corporation's executives.[46] Whatever the specifics of Dancy's relations with Ford and his company—and unfortunately the materials that have survived in the Detroit Urban League Archives are virtually silent on the subject*—when it came to trade unions Dancy was among the most consistently anti-labor executives who headed the League's local affiliates. In 1921, for example, during a metal workers strike at the Timken Axle Company the Detroit League's industrial secretary, whose salary was paid by the Employers Association, supplied black strikebreakers and escorted them through the picket line.[47] Dancy was convinced that if trade unions had had any influence with the Ford Motor Company, blacks would not have achieved their favorable position at the Rouge plant. In his opinion, since Detroit was an "open shop" town where unions had little chance of success, blacks should not waste time trying to join them, especially because labor leaders had made it abundantly clear that only whites were wanted. As he said in 1934, "Of one thing I am convinced, and that is that the local [AFL] president is not warm toward Negroes and I am against him and have told him so to his face."[48]

By the 1930's Dancy's views differed sharply from those of the Urban League's national office. Originally the organization had been ambivalent toward the labor movement—urging blacks to

---

* It is difficult at this point to distinguish between image and fact in Dancy's relationship with Henry Ford. NUL executive secretary Eugene Kinckle Jones was actually under the impression that Dancy had played a key role in inaugurating Ford's employment policy regarding blacks. (Jones to Dancy, March 3, 1931, DUL Box 1.) However, Dancy, in his autobiography, while emphasizing the kindly treatment he received from Ford, specifically mentions only two meetings with him (Dancy, *Sand Against the Wind* [Detroit, 1966], 138–40) and takes no credit for having anything to do with Ford's personnel practices.

join unions, seeking unsuccessfully to convince the AFL to eliminate racist practices, yet simultaneously endorsing the use of black strikebreakers as a last resort. In 1934, however, following the National Industrial Recovery Act's recognition of collective bargaining, and convinced that unions were to become an influential force in American society, the League's New York headquarters began establishing Workers Councils across the country to stimulate "labor consciousness" among black industrial workers.[49] But in Detroit Dancy and his board refused to cooperate. Lester Granger, director of the national office's Labor Bureau, decided to come anyway without the local affiliate's help. But upon arriving in 1935 Granger found that Wilbur Woodson, pressured by Donald Marshall, reneged on an earlier agreement to allow him to hold a meeting at the YMCA. Granger rescheduled the event for the black YWCA, but not surprisingly the Detroit Workers Council which he organized disintegrated within a few months.[50] And even after the National Urban League began working with the fledgling CIO, Dancy's position remained unchanged.

The Detroit NAACP, although it generally left labor matters to the Urban League, was dominated by black business and religious elites who articulated a typical middle-class outlook and were ever-conscious of their community's dependence on Ford. Organized in 1912,[51] the branch maintained exceedingly close ties with St. Matthew's and the Second Baptist Church. Among the largest NAACP branches in the country (with 1800 members in 1935)[52] the Detroit affiliate relied heavily on the preachers during membership drives—kickoff meetings for the annual campaigns were ordinarily held in these two churches, and their pastors, like many others, used the pulpit to help the NAACP leaders build their membership.[53] St. Matthew's rector, Robert Bagnall, was branch president in 1919–20, before joining the Association's national staff, while Rev. Robert Bradby led the branch in 1925–26. Then, for a dozen years beginning in the late 1920's the local organization was headed by executives of Detroit's leading black insurance enterprise, the Great Lakes Mutual Insurance Company.[54] The latter's guiding spirit, Louis T. Blount (a prominent leader and future president of the Booker T. Washington Trade Association), argued as NAACP president during the 1930's that the automobile work-ers union was doing little for blacks and that Henry Ford's record had been impressive "under the open shop plan."[55]

Blount's opinion was probably partly influenced by the fact that Henry Ford's son, Edsel, who also maintained friendly contacts with the local Urban League, had made substantial financial con-tributions to the Detroit NAACP and the Association's national headquarters for more than a decade. Although NAACP mem-bership and financing came overwhelmingly from the black com-munity, the Association's national office had deliberately enlisted prominent whites as members and donors. Thus in Detroit, Judge Ira W. Jayne had proven a devoted booster, recruiting among a broad spectrum of influential whites—from Henry Ford's early partner, Mayor James Couzens, to Mrs. Horace Dodge. In addi-tion, national board chairman Mary White Ovington had long known Mrs. Edsel Ford's family,[56] and Edsel Ford indeed became one of the Association's largest single contributors. Commencing with hundred dollar annual gifts around 1922, he stepped up dona-tions until by 1930–32 they amounted to $1000 a year. Although these abruptly ceased soon afterwards, they must have strength-ened the NAACP branch leaders' view of Ford and his company as benefactors of the race.[57] In short, like the Detroit Urban League, the local NAACP branch, in espousing vigorous pro-business and anti-union policies, by the mid-1930's was diverging sharply from the position of its national office.

Thus blacks' traditional skepticism about labor unions had been vastly reinforced by the opportunities offered by Detroit corpora-tions such as Dodge, Bohn Aluminum, Midland Steel, and Ford. In particular, Ford's system of recruiting and managing his labor force had won him support throughout all strata of Detroit's black community that was unique in American industry. As late as the middle of the Depression decade, the Motor City's black leaders and spokesmen—like the overwhelming majority of black

workers—remained fearful of organized labor; as a careful investigator observed, "the philosophy permeating the entire Negro
community . . . could be summed up in the phrase, 'Beware of
unions.' "[58] Substantial black support for the UAW would not
emerge before the early 1940's, and even though a small band of
veteran black radical organizers had existed since the advent of the
Depression, it was not before 1936 that the first significant voices
on behalf of the union appeared among the city's Negro elite.


## 3

As already suggested, on the national level, black leaders and race
advancement organizations were generally considerably ahead of
Negro opinion in Detroit in supporting the new industrial unions.
Enthusiasm for the CIO was to be found across a broad spectrum
of opinion—from the National Urban League, with its connections
with white business, on the right, to the new and aggressively pro-
labor National Negro Congress, with its communist connections on
the left. However, since neither of these two organizations possessed a substantial membership base among blacks, the NAACP
best revealed the fundamental shift in the views of black Americans toward trade unions.

From the NAACP's beginning it had permitted the Urban
League to assume nearly the entire responsibility for employment
problems, and quite deliberately concentrated on the battle for
constitutionally guaranteed rights.[59] Yet the Association had not
been entirely indifferent to union discrimination; on several occasions it had provided assistance to black railroad workers, and
periodically pressed the AFL to moderate its racist practices. After
the bitter East St. Louis race riot of 1917, in which labor animosity
toward blacks had played such an important role, the Association
worked closely with the Urban League in a futile effort to persuade
AFL leaders to help dismantle the discriminatory barriers erected
by the craft unions.[60] A decade later, with nothing accomplished,
NAACP Secretary Walter White reaped considerable publicity

from a confrontation with John P. Frey, secretary of the AFL Metal Trades Department, who publicly defended the Federation on the grounds that the race problem was rooted in the prejudices of the larger society. But the exchange failed to modify the craft unions' practices.[61]

With the coming of the Depression the NAACP experienced rising demands to reorient its activities and attack the economic problems of the black working class. These came from various sources: Socialists like A. Philip Randolph and Howard University economics professor Abram L. Harris, who for years had considered the NAACP approach too narrow; the newly invigorated Communist party, who denounced middle-class "misleaders" of the Negro people like Walter White; and most important, a group of younger black intellectuals such as Professor Ralph Bunche of Howard's Political Science Department and Dean Charles H. Houston of its Law School—individuals who were impatient with the gradualism of their elders and deeply influenced by the leftward trend widespread among American intellectuals during the Depression. Responding to these pressures, the NAACP Board in 1934 asked Harris to chair a committee to consider new directions for the Association, and the following year approved its recommendation that the organization emphasize programs seeking economic justice for the Negro and attempting "to get white workers and black to view their lot as embracing a common cause."[62] Although no concrete program was developed to implement the committee's call for blacks to join the ranks of organized labor, the Harris Report signaled the beginning of an important policy shift that would become very evident in the Association's subsequent relationships with the CIO and the UAW.

During the discussions over the Harris Committee's work, the NAACP, supporting a protest spearheaded by Brotherhood of Sleeping Car Porters president A. Philip Randolph, was engaged in a vigorous confrontation with racist AFL craft unions. Among white AFL leaders, support for the blacks' effort came from those who were agitating for industrial unionism and who in the autumn of 1935 formed the Committee for Industrial Organization (CIO). Hopeful over the new trend, the NAACP officially endorsed the CIO the following year; at the same time the Association also sought to press CIO leaders to implement their professed commitment to interracial working-class solidarity.

In the summer of 1934, at the very time when the AFL was first facing the demands of John L. Lewis and others for organizing unskilled workers in the mass production industries, the NAACP, backing Randolph's call for an investigation of racist practices in the craft unions, had taken the unprecedented step of picketing the Federation's national convention. The AFL responded by appointing a committee, which included Lewis's close associate, John Brophy, to look into Randolph's charges. The committee held hearings at which expert witnesses like the NAACP lawyer Charles H. Houston effectively documented AFL discrimination. Nevertheless the strongly worded majority report urging remedial action was pigeonholed by the same stormy 1935 AFL convention that also rejected a resolution calling on the Federation to organize industrial unions. Brophy, who only a few weeks later would be named by Lewis as director of the newly established CIO, angrily denounced the AFL's refusal to tackle the racial discrimination within its ranks.[63]

It is scarcely a coincidence that the racial issue achieved salience in the Federation at the very time the organization was splitting over the question of industrial unionism. For blacks were overwhelmingly found among the ranks of the lower-skilled workers in the mass-production industries which the AFL typically failed to organize. Nor is it surprising, in view of the United Mine Workers' almost unique tradition of interracial solidarity, that its president John L. Lewis and his CIO should have been so prominently identified in the minds of many blacks with their own struggle for economic justice. Yet curiously, although Lewis, Brophy, and other CIO leaders believed in the necessity of including blacks in the new industrial unions, neither this fact nor the discrimination faced by black workers were topics that loomed large in their deliberations.

Thus during the 1930's neither the problems of Negro workers nor the importance of fostering an interracial labor movement are mentioned anywhere in the minutes of the original Committee for Industrial Organization, or of the Executive Board set up in 1938 by the new federation, the Congress of Industrial Organizations. It is true that the CIO's constitution provided for organizing "the working men and women of America regardless of race, creed, color, or nationality," and annual conclaves routinely passed vague resolutions denouncing employers for undercutting unionization by arousing racial, religious, and ethnic antagonisms. Yet only occasionally did convention minutes contain a discussion of efforts to recruit blacks or of the need for black-white working class solidarity, while in the Congress's official newspaper there were only the sparsest references to organizing among blacks.[64]

A small number of black organizers were employed as the CIO went about building unions in industries like steel, but when pressed by race advancement leaders to do more about black recruitment or to end discriminatory practices within the new unions, CIO leaders usually counseled patience until the basic task of firmly establishing the industrial unions had been accomplished. Thus shortly after the establishment of the CIO, when Walter White urged John L. Lewis not to forget the plight of blacks as the AFL hypocritically did in burying the report of Brophy's committee, Brophy himself replied for his boss, "As we get further along with our problem, I shall be glad to give some attention to the matter of racial discrimination." Similarly nearly two years later the National Urban League's industrial secretary, T. Arnold Hill, while reiterating the League's "wholehearted support" for the CIO's organizing drives, charged leaders in the Steel Workers Organizing Committee and other CIO unions with being "short-sighted" for taking insufficient interest in reaching black workers.[65]* It was not until 1940, amidst the growing agitation of

---

* Just a few months earlier Philip Murray, head of the Steelworkers Organizing Committee, had described the discouraging results in reaching black workers, despite the employment of Negro organizers and the cooperation of the National Negro Congress, National Urban League, and NAACP. He pessimistically con-

black advancement groups for jobs in war industries, and with John L. Lewis seeking to attract these organizations into his anti-Roosevelt political coalition, that the CIO issued its first educational pamphlet on *The CIO and the Negro Worker*, or that the CIO president agreed to speak at conventions of Negro organizations.[66]

CIO leaders consistently placed the entire responsibility for racial discrimination on its two enemies—management and the AFL—and failed to come to grips with the racism endemic among rank-and-file whites. Instead Negro workers and civic leaders were blandly assured that the CIO had settled the racial issue in the house of labor. Lewis informed the NAACP's 1940 annual conference that in his federation there were "many Negroes . . . high up in the ranks of leaders," and that "the problems of the Negro people are the problems of all American wage earners." Like the Congress' black sympathizers, he pointed out "That *is* why the CIO organized all workers without racial discrimination . . . and seeks equal economic opportunity for Negro workers." The following year the CIO convention's resolution on "Unity of Negro and White Workers," maintaining that "reactionary employing interests" discriminated against blacks to weaken labor's potential power, proudly asserted that the CIO from its beginning consistently opposed racist practices: "One of the great contributions which the CIO has made to the strength of organized labor in the United States has been to break down the barriers which have existed in the past between Negro and white workers in labor organizations."[67]

Even though they failed to eliminate discrimination, the industrial unions did certainly inaugurate a major shift in the relationship between Negroes and the labor movement by recruiting black workers. Yet curiously, while this development loomed large in black perceptions of the CIO, the surviving records of the orga-

cluded: "It is our conviction . . . that the organization of the negro [sic] steel workers will follow, rather than precede, the organization of the white mill workers." (Statement by Philip Murray, November 8, 1936, CIO Archives, Box A7-33.)

nization during its formative period and the scholarly literature on the early CIO and its leaders are virtually silent on racial matters.* There were probably several reasons for this. Because the early CIO leaders accepted without question the importance of including black workers, no discussion of the issue was required. On the other hand, while some left-wing activists in the CIO were personally dedicated on ideological grounds to the cause of racial justice, individuals like Lewis, Philip Murray, and Sidney Hillman, fully aware of management's propensity to exploit racial cleavages among their employees, were committed to recruiting Negroes for very practical reasons. But the paucity of references to racial issues in the CIO's discussions suggests that the leaders attached low priority to fighting the racially discriminatory employment and promotion policies pervading industry since long before the rise of the CIO. While criticizing management for manipulating the racial prejudices of the white workers, they themselves felt constrained by the prevalence of such attitudes, and hesitated therefore to take up in any aggressive way the specific grievances of the black workers. All in all, the relationship between black workers and the new industrial unions was characterized by considerable ambiguity and inconsistency; the individual unions varied greatly in the extent to which they concerned themselves with the problems of the black workers, and Negroes found the result far from perfect. Thus although CIO leaders broke significantly with AFL practice on racial

* Unfortunately no definitive statement on the practices of CIO unions regarding blacks and racial discrimination can be made at this time. To our knowledge no detailed, scholarly investigations of the dynamics of race relations within the CIO have been published. Even the standard works on the subject of blacks and organized labor speak in general terms about the CIO and a few individual unions, but none of these books makes a systematic analysis in any depth. This is true both for the studies specifically devoted to black labor and for the histories of individual unions. In general, the picture emerging from the literature is that the United Packing House Workers of America has been the most equalitarian in its practices, while the United Steelworkers of America was among the CIO unions that dealt least successfully with racism in industry. Yet there remains a real need for detailed studies examining with precision the ways in which the various industrial unions handled the grievances and problems of their black members.

matters, their appeal to blacks was low-keyed and based primarily, not on abstract ideals of racial justice, but on the solid realities of organizing strong unions in the mass production industries. Nothing more vividly demonstrates this than the blacks' experience in the UAW.*

Nevertheless it was the CIO leaders' commitment to organizing blacks along with the masses of other semi-skilled and unskilled workers that aroused the enthusiasm and hope of a number of Afro-American leaders and spokesmen. The national NAACP, like the National Urban League, saw in the CIO enormous potential for social change and officially endorsed the nascent Committee for Industrial Organization at the Association's 1936 annual conference: "We urge support and active participation in the effort for organization of industrial unions in the American labor movement without regard to race or color."[68] This NAACP decision came at a crucial juncture in the history of both organized labor and the black protest movement. On the one hand, within a few months the rupture between the CIO and the AFL was complete. And on the other hand, the NAACP resolution was part of a groundswell of sentiment among many younger black intellectuals and spokesmen that had earlier in the year crystallized in the formation of the National Negro Congress (NNC).

Essentially the creation of John P. Davis, a black lawyer and an activist with intimate ties to the Communist party, the Congress was a broad coalition of fraternal, civic, and church organizations, and enjoyed the warm support of important non-Communist spokesmen. Ralph Bunche, for example, worked closely with Davis in creating the new organization, and A. Philip Randolph served as its national president. Financed in part by John L. Lewis

---

* Recent scholarship, stressing the pragmatic rather than the social reformist character of CIO leadership, has influenced our interpretation. See especially David Brody, "Labor and the Great Depression: The Interpretive Prospects," *Labor History* 13 (Spring 1972): 231–34; and Brody, "The Emergence of Mass-Production Unionism," in John Braeman *et al.*, eds., *Change and Continuity in Twentieth-Century America* (Columbus, Ohio, 1964), esp. 240–42. Also very helpful in clarifying our thinking were interviews with David Brody, Dec. 31, 1977, and Walter Galenson, Dec. 17, 1977.

and the CIO, the NNC from its inception made support of the new industrial unions central to its platform and program. Especially notable was the assistance it lent to the CIO's drive in the steel and tobacco industries in 1936–37. Not operating essentially as a membership organization but as an umbrella group that sought to include mainstream organizations, Davis and the Congress were accorded considerable respect by black moderates during the "Popular Front" period. But Walter White was skittish about cooperation with the NNC, both because it posed a threat to the preeminence of the NAACP in black protest activities and because of the prominence of Communists in its affairs. White was not alone in his views, and with the NAACP and others reluctant to participate in the NNC's work, the latter generally failed to obtain the depth of support it needed, and functioned both nationally and locally largely as a paper organization. Finally in 1940, when the communist influence became more evident than before, Randolph, Bunche, and others departed in disillusionment.[69]

In Detroit, of course, with the mainstream black leadership so conservative, the energetic Congress chapter was unable to create a broad base, and prior to the Second World War operated on the periphery of black community organizations. (Even during the war its leading spokesman would function primarily as the head of other ad hoc coalitions rather than through the NNC.) Accordingly among Motor City blacks the highly vocal pro-union local NNC was scarcely more helpful to the fledgling UAW than were the anti-labor Detroit affiliates of the Urban League or the NAACP. Instead it was to a tiny but respected minority of prominent professional and business men that the United Automobile Workers would have to look for support as Detroit's Negro community moved reluctantly and cautiously toward working with the UAW and the CIO.

## 4

NAACP Secretary Walter White was acutely aware of the dilemma facing Detroit's Negroes when the AFL, encouraged by the collective bargaining provision of the National Industrial Recovery Act of 1933, began organizing auto workers. Black interests "are indissolubly linked with those of the working classes," he asserted. Yet unions were usually hostile, and in the Motor City the open shop had provided blacks with unusual opportunities. "Our sympathy," White concluded, "would be with organized labor if only organized labor would permit this."[70]

Actually the recruitment of blacks had not been entirely ignored by labor organizations in the auto industry. Over the years the most sustained organizing efforts—though these never posed a serious threat to the manufacturers—had been carried out by the Auto Workers Union (AWU), which, after it passed from Socialist to Communist control in the late 1920's, espoused an explicit ideology of interracial unionism. It employed blacks as organizers, aggressively sought to enlist Negroes as members, yet found that blacks were even less interested than white workers. Although the AWU seemed to enjoy something of a temporary resurgence in 1933 during an unsuccessful strike at the Briggs Manufacturing Company, there is no indication that the rather large black work force there played a significant role, and the union itself was dissolved by the end of the following year.[71]

Meanwhile, given the strategic position that blacks occupied at Ford, William Collins, the organizer whom AFL president William Green had dispatched to Detroit in mid-1933,[72] found his overtures stymied both by black skepticism and by the Ford Company's countermeasures. It may have been only coincidence, but the organizer had scarcely arrived in town when Henry Ford asked Tuskegee Institute president, Robert R. Moton, to interrupt his summer vacation and come to Detroit. Ford personally conducted him on a well-publicized tour of the Rouge plant, while the industrialist's favorite black clergyman, Father Daniel, entertained Moton as his houseguest and arranged a banquet in the black educator's honor.[73] Over the following months Donald Marshall persistently warned blacks of the dangers of joining a union. Speaking at the black YMCA, for example, he recounted the benefits that

Henry Ford had bestowed, and declared that, if the AFL should ever organize the industry, black employment would be doomed. Although at other auto plants there were some blacks who believed that unionization could help them, other Detroit black leaders echoed Marshall's sentiment, and overall Collins found that he elicited a negative response.[74]

Meanwhile in New York, Walter White, at the time actively battling the national AFL leadership, was also deeply disturbed. By March 1934, when developments in the Federation's Detroit drive had reached the point where a collective bargaining agreement under the NIRA seemed imminent, White journeyed to Washington to seek assurances from Assistant Secretary of Labor Edward F. McGrady that blacks would be protected. Telling McGrady, a former AFL official, that under the open shop blacks had attained their "greatest industrial progress," White was solemnly assured that unionization would not bring discrimination with it. Actually, White had little cause for concern; not only did the weak settlement—secured through federal intervention—leave the AFL in Detroit virtually powerless, but in fact by the mid-1930's even the Federation's leadership clearly understood that unionization of the auto industry required an appeal to blacks too. Indeed, although few Negroes decided to join, when AFL federal locals in the various factories merged to form the United Automobile Workers of America in 1935, the union's constitution explicitly called for uniting all the workers "into one Organization, regardless of . . . race. . . ."[75]

The relationship between the union and the black auto workers did not, however, improve in the following months. Thus when the local at Flint's Buick plant sought to enroll blacks and even elected two to the executive board, the bulk of the Negro workers remained indifferent, and Flint's black civic leaders actually condemned the two new board members "for betraying the race."[76] Neither the UAW's affiliation with the Committee for Industrial Organization in 1936 nor the emergence that same year of a new pro-CIO younger leadership cadre among Detroit blacks produced any immediate changes. Yet ultimately both developments would have a crucial impact. Inspired by the reform tendencies of the New Deal era, impressed with the record of John L. Lewis's United Mine Workers and the way in which the new industrial unions explicitly encouraged the recruitment of black workers, this handful of spokesmen eagerly urged the Negro auto workers to join the UAW.

1936 would in fact prove in the long run to have been something of a turning point in the history of the relations between black Detroit and the UAW. In the spring John P. Davis was finally able, after at least one failure, to establish a viable chapter of the NNC, headed by a young attorney recently graduated from the University of Detroit Law School, LeBron Simmons. Though from the beginning the Detroit NNC was an ardent supporter of the UAW, its alleged Communist connections limited its influence, and not until 1941 would it be able to attract to its leadership an individual of prominence and substantial influence in Detroit's Afro-American community.[77]*

Far more influential, though at first they also had little impact on Detroit blacks' thinking about trade unions, was a triumvirate of business and professional men identified with the New Deal and the Democrats: a politician, Charles C. Diggs; a minister, Horace White; and a newspaper editor, Louis Martin. Of them Diggs, who had arrived in Detroit in 1913 and established a highly prosperous undertaking business in 1921, was the only one who was middle-aged in the 1930's. By 1932 he had emerged as a leader in Democratic ward politics, and four years later, when Detroit blacks decisively shifted their allegiance from the Republicans to the Democrats, he was elected to the state senate. Representing a district

---

* In 1939, in testimony before the House Un-American Activities Committee, the ex-Communist and former UAW organizer William Odell Nowell, testified that he and other blacks whom he named as Communists—Paul Kirk, Ed Williams, and Lonnie Williams—had organized the Detroit NNC at the express instructions of the Communist party. (Statement of William Odell Nowell, in U.S., Congress, House, 75th Congress, 3rd Session, Special Committee To Investigate Un-American Activities and Propaganda in the U.S., *Hearings*, vol. XI [Washington, 1939], 7029.)

composed primarily of Polish and black auto workers—and indeed his constituency, which included the town of Hamtramck, actually had a slight majority of Poles—Diggs proved to be a vigorous champion not only of civil rights laws but also of New Deal reform legislation and the CIO.[78] Equally enthusiastic about the possibility for social change inherent in industrial unionism were Martin and White, young men in their twenties who both arrived in Detroit during 1936. Martin, fresh from his undergraduate studies at the University of Michigan, became editor of the new weekly, the Michigan *Chronicle*. A subsidiary of the Chicago *Defender*, it replaced the Detroit edition of that Republican organ; since the other two Detroit black newspapers were also Republican, Martin with his New Deal and union sympathies consciously developed for the *Chronicle* a new constituency. Horace White, a graduate of Oberlin College's Divinity School, became pastor of Plymouth Congregational Church. He appealed especially to a younger and well-educated group and vigorously involved himself in a wide range of local civic activities, including membership on the NAACP branch's executive board. Both men were deeply interested in politics, White being elected to a term in the Michigan House of Representatives and Martin joining the staff of the Democratic National Committee in 1944.[79]

Thus by the opening of 1937, amid the social ferment of the Depression and the New Deal, the seeds of future change had been planted. Yet for the present most of the black workers and spokesmen alike remained skeptical of the nascent UAW, and black participation in it remained slight.

# II

## *From the Sit-downs to the Ford Strike:*
## *Blacks and the Union, 1937–1941*

Given the conditions already described, it is not surprising that
during the period of the UAW's great organizing drives between
1937 and 1941 Detroit's blacks exhibited considerable resistance to
unionization. The UAW, having received only negligible black
support in the famous sit-down strikes against the automobile industry in late 1936 and early 1937, decided to make a serious appeal to Negroes when it turned attention to unionizing Ford a few
months later. Black organizers were hired and a propaganda campaign was mounted to destroy the negative image of the union
held by Ford's Negro employees. But because of the company's
countermeasures the Ford drive faltered among workers of both
races and soon collapsed amidst the union's debilitating factional
conflict in which the new Negro organizational setup, caught in the
crossfire, was destroyed. Meanwhile, the black community remained highly polarized, and the UAW's efforts to influence the
city's black leaders made no greater headway than the campaign
among the black workers—a situation epitomized by a bitter clash
at the NAACP's 1937 national conference in Detroit. Both
Chrysler in 1939 and Ford two years later exploited this pervasive

anti-UAW sentiment, using black strikebreakers to try to defeat the union. Yet these attempts actually boomeranged and drew black spokesmen closer to the UAW. Moreover by the time of the 1941 Ford strike the union found itself the beneficiary of a perceptible rise in pro-UAW feeling among Detroit's blacks. This strike proved to be a pivotal event in the history of the UAW's relationship with black Detroit; yet paradoxically the union's victory demonstrated not only the existence of this growing black support, but also the considerable distance that yet remained before the loyalty of most of the black workers would be won.

1

Although black participation of the sit-down strikes was minimal, ironically in the first one in Detroit—the successful confrontation at the Midland Steel Frame Company at the end of 1936—Negro workers were very active. At the time, blacks, many of them recruited in a recent expansion of Midland's operations, comprised about one-third of the employees, and because they worked in an unusually broad range of job categories in close interaction with white workers, the setting was conducive to interracial cooperation. Not only did the men of both races act together, with a black assembler, Oscar Oden, serving on the bargaining committee, but the wives on the outside jointly prepared food which they passed up through the factory windows.[1]

Yet in subsequent sit-downs blacks mostly left the plants, neither joining nor actively opposing the strikers, and by and large these strikes were won virtually without black support. At the lengthy sitdown strike at Bohn Aluminum Plant #3 that began December 10, of the hundred Negroes employed only three or four remained in the factory.[2] At General Motors, scene of the major strikes in January and February 1937, black participation was negligible except for the Buick foundry in Flint. UAW leadership actively sought Negro support for this attack on the industry's largest producer, and in an interview with a reporter from the influential black weekly, the Pittsburgh *Courier,* president Homer Martin and vice-president Wyndham Mortimer vigorously assured blacks that they would be protected in their jobs. Citing the union constitution's anti-discrimination clause, Martin asserted: "Negro workers have all the benefits and rights of our union. . . . We will go so far to protect them as we will white workers. We feel very, very strongly on this matter. We don't segregate." Maintaining that there must be no discrimination in the implementation of the union's seniority demands, he continued: "The Negroes in the automobile industry must join us in our fight. We must solve together, not pitted against each other, all discrimination." Nevertheless, although a few did indeed join the sit-downers, at Chevrolet Gear and Axle most of the blacks actually sided with those whites who opposed the sit-down strike, and, in general, as NAACP Assistant Secretary Roy Wilkins stated after touring Michigan in February, "While some Negro workers in General Motors plants have joined the United Automobile Workers of America and some took part in the sit-down strikes in Flint, many more are hanging back, asking the usual question: 'Will the union give us a square deal and a chance at some of the good jobs?' "[3]

A similar pattern emerged at the month-long Chrysler sit-down strike in March and early April. Since Chrysler was the industry's second-largest employer of blacks, it is not surprising either that the union bent every effort to enlist them, or that the blacks exhibited considerable loyalty toward the company. Moreover, unlike the situation at Midland Steel, Chrysler's blacks, virtually confined to the foundry where they formed the overwhelming majority of the work force, did not interact much with the white workers. At Chrysler's Dodge plant the UAW distributed leaflets exhorting blacks to "join with us" in fighting a racist company that actually rejected many Negroes at the hiring gate and exploited the race issue to promote divisiveness. Clashes, however, broke out between the white unionists and Dodge's blacks. In one instance Negro workers, seeking to pick up their paychecks, "had to club their way through the strong guard stations [of strikers] at the gate." Although a few like Samuel Fanroy, a chief steward in the paint shop at Chrylser Kercheval and a member of the plant's strike committee, were deeply committed to the union, as elsewhere most refused to take sides, quietly slipping out of the factories where possible. Fanroy repeatedly urged his four hundred black co-workers to stay inside, but most of them gradually disappeared, and when the sit-down finally ended only three remained.[4] The story at Briggs, another firm with a substantial proportion of black workers, was similar. With most of them concentrated in one department at the Mack Avenue plant, there was practically no interaction between them and the largely southern white work force; and the youthful UAW organizer Emil Mazey, who would later chalk up a good record for supporting the interests of his local's Negro members, must have found the task of getting the Negroes to join the sit-downs a frustrating experience.[5]

Like the black elite in cities across the country,[6] Detroit's Negro leadership overwhelmingly sided with the manufacturers. However, what the minority of pro-labor spokesmen lacked in numbers they more than compensated for in their ability to raise the issue of trade unionism and get it discussed. Thus at the height of the sit-downs YMCA secretary Wilbur Woodson sponsored a debate between Horace White and Donald Marshall. Addressing the overflow crowd, Marshall charged the UAW with communist domination and a lust for power, while White flayed auto manufacturers for paying starvation wages and denounced critics who said that the UAW would expel blacks once the sit-downs were won. Conceding that the UAW was not perfect, White remarked that the same could be said of political parties, but that didn't stop blacks from voting on election day: "The Negro should not stand on the outside and look in; but should step in and join." Nationally, leading black spokesmen were also highly divided. Even some who sympathized with the new interracial industrial unions were so deeply aware of the white workers' prejudices that they recommended a stance of watchful waiting. During the GM strike the Pittsburgh *Courier*, hoping that the company's white employees might be experiencing "a change of heart" toward blacks, nonetheless inquired how far Homer Martin and the new UAW could be trusted to follow in John L. Lewis's footsteps and see that blacks received a fair share of employment when the strike was settled.[7]

Similarly the NAACP, even though it had endorsed the CIO at its annual conference the previous year, refused unequivocally to approve the UAW. After Wilkins returned from his Michigan trip and discussed with Walter White "what ought to be the attitude of Negroes toward the CIO and UAW," the Association's press release pointedly noted: "Many [sic] are joining up, hoping for the square deal promised by John L. Lewis," but "Everywhere in Michigan colored people are asking whether the new C.I.O. union is going to permit Negroes to work up into some of the good jobs or whether it is just going to protect them in the small jobs they already have in General Motors." Soon afterwards, when the NAACP heard rumors that at Dodge the UAW was demanding seniority rights only for whites, and at Ford was creating a separate black local, the Association protested directly to Homer Martin. In denying these reports Martin reiterated that the UAW stood for the "full protection of the Negro worker in every way," with absolutely no segregation or discrimination whatsoever. Satisfied that the union was committed to the CIO policy represented by Lewis and John Brophy, the NAACP gave wide publicity to Martin's reply.[8]

Thus in the spring of 1937 after the main wave of sit-down strikes had brought contracts with most of the industry, and as the UAW was preparing to begin an organizational drive against Ford, only the most limited advances in winning black support had been achieved. Negro workers, unconvinced that membership in the UAW would bring any benefits, were "still reluctant to cast their lot with the union";[9] even the national NAACP had expressed skepticism of the UAW's intentions, and in Detroit the sit-downs garnered no new friends among the local black leaders.

2

During the year following the sit-down strikes, the UAW was engaged in its first. major drive against the industry's most intransigent employer: the Ford Motor Company. The union, facing the calculated intimidation of Harry Bennett's notorious Service Department, was too weak to mount a sit-down and therefore confined itself to propagandizing among the company's employees. Given the importance of blacks at the gigantic Rouge complex, the union now made the recruitment of black workers a central concern, exerting special efforts to attract them and their community leaders. For the first time Negroes were placed on the salaried international staff, and conscious steps were taken to increase the presence of blacks in the leadership of some of the locals. In the short run at least, these efforts proved futile. Henry Ford's earlier philanthropy and his connections with black preachers and other leaders now paid off handsomely. Few of his black employees were willing to join the union. Although the Ford drive was in disarray by the spring of 1938, the issue of unionism had at least been raised and widely debated in the Motor City's black community.

Even when the sit-downs were still at their height, the Ford Company had begun girding for the struggle, and its strategy included specific plans for utilizing the loyal black workers. As early as January 1937, "realizing that its colored employees could be relied upon," the Company's Service Department for the first time recruited blacks as armed guards—handpicking large, strong men from various departments in the Rouge plant, and arming them with blackjacks and other similar weapons. A confrontation was not long in coming. When the union, seeking national publicity, dramatized its campaign by having several top leaders distribute leaflets at the Rouge gates in violation of a local ordinance, the company, as anticipated, reacted with violence. In the famous "Battle of the Overpass," union officials were brutally assaulted by Ford Servicemen, their ranks now augmented with the recently recruited blacks. Most of the attackers were actually whites, but

Negroes were prominently involved, and the pro-Ford Baltimore *Afro-American* even described one black who knocked down four unionists as "the uncrowned hero of the pitched battle." On the other hand several Negro unionists were among those beaten up and called "black bastards" by the white Servicemen. While the incident reaped considerable press coverage for the UAW, it also spotlighted the substantial support that Ford enjoyed among his black employees. [10]

In seeking to enhance its appeal to black workers at the Rouge, the union in April 1937 appointed its first paid black organizer. The man chosen for this position was Paul Kirk, a crane operator at the Michigan Steel Casting Company. Son of an Alabama preacher, Kirk had come to Detroit in 1929, where he joined the union seven years later (1936), became closely involved in National Negro Congress activities, and was elected recording secretary of the half black Michigan Steel Casting Local 281. So that no one could miss the point, the union announced that Kirk's selection "further substantiates" the UAW's constitutionally mandated policy of non-discrimination. In theory Kirk was responsible to a special non-salaried "Sub-Committee for Organization of Negro Workers" created soon afterwards, and chaired by the black sit-down striker from Chrysler, Samuel Fanroy. [11]

More black organizers were added during the summer, and just before the UAW convention it was announced that there were six on the International staff—three full-time and three part-time. Heading this group and soon replacing Paul Kirk was Walter Hardin, a man with long experience in radical circles and the labor movement. [12] Born in Tennessee, he had moved to Pennsylvania, joined the IWW, and then taken an active part as a member of the Amalgamated Association of Iron, Steel, and Tin Workers at Johnstown during the 1919 steel strike. Subsequently he became a Communist, and in 1929 moved to Pontiac, Michigan, where he worked in several foundries. There during the early 1930's he served as an organizer for the Communist-dominated Auto Workers Union and as a leader in the Communist-sponsored hunger marches, anti-eviction demonstrations, and Unemployed Councils. His participation in these activities was so prominent that in November 1931 he was abducted and horsewhipped by right-wing vigilantes. Over the next few years Hardin quit the party and obtained a job at the Pontiac Motor Company, where he was when Homer Martin made him an organizer in 1937. A tall, muscular man weighing about 200 pounds, Hardin had a big voice that made him a superb platform speaker. One associate recalled Hardin as "a great speaker. Whites found him absolutely impressive—you could almost place him in the category of an orator, he was that impressive. He could certainly shake up an audience." Another co-worker remembered, "He was the most convincing speaker I've ever seen in my life. He could move white union audiences because they respected his long fight for working people." In a feature article published in 1939 the *CIO News* called his record "an inspiration to both his colored and white brothers": "Kidnapped and flogged, clubbed on the picket line, threatened with 'bodily violence' a score of times and victim of other anti-labor uprisings. . . . His courage in refusing to be bullied by vigilante mobs symbolizes the driving spirit of the CIO. . . ."[13]

The development of the salaried black organizing staff had been in part a response to the prodding from blacks themselves,[14] and at the UAW national convention that met shortly after Hardin's appointment, Negro unionists pressed for the hiring of further black organizers. One delegate asserted that few black Ford workers had joined the UAW "because of the indisputable fact that enough negro [sic] organizers have not been appointed. . . . I am proud of being a black man and I say that a black man can contact and approach another black man better than a white man. He knows the feelings, the desires, the needs, the sufferings of the black man." Charging that employers would use black non-union labor to drive down wages unless the UAW made special efforts to reach racial and ethnic minorities, the convention called for "hiring additional Negro organizers and clerical workers who are acquainted with the special problems of the Negro race, so that they may enjoy the benefits of organized labor."[15]* Within weeks after the convention, the International Executive Board decided to assign the Negro work higher priority, and in October the Sub-Organizing Committee was replaced with a Committee in Charge of Organizational Work Among Negroes, directly responsible to the International President and Executive Board. Hardin, who was simultaneously elevated to membership on the Ford Organizing Campaign Committee itself, directed the new setup. At the same time the black staff was expanded with the appointment of two additional full-time organizers—William Nowell and Frank Evans. Hardin also had the assistance of three part-time organizers in the outlying cities of Flint, Saginaw, and Pontiac; and at the opening of 1938 a fourth full-time organizer, Joseph Billups, was added to strengthen the staff in Detroit, while a black woman, Magdalene White, was hired to assist in research and publicity.[16]

Like Hardin, two of these two organizers—Nowell and Billups—had emerged from a radical past in the Communist party and the old Auto Workers Union. William Odell Nowell, born in Georgia in 1904, had arrived in Detroit as a young man in 1923. Joseph Billups, the son of a Mississippi preacher, had been a miner and a steelworker before obtaining a job at the Ford foundry in the late 1920's. In the latter part of the decade both were active in the AWU's Ford local and joined the Communist party. In 1930 the

---

* Although from the beginning the clerical work at the Negro Sub-Organizing Committee's office was handled by a black secretary (*Defender*, April 27, 1937; see also Paul Kirk to John P. Davis, July 16, 1937, NNC Archives, Reel 1187), the hiring of black clerks was to be a point that white UAW officers would ignore for years. In 1938 Emil Mazey, president of the Briggs local, was the first to hire a black secretary in a local union office. The white secretaries vehemently objected, but quieted down when firmly told that they would be fired if the Negro woman were not treated as an equal. (Michael D. Whitty, "Emil Mazey: Radical as Liberal" [Ph.D. dissertation, Syracuse University, 1968], 127; *Chronicle*, Feb. 23, 1957.) In late 1943 Walter Reuther recalled, "The first Negro employed there [at International headquarters] came as a result of [Horace] Sheffield's vigorously calling the matter to Dick Leonard's attention about sixteen months ago. Whereupon, Leonard prevailed upon Eddie Levinson, the publicity director, to request her as his secretary, in which capacity she served ever since." (*Chronicle*, Oct. 2, 1943.)

two men ran for political office on the Communist ticket—Nowell
for Congress and Billups for governor; and during the early years
of the Depression Nowell was named to a number of local party
posts, while both men were prominently involved in Communist-
sponsored organizations—the Trade Union Unity League, the
League of Struggle for Negro Rights and the Unemployed Councils and Tenants Leagues. Nowell, however, had, unlike Billups,
left the party at the end of 1936.[17]

On the other hand both Evans and the part-time organizers
were all "nonpolitical men." Frank Evans, born in 1908, the son of
an Alabama sharecropper, moved to Cleveland in 1927, working in
various foundries as a molder's helper. An active member of an
AFL Molder's Union local, whose organizing efforts had been consistently undermined by the cleavage between the white skilled
workers and the mainly black helpers, Evans during 1936–37
played a leading role in bringing his fellow workers of both races
into the UAW, and mobilizing them for a successful strike. A delegate to the 1937 UAW convention, Evans found himself "enthused
because this union was not only organizing blacks but even electing blacks as delegates to the convention," and several weeks later
was delighted to accept Martin's invitation to become a staff member.[18]

Of the three part-time men, Buick foundry worker Henry Clark
of Local 156 would be active for only a few years, but the other
two—Rev. William Bowman and especially Oscar Noble—would
be the most enduring of the blacks who joined the UAW staff at
this time. Bowman, born in Arkansas in 1900, had come to Michigan in 1925; a molder at the Chevrolet Grey Iron factory in
Saginaw since 1926, he was also pastor of Christ Community
Church. A magnetic personality with a following among his fellow
black foundry workers, Bowman early became a member of the
local UAW's executive board. Unlike Bowman, who had no background in trade unionism, but was simply hopeful that the new industrial unions would indeed be different from the old craft organizations, Noble, born in Jacksonville, Florida, in 1914, was the son

of a bricklayer and AFL union member. He had arrived at Pontiac as a small child during the World War I black migratory wave to the Northern automobile cities. By the time he was twenty-one, Noble was operating a molding machine in the Pontiac Motor Company, one of two black machine operators in the entire plant. Like Evans, Noble possessed unusual interpersonal skills that appealed to men of both races. His firm and dedicated but tactful manner, his willingness to take up workers' grievances with management, and his ability in this delicate task made him a natural spokesman for both blacks and whites. Not surprisingly in 1937 he served on the early city-wide strategy committee set up in Pontiac during the organizing drive there, and was subsequently elected chairman of the union local's foundry unit and member of the plant bargaining committee.[19]

Clearly the obvious necessities of the Ford drive and the demands of black UAW members had together prompted the union to hire black organizers and develop an organizational structure geared specifically to recruiting Ford's Negro employees. That a high proportion of this early group of black organizers had a background of previous Communist activism was not accidental. For as with whites, the CIO unions found that such men provided a rich source of expertise, dedication, and ability. Thus back in November 1936 out of the nine whites who constituted the UAW's organizing staff in Michigan five had been Communists, and three of them came out of the Communist-dominated Auto Workers Union. Similarly at least three of the new black organizers—Hardin, Nowell, and Billups—had been Communists who had obtained their experience organizing for the AWU.[20] Yet neither was it an accident that nearly all of the black organizers appointed by Homer Martin were individuals who had either shed their Communist connections or never had any in the first place. For the development of the "Negro Department" and the political leanings of its personnel were also strongly influenced by another factor—the schism over Martin's leadership that was emerging and that would by the spring of 1938 force the suspension of the UAW's organizing drive at Ford's.

By the summer of 1937 the UAW's several cliques and factions had coalesced into two rival groups: the Progressive Caucus headed by Martin and Richard Frankensteen, and the Unity Caucus led by Wyndham Mortimer, Ed Hall, and Walter Reuther. Although in both caucuses non-political types constituted the majority, intertwined with the personality clashes and differences over programmatic and tactical issues was an ideological struggle among sectarian Marxists. Homer Martin had come under the influence of Jay Lovestone, the former general secretary of the CP who had been expelled in 1929 for right-wing deviationism, while the opposing Unity Caucus, including both the UAW's Communist contingent and Reuther's Socialist associates, exemplified the "united front" strategy employed at the time by the CP.[21] For Martin, who had appointed "Lovestoneites" to key positions on his staff, the struggle became a crusade against a Communist conspiracy, and in this context changes in the UAW's Negro organizational work revolved around people's political affiliations, real or imagined. Whether or not certain black organizers and their friends in the National Negro Congress were actually Communists, Martin and his Lovestoneite associates certainly believed they were.

In any event there were charges and sometimes empirical evidence connecting the individuals in the original Negro Sub-Organizing Committee created in early 1937 with Communist activism, and certainly nearly all of them had close relations with the NNC. Testifying at Congressional hearings in 1938–1939, both a former president of Briggs Local 212 and William Nowell, the ex-Communist who had become a Lovestoneite, charged that NNC leaders John P. Davis and LeBron Simmons, UAW Organizer Paul Kirk, and Samuel Fanroy and Lonnie Williams—respectively chairman and secretary of the Sub-Organizing Committee—were all members of the Communist party. Nowell even listed Kirk as former head of the "Communist fraction" within the UAW [22] Williams, a Ford foundry worker whom Kirk was anxious to add to the UAW staff as an organizer, had been, like Nowell and Hardin, prominent in the Communist-led Unemployed Councils and League of Struggle for Negro Rights during the early 1930's.[23] Nowell also recalled that both Williams and Kirk had worked with him in setting up the Detroit NNC under instructions of the CP's Central Committee. Kirk, while on the UAW staff, consulted quite closely with John P. Davis,[24] and most members of the Negro Sub-Organizing Committee were actively involved in the local NNC.*

Only the fact that Homer Martin and others in his Progressive Caucus viewed the personnel of the original Sub-Organizing Committee and the NNC as Communist-dominated can explain the changes already described in the black organizational work during the summer and autumn of 1937. The selection of Hardin rather than Kirk's candidate Lonnie Williams as the second salaried black organizer, occurring as it did amidst the growing tensions between the two caucuses, represented the hiring not only of a highly experienced individual but also of an ex-Communist who had even joined Jay Lovestone's Independent Labor League.[25] † Reflecting

---

* Sub-Organizing Committee vice-chairman L. B. Spradley, of Hudson Local 154, was active in the local National Negro Congress's trade union section. (Untitled interview with LeBron Simmons, n.d., in William McKie Papers in the Nat Ganley Collection, Series VI, Box 33; Spradley and Simmons to Frank X. Martel, September [no date], 1938, in the Wayne County AFL Archives, Box 12; letterhead of Michigan Division, NNC on Simmons to Davis, June 12, 1939, NNC Archives, reel 1191.) Both Kirk and Fanroy remained actively identified with the National Negro Congress for years. (Letterhead, Detroit Council NCC, 1945, on Shelton Tappes *et al.* to Mr. Novak, March 13, 1945, in Association of Catholic Trade Unionists Archives, Box 29.)

† John P. Davis could only have been disappointed when Hardin rather than Lonnie Williams was added to the staff. (See Kirk to Davis, July 16, 1937, NNC Archives, reel 1187.) Yet with the situation seemingly fluid and with the NNC sponsoring a conference in August on behalf of the UAW, Davis did not give up easily. He urged Kirk to wangle him a speaking invitation at the UAW convention, hoping that Martin's office might accept the argument that the black leader's appearance would garner valuable publicity for the union in the Negro press. As Davis explained to Kirk, his presence on the program "will enable us to control the

the fact that Martin emerged from the Unity Caucus's challenge to his power at the 1937 convention still in control of the staff apparatus were both Kirk's disappearance from the scene soon afterwards and the restructuring of the Negro organizing work. In publicizing the latter action, Martin's staff, utilizing the circumlocutions and oblique references to Communists so characteristic of the Progressive Caucus, explained that the step was calculated "to guard against any tendency that might arise out of erroneously related committees to direct the work among Negroes away from the general apparatus." Or, as Hardin put it, the reorganization was needed "due to the very loose and 'outside' organizational relation of the former Sub-Organizing Committee to the general union setup."[26] Thus the appointment of the two former Communists-turned-Lovestoneites, Hardin and Nowell, and of the highly able non-political Frank Evans must have been calculated moves on Martin's part. And although Joseph Billups, a known Communist, was indeed added a few months later, he was regarded at the time as not highly sectarian but very loyal to the union; moreover, he had excellent connections with recent migrants to the "Black Bottom" slums that no other organizer could reach.[27] In short, the Negro organizational structure, once seen as a center of Communist influence in the union, had now come under the control of anti-Communists. As an agency dominated by Martin loyalists it would, in the following months, be subjected to attack from the Unity Caucus and ultimately destroyed.

With this growing "Negro Department," as it soon came to be called informally, the UAW continued during the summer and fall

trend of discussion which the Negro question takes at the convention." (Davis to Paul Kirk, August 15, 1937 *ibid.*, reel 1187.) But the invitation was not forthcoming, and although Davis wanted to make the automobile industry the NNC's "next point of concentration," clearly Martin had closed off cooperation with the Congress. In a final effort Davis wrote John L. Lewis of his hopes for a future tie with the UAW, complaining that "Through no fault of our own (and of this I am absolutely certain) our relationships with Brother Homer Martin have not been as cooperative as we would have liked." (Davis to Lewis, Oct. 19, 1937, CIO Archives, Box A7A16.)

of 1937 to give more attention to "bringing . . . the recruiting of
Negro workers abreast of recruiting in general." The black organizers enthusiastically created a network of neighborhood committees to contact black Ford workers.[28] The company, of course,
countered with a combination of propaganda and intimidation
which the Negro organizers found hard to combat. Ford's Loyal
Workers Club filled black churches to capacity for mass meetings.[29] and as the UAW drive's director, Richard Frankensteen,
recognized, the main difficulty in organizing blacks lay in Ford's
constant reiteration of the superior treatment they received at the
Rouge. Yet "the intensified terror" of the Service Department also
posed a grave problem. "As bad as it is in relation to white workers, the terror used by the Negro Servicemen has been much
greater." On several occasions integrated UAW groups seeking to
distribute literature at Inkster were driven out by armed blacks
wearing Ford Service Department badges. There were even reports of Ford Servicemen tampering with workers' mail and demanding that employees inform the company about the UAW's
recruiting activities. The black organizers stood up to this
challenge. Once when a black Ford Serviceman stormed into a
meeting being held by Evans and Billups, the two coolly ordered
him out.[30]

Supplementing the work of the black organizers, the union
beamed a persistent propaganda campaign at Ford's Negro employees. Articles specifically addressed to blacks were published in
the union's official organ, the *United Automobile Worker;* columns
first by Kirk and then by Hardin appeared there and in the black
weeklies.[31] Before leaving the UAW organizing staff, Kirk arranged a conference co-sponsored by the Michigan NNC and the
Communist-oriented Workers Alliance, International Workers
Order, and WPA Union. Panel sessions at this meeting explored
the various aspects of black-union relationships and what blacks at
Ford could gain by supporting the UAW, while the featured
speaker, NNC president A. Philip Randolph assailed Henry Ford
and vigorously declared: "The time has come when the Negro has

to decide between organized labor and organized capital. The day the Negro depended upon the 'good, rich white man' is gone—and gone forever! . . . There must be solidarity among workers—white and black—to build industrial democracy in America."[32] More to the point, the Ford Organizing Committee widely distributed pamphlets "to educate workers on the vital necessity of solidarity regardless of race," sponsored special radio programs pitched to black audiences, and arranged "outdoor twilight meetings at the Negro districts" featuring baseball games, band concerts, and pro-union speeches.[33]

In this propaganda drive the union stressed that Ford had no love for the blacks, since they were actually underrepresented in better-paying jobs at Rouge and virtually absent except as janitors at other Ford plants. As Hardin said, Ford's "exceptionally liberal policy" was "an illusion."[34] Blacks were reminded that they shared with white Ford workers notorious grievances such as the speedup and the surveillance of Harry Bennett's Service Department. (Donald Marshall was dubbed a "high salaried spy master.")[35] Kirk, pointing to Ford's arbitrary layoff and hiring system, promised black workers that under collective bargaining their seniority would be protected. Black workers were urged to follow their own self-interest and cease accepting the black bourgeoisie's pro-Ford arguments. In Kirk's view the union provided "the greatest opportunity for the realization of economic equality for the Negro worker . . . in the history of America." Hardin denounced black leaders who, "blind to the birth of a new labor movement possessed of new ideals and new methods," "stand on the side of industrial feudalism and against the Negro and white workers." Finally, blacks were advised to see through the Ford company's duplicity of posing as friend while playing them off against the whites in a "divide and rule" policy. Warned the UAW's official organ: "You Negro workers must realize that King Henry is merely fattening you for the slaughter—buying up loyalty with petty favors in order to promote conflict. . . . You other workers . . . must realize that Henry has you figured out for saps; Henry wants to keep you 'burned up' over the Negro workers to prevent you from uniting with them into the UAW and ending Ford's industrial slavery." When a predominantly white UAW local in Chicago elected a black man as its president, the *United Automobile Worker* greeted this unprecedented event by quoting the white unionist who nominated him: "To me color does not count."[36]

These efforts notwithstanding, UAW leaders were well aware that, to win the black workers' allegiance at Ford and elsewhere, much more was needed. 1937 union membership statistics revealed the scope of the problem. It is likely that somewhat over half of the blacks in plants covered by contracts had joined the UAW, but white support was far higher. There was, it is true, considerable variation, yet Henry Clark's success in organizing nearly all the Negroes in the Flint foundries was clearly atypical. Thus, for example, at the Dodge Motor Company over 75 percent of the whites but only 65 percent of the blacks were in the UAW; at Murray Body, nearly 80 percent of the whites but only 50 percent of the blacks; while at Bohn Aluminum, the figures were 95 percent and 50 percent respectively.[37]

Union leaders understood the reasons why so many blacks held back. At the Rouge of course there were the unique problems stemming from the Ford Motor Company's policies. But in addition there was the whole array of issues reflecting the blacks' subordinate position in the industry: the prejudices of white workers; the black concentration in the least desirable jobs; the underrepresentation in union offices; and the fears that the union's seniority clauses would be manipulated to the blacks' disadvantage both in the industry's periodic layoffs and rehirings as well as in the matter of promotions. As a UAW official later conceded, with management controlling the hiring of new personnel, the union was in no position to demand the employment of more blacks, and in most cases the earliest contracts "froze the existing pattern of segregation and even discrimination. Seniority rules, necessary to protect job security, gave white workers a faster claim to the unskilled and semi-skilled jobs they already had."[38] In short Negro automobile workers tended to suspect that unionization would actually undermine their foothold in the industry rather than protect it.* Indeed a reporter for the Associated Negro Press, writing on the eve of the Ford organizing drive, stressed that exclusion from the better jobs made blacks skeptical of the union's anti-discrimination promises, and he pointedly asked, "Can and will the union bring enough pressure to bear on these giant corporations to cause them to change their policies?"[39]

As UAW officials realized only too well, remedying this problem involved modifying the attitudes of white workers as well as management, and white union leaders were not prepared to stick their necks out. Not surprisingly, Kirk and Hardin, anxious to recruit blacks, were reluctant to openly criticize the white workers or the union. Yet even they at times voiced reservations. Kirk, praising white Dodge workers for having recently obtained a promotion for a Negro previously denied it because of their opposition, observed:

*Thus there were even cases in which black workers, suspicious of the way in which seniority provisions might be applied, pressed not for plant-wide seniority, which would theoretically open the more desirable and highly skilled jobs to them, but for departmental seniority, which protected them in the narrow range of jobs to which they were restricted by most employers. For example at the Kelsey-Hayes Wheel Corporation, during the organizing campaign of 1937, blacks actually proved reluctant to join until their traditional status in the foundry was made secure. The local's organ reported: "The foundry boys don't have to be backward about joining the union. The foundry will be treated as a separate unit in the matter of seniority. Jobs within the foundry will not be affected by the general seniority rule." (See column entitled "Kelsey Hayes Picket" in West Side *Conveyor*, Aug. 3, 1937.) This is evidently the unidentified Detroit foundry described by Robert C. Weaver in "Detroit and Negro Skill," *Phylon* (Second Quarter, 1943): 135. Black experience after the 1938 recession lent some support to those blacks who espoused this position. Bumped during the economic downturn by whites who had had better positions and longer service, blacks sometimes discovered that when industrial expansion occurred again, management and local union officials violated the union contract in order to avoid placing blacks of high seniority in the better jobs to which they were entitled but from which they had hitherto been excluded. See Herbert R. Northrup *et al., Negro Employment in Basic Industry: A Study of Racial Policies in Six Industries* (Philadelphia, 1970), 60. On the other hand, those black union leaders who fought for plant-wide seniority were vindicated when the changing job opportunities associated with the rise of defense production made the disadvantages of departmental seniority very clear. (See Chapter III below.)

"Only when the Negro member has been guaranteed the right to perform any jobs for which he is qualified, will we be able to march forward as one united body." Hardin could speak similarly on the importance of developing "the proper enlightenment in the local union necessary to solve the many difficulties of the Negro workers in the shops," and once he even pointed up the UAW's dereliction: ". . . insufficient measures have been taken to break down the discriminatory policies of factory management . . . such as refusing promotion to better jobs, relegation of the most difficult and unsanitary work to Negro workers exclusively etc. . . ."[40]

White union leaders preferred to speak as if the difficulties were caused solely by management. Vice-President Richard T. Frankensteen once declared: "Sell[ing] unionism to the Negro workers" was difficult "because of the usual employer tactics of setting white man against Negro. . . ." Officials in Packard Local 190, concerned about black reluctance to join, yet unwilling to censure the white workers for their racism, warned: "Negro workers must understand that the UAW is their Union and if they want their problems taken up and adjusted they must join the Union." Yet in actual fact, UAW leaders were well aware that the union had not put its own house in order, and occasionally men in both caucuses addressed themselves to the issue. Thus Frankensteen himself, at the time a prominent Martin partisan, told black shop stewards that he recognized "the need for more educational activity among the white workers in the local unions on the problems confronting the Negro workers in the shop. . . ." And Martin's opponent, Vice-President Wyndham Mortimer, was even more explicit when in the pages of the *United Automobile Worker* he lectured the white membership about the divisive race prejudice inside the union: "Since it is the white worker that is the offender . . . the white worker must demonstrate his sincerity not by words but by his actions. We must demand that all discrimination in the matter of jobs must be abolished and Negroes be given an opportunity to engage in the skilled trades along with white workers." Employers, using the "foolish yarn about race superiority . . . so the

thoughts of the white workers will not dwell on the bread and but-
ter phase of the problem," were responsible for job discrimination.
But, he admitted, "as leaders of the labor movement we are not
doing anywhere near our duty to all workers if we do not fight
against this practice with every ounce of energy we possess."[41]

Another touchy matter was the question of black participation in
the locals' social affairs. On a number of occasions, white worker
antagonism to the presence of blacks and/or the refusal of certain
establishments to serve them, compelled locals. to dispense entirely with dances and picnics. Problems arose for example at
Chevrolet plants. Many whites objected to including blacks in a
1937 summer picnic, "but after several meetings the union went
on record against any discrimination. Negro members were placed
on the Picnic Committee and colored union members were given
tickets to sell."[42] Two months later, however, trouble arose again
when black members were barred from a dance sponsored by the
Chevrolet Gear and Axle local. Black workers and the Michigan
NNC held indignation meetings, and in the pages of the *United
Automobile Worker* Hardin predicted disastrous repercussions for
the drive to recruit black members at Ford. Representing the International he helped resolve the problem, however. After a
stormy session the local's executive board reaffirmed the UAW's
non-discrimination policy and promised to better supervise its social events.[43]

One measure of the acceptance of blacks in the union was their
presence in elective offices. While at the national level blacks held
no such positions, by the summer of 1937 Hardin could assert that
"in almost all locals having one hundred or more Negro members"
at least one black won some elective office.[44] Most of these individuals were stewards elected from predominantly black departments, but there were also occasional instances of blacks occupying
prominent posts in overwhelmingly white settings. Altogether
there were some twenty-five shop stewards. Seventeen of them
were in the Chrysler factories, including the chief stewards in the
foundry and cleaning departments at Dodge, and Samuel Fanroy,

chief steward in the sanding department of Chrysler Kercheval, who also sat on his local's executive board and on the UAW's district council. The chief stewards at two plants of Bohn Aluminum were blacks, and at Cadillac there was a Negro chief shop steward who was also assistant chairman of the strike committee. At Midland Steel, Oscar Oden continued on the bargaining committee, and in addition, when the plant's new Local 410 was created in the spring of 1937, a black hilo driver was elected to the executive board. One of the earliest union supporters at Briggs, Leonard Newman, was similarly elected to Local 212's first board of trustees. At Michigan Steel Casting, with its half black work force, both the recording secretary and chief negotiator were blacks, as were the heads of two of the local's important committees. On the other hand, at Pontiac Motor Company, where blacks composed only 400 of the 8500 employees, Oscar Noble was chairman of the foundry unit and a member of the plant bargaining committee,* while at another GM subsidiary, the Grey Iron foundry in Saginaw, not only was William Bowman on the executive board, but Boss McKnight was elected vice-president, although only about 600 of the plant's 4700 employees were Negroes. Finally in a unique instance during the autumn of 1937 the predominantly white local at the National Malleable and Steel Casting Company in Chicago elected William Sneed its president; not until 1944 would a UAW local in Detroit elect a black man as its president.[45]

Yet the total number of such officers was very small, and only a handful were elected from mainly white constituencies. That the number was even this large partly reflected conscious efforts in some locals after the sit-down strikes to encourage black membership and participation. Moreover, the International was anxious to guarantee that there was at least some black representation at

---

* Noble represented Plant No. 6 on the nine-man Pontiac bargaining committee. His constituency was overwhelmingly white; Plant No. 6 included the foundry, but even in that department blacks were no more than 25 percent of the workers. At the time he was elected to this post early in 1937, interest in the union among black workers at Pontiac was so slight that he and Hardin were the only Negroes present at the meeting. (Interview with Noble, March 16, 1978.)

the 1937 convention. A letter that went out over Paul Kirk's signature, urging the locals to "elect at least one Negro delegate" in the name of "unity of all workers," was ignored but subsequently additional elections were mandated and several blacks were chosen unanimously. Thus for example at the Romeo Foundry near Rochester, Michigan, where there were 13 black employees and 365 whites, a white pattern-maker was replaced by a black laborer.[46] At the Kelsey-Hayes Wheel Corporation, the plant committee decided that one of its sixteen delegates would be a black, and Doyle Buckman was duly elected—the one black on the large 95-man delegation from the Reuther stronghold, Local 174. And from Briggs Local 212 came two delegates, trustee Leonard Newman and Leon Bates, who would figure prominently in future years.[47]

Meanwhile the union proved unable to expand its beachhead in the larger black community. As Louis Martin observed, "the prevailing sentiment among race people in Detroit favors Ford policies" rather than the UAW. Epitomizing that fact was the way in which Bradby and Daniel had responded immediately after the Battle of the Overpass when they informed top Ford officials that the Company could "count on our group almost one hundred per cent."[48] Public support for the UAW of course was consistently voiced by State Senator Diggs, Horace White, and Louis Martin's *Chronicle*. White was a frequent speaker at mass meetings, always preaching a social gospel and contending that the church was doomed if it failed to reach out to the working class.[49] The Detroit chapter of the NNC was also very active on the union's behalf. Its trade union committee conducted organizing sessions in black workers' homes, and John P. Davis proudly reported to the Congress's national convention that the Detroit group had "distributed leaflets, held mass meetings, [and] furnished volunteer organizers. . . ."[50] None of these efforts, however, appeared to have a significant impact upon Ford workers or many other blacks in Detroit. Mainstream black organizations like the NAACP refused to endorse the conference, addressed by A. Philip Randolph, that Kirk had arranged with NNC assistance. Even the agitation of a man like Horace White rankled Ford loyalists; one long-time Rouge worker denounced the Congregationalist cleric as a meddling newcomer to the city, ignorant of conditions at Ford: "Mr. Ford is not a god, but he has been a savior to thousands of Negroes by giving them employment according to their ability when union shops are closed to them." [51]

Highlighting the debate—and the bitterness—which the UAW's Ford Organizing Drive produced among Detroit's Negroes were events at the NAACP annual national conference that opened in the Motor City at the end of June 1937. With labor and economic issues naturally ranking high on the agenda, Assistant Secretary Roy Wilkins had arranged for Paul Kirk, John P. Davis, and UAW president, Homer Martin, to speak. (To assuage labor's opponents, John C. Dancy was invited to discuss the Ford Company's policies, but unfortunately no record of his remarks survives.) [52] As the time for the conference approached, Homer Martin's scheduled appearance generated a serious controversy among local NAACP members. Father Daniel and other ministers publicly rebuked the Association's national office for inviting the UAW president, and pressure was exerted on the pastor of the Ebenezer A.M.E. Church to cancel the arrangements made to use his church for that session. Both Wilkins and Walter White, aware of the strong pro-Ford sentiment in the branch, actually capitalized on the anticipated clash and released a press statement predicting "a sharp debate over union labor policies and the future of Negro workers," which the black weeklies duly carried. On the Sunday before the conference opened, when White's special assistant, Juanita Jackson, appeared at several churches and indicated that Homer Martin was still on the program, "the congregations responded with very audible boos and cat calls." Upon arriving in the city Wilkins and White were confronted by a delegation of "angry and belligerent" ministers who threatened a boycott, but White "curtly told them that the law compelling anyone to attend an NAACP meeting had long since been repealed." Unperturbed, Wilkins predicted that the controversy "should add interest" to the proceedings.[53]

At the lively sessions both John P. Davis and Charles Diggs urged support for the CIO out of racial self-interest—the state senator championing a "strong alliance" with the new labor movement to cash in "on the benefits it is certain to reap." Homer Martin, prominently featured at an evening program, delivered a ringing evangelistic appeal. Announcing that, like Jesus Christ, "I come to you tonight representing the poor, the oppressed and the exploited people, both colored and white," the former Baptist preacher assured the delegates that the UAW was absolutely committed, on both practical and moral grounds, to protecting black workers. "I am sure," he continued, "it would do your hearts good, just as it does my heart good, to go into a union meeting and find that white and colored workers sit together, converse together, vote together, work together on committees and in meetings. . . . The elimination of prejudice against the Negro people is to me a definite part, not only of a wise labor movement . . . but a part of Christianity itself. . . . We propose, not only as an economic measure, but also as an ideal, to drive from the minds of the workers of this country the antiquated prejudices that have thrown them at each other's throats."[54]

Davis's and particularly Martin's presentations "opened the floodgates of acrimonious criticism" on the convention floor. Especially rankling was the notion that the UAW president had anything in common with Jesus Christ. Feeling ran so high that NAACP field secretary, William Pickens, in effect challenging his national officers, leaped to Henry Ford's defense, demanding to know "just what grievances if any," blacks had against him.[55] The conference's resolutions committee was nearly torn apart in a three-day fight over the question of whether to endorse the CIO. Ford sympathizers who swamped the committee angrily rejected the labor resolution which the national office had prepared. Even though it had urged that black workers "appraise critically the motives and practices of all labor unions," the proposed statement's reaffirmation of the 1936 convention's endorsement of industrial unionism as "the greatest hope" to black and white workers, was anathema to the majority. After "turbulent discussions" the conference eventually approved an amended version that pointedly condemned discrimination by labor organizations and omitted all praise for the CIO.[56]

Walter White tried to stand above the battle; in his address at the closing mass meeting he touched on many topics but said nothing about labor. Yet Wilkins, having borne the chief responsibility for planning the conference, returned to New York resentful against Bradby and Daniel, who from their pulpits had denounced Martin's speech, criticized the NAACP, and defended Henry Ford. Using the editorial pages of the NAACP's *Crisis*, Wilkins informed "the very small clique of Detroiters" who demanded that the Association's national office mind its own business and cease interfering in the Motor City's affairs, that it was indeed the organization's business to formulate a program for the millions of economically disadvantaged blacks, and added: "If the two greatly disturbed divines in Detroit feel called upon to attack their one great national organization because of their love for what Mr. Ford has done for Negroes in Detroit, we invite them to Mr. Ford's plants in Edgewater, N.J., Chester, Pa., Atlanta, Ga., Kansas City, Mo., and St. Paul, Minn. [where blacks were limited to janitorial work], and ask them if they will find anything in those places to cause them to don the garments of the Lord and preach a holy defense of the 800 million-dollar Ford Motor Company. The spectacle of poor preachers, ministering to the needs of poor people whose lot from birth to death is to labor for a pittance, rising to frenzied, name-calling defense of a billionaire manufacturer is enough to make the Savior himself weep."[57]

Wilkins's editorial "created quite a furor" locally, and the two ministers vigorously defended themselves. Warning that "We can't afford to have Ford close down on us. Where would we go?" an angry Rev. Everard W. Daniel preached against the local NAACP branch for having allowed White and Wilkins to ignore Detroit leaders and schedule Homer Martin's appearance. The following Sunday Daniel shared his pulpit at St. Matthew's with Ford's black personnel man, Donald Marshall, who delivered an even more pointed attack to the capacity crowd. Charging Communist influence in both the UAW and NAACP, he impugned Roy Wilkins's honesty and integrity and insinuated that the union supported segregation in auto plants it had already organized. Significantly it was not the Detroit NAACP, dominated by its pro-business leadership, but men like Louis Martin and Rev. Horace White who defended the national office and its right to invite the UAW president.[58]

For their part the UAW leaders were upset by the convention's negative labor resolution, fearing that the Association's conclave would have an unfortunate impact on the attitudes of black workers and leaders alike.[59] The union's disappointment was of course especially deep just because of the way in which the Ford Company was now benefiting from the strong ties it had established with the clergy and other black leaders.

That Ford company personnel were not above deliberately exploiting this connection became evident in the case of William Peck, the conservative but independent-minded pastor of Bethel A.M.E. Church, who was one of the very few ministers willing to open his church to pro-union speakers. As early as February 1937, after Howard University's president, Mordecai Johnson, told a Bethel audience that Negroes should not be afraid to join friendly labor organizations, an infuriated Donald Marshall threatened to hire no more Bethel members unless Peck denied his church's facilities to such persons. At first Peck ignored Marshall; during the summer the UAW obtained the church for the two-day conference co-sponsored by the NNC, featuring the militant union leader A. Philip Randolph. No sooner had the plans for Randolph's appearance become known than Marshall took steps to prevent it. Foremen at the Rouge plant threatened to fire Bethel members, but Peck nevertheless allowed the meeting to go on as scheduled.

Rumors of actual dismissals again circulated in the black community. Finally, feeling unable to continue jeopardizing the jobs of his congregation, he gave in and closed his church to programs critical of Ford. Thus in January 1938, when Mordecai Johnson made a return visit to Detroit, he was barred from Bethel. Forced to use a municipal auditorium, the president of Afro-America's finest institution of higher education lashed out at Ford and the controlled black churches while warmly lauding the UAW. From his pulpit the following Sunday Father Daniel rushed to Ford's defense, assailing Johnson and his UAW supporters: "They did not come to me for the use of this church," he announced. "They know that this is not the place to come with that piffle."[60]

These incidents involving Bethel were not isolated ones. When a West Side neighborhood group requested Horace White as its annual Emancipation Day speaker on January 1, 1938, the invitation was withdrawn after every church in the area refused its facilities. In silencing criticism Donald Marshall was so transparently manipulating the Ford Company's relations with the churches that even the conservative Detroit *Tribune* reported certain incidents such as this one, and admitted: ". . . in many local church congregations there are not a few who are in the employ of the Ford plant and other industrial concerns and they do not wish to run the risk of losing their jobs by directly or indirectly affiliating with the advocates of unionism." Horace White denounced this intimidation in an article for *Christian Century* entitled, "Who Owns the Negro Churches?": "The one organization through which the Negro ought to feel free to express his hopes and to work out his economic salvation cannot help him because the Negro does not own it—it belongs to the same people who own the factories. . . . The leadership of the Negro people is still in the hands of the clergymen and will be there for years to come, and these clergymen [with few exceptions] are at the moment leading for the industrialists rather than for the welfare of the Negro. While that situation exists . . . the Negro worker will be a tool in the hands of the controllers of industry—his fellow laborers will look upon him as an enemy."

But the most devastating commentary came not from union sympathizers like White in Detroit but from the well-known and iconoclastic black journalist George S. Schuyler, who compared conditions at Ford's to southern slavery. Calling the Rouge plant "an industrial plantation," he explained: "Since every Uncle Tom's Cabin must of course have an Uncle Tom, it need occasion no surprise that there are any number of Uncle Toms in the Ford setup. Nor is it surprising that these Uncle Toms are to a large degree gentlemen of the cloth, reverend gentlemen who are eager to sell out their people for filthy lucre. . . . They, in their zeal to serve their master, are quite willing to do anything that will antagonize white and colored workers. . . . they are busy arraying blacks against the white workers by urging the former not to join with the latter. One can imagine what this will lead to when all the white workers are organized, as they soon will be, and the Negro workers are not. . . . Are not these so-called leaders either knaves or fools?"[61]

Eight months after the commencement of the Ford drive, the union had made no visible progress in changing the sentiments of black Detroiters. As Louis Martin put it, local race leaders remained "afraid of the C.I.O. . . . [and] a great many of the Negro leaders and preachers are telling them [the workers] not to trust the union."[62] Moreover, by the spring of 1938 the company's resistance to the UAW had clearly paid off. The organizing drive and the recruitment of blacks alike were faltering, the economic recession forced substantial staff reductions,[63] and all these problems were compounded by the climax of the bitter factional fight, in which the campaign for black support suffered severely.

## 3

The factional struggle between Homer Martin's Progressive Caucus and the Wyndham Mortimer–Walter Reuther Unity Caucus only incidentally involved the question of organizing black workers, yet the schism seriously damaged that effort. The Negro Department was dismantled, and the work of recruiting blacks received lower priority; in addition the black unionsts' attempt to advance black interests by exploiting the desire of the two competing factions to attract Negro support accomplished nothing. Then, after its defeat and expulsion the Martin faction engaged in a dangerous though futile ploy to undermine the victorious Unity Caucus by encouraging blacks to act as strikebreakers in the Chrysler strike of 1939. Although an important consequence of this incident was a small but valued increment of support for the union among the city's black leaders, by and large the UAW did little to tackle the grievances of its black members. Indeed, not until the end of 1940, when the campaign to unionize Ford was renewed, would there again be a serious drive to organize black workers.

The Ford campaign suffered when its head, Vice-President Richard Frankensteen, having deserted Martin to join the Unity Caucus, was dismissed by the UAW president in the spring of 1938. Amidst the intense power struggle over the following summer that produced, first, Martin's expulsion of four vice-presidents and Secretary-Treasurer George Addes and then their restoration at the intervention of top CIO officials, the Negro Department came under attack. Staffed largely by Martin loyalists, the black organizational setup was a target for the Unity Caucus, which ironically included the very people who had comprised the original Negro Sub-Organizing Committee. Hardin, suspected by Martin of playing both sides, departed early, his exit precipitated by a personal feud with one of Martin's chief supporters on the International Executive Board.[64] By autumn, Martin's opponents were able to force the dissolution of the Negro Department.[65] Martin, however, promptly rehired on his organizing staff the two Negroes most loyal to him—William Nowell and Frank Evans. The UAW president also attempted to compensate for the change by establishing a small biracial National Coordinating Committee on Race Relations (including Nowell and Evans) to cooperate with the Ford Organizing Drive. But this gesture was futile, with Martin's opponents such as Addes and Frankensteen sniping at it during UAW Executive Board meetings, demanding both its dissolution and the firing of the pro-Martin black organizers. The latter were denounced by Paul Kirk, Joseph Billups, and other blacks in the Unity Caucus as "false leaders on the road to company unionism."[66]

Only rarely do the surviving sources illuminate the role of blacks in the intense day-to-day maneuvering in which both sides engaged during this period, as when, for example in early 1939 the anti-Martin leadership of the Dodge Main Local 3 found that his forces had packed a membership meeting with previously inactive blacks. Given the collapse of the black recruitment drive and the rank-and-file Negro workers' ambivalence toward the UAW in the first place, not surprisingly many black members stopped paying dues.[67]* Yet it is clear that with both the Unity and Progressive caucuses vying for the support of the Negro workers, the black unionists' dissatisfactions about job discrimination in the plants and the lack of officeholding in the UAW became issues in the factional struggle. Actually these issues, raised by Negroes from both groups cut two ways. On the one hand, black spokesmen on both sides, charging their opponents with foot-dragging about the black workers' welfare, gave the subject considerable emphasis in appealing to rank-and-file blacks for support. At the same time blacks in both camps, hoping to capitalize on the exigencies of the situation, pressed their own leaders for action to end the racist practices of employers, and provide greater black representation among the union's staff and elected officers.

In theory, of course, the white UAW leaders in the two factions were all in favor of equality. Back in 1938 both Martin and his opponents on the Board had reaffirmed the union's non-discrimination policies and instructed international representatives and local negotiating committees to see that blacks in the plants were

---

* It should also be noted that following the initial euphoria of the sit-down strikes and the rise of internal factionalism, many white unionists also became delinquent in paying their dues. (See Ray Boryczka, "Militancy and Factionalism in the United Auto Workers Union, 1937–1941," *The Maryland Historian* 8 [Fall 1977], 14–15, and Boryczka to authors, October 20, 1978.)

treated exactly like whites. But since concrete efforts to grapple
with the black workers' grievances had proven negligible, they became issues around which black spokesmen in each camp—blaming their opponents for the sad state of affairs—sought to rally support. In the autumn the pages of the Martin-controlled *United
Automobile Worker* carried strong statements by blacks like Frank
Evans, who asserted that the UAW should directly challenge the
discriminatory employment policies of the auto manufacturers,
elect a black to the International Executive Board, and give Negroes greater representation in running the locals.[68] Negroes in
the Unity Caucus argued similarly. Thus Percy Key, a worker at
Cadillac who had been beaten severely by the police in the Federal Screw strike of 1938, and who had recently been elected to
the board of Reuther's West Side Local 174, urged black workers
to join the union, arguing that, if enough did, it would be feasible
to elect a Negro to the International Executive Board.[69] Similarly,
the Unity Caucus's outspoken supporters, LeBron Simmons and
the Detroit NNC, not only backed Martin's opponents but also
argued that a black seat on the executive board would draw Negroes into the UAW.[70] A few weeks later, at a time when Homer
Martin's opponents were assiduously bending every effort to undermine the base he retained in the locals outside of Detroit,[71]
black union leaders from Pontiac, Flint, and Saginaw met to rally
Negroes to the Mortimer-Reuther caucus. Spurred on by speeches
from Detroit's militant left-wingers, Joseph Billups of Rouge Local
600 and Local 281's recording secretary, Paul Kirk, the conferees
denounced Martin and his "tools" William Nowell and Frank
Evans for failing to remedy black grievances, and demanded action
by the International on promotions, seniority, and increased representation in union offices. This gathering was especially significant
because it indicated that highly influential black unionists, such as
William Bowman at Saginaw, Henry Clark at Flint, and Walter
Hardin and Oscar Noble at Pontiac, were now supporting the
Unity faction.[72] Noble was in fact later credited with playing "a

dominant role in holding 10,000 GM workers in the CIO after the Homer Martin split." [73]

Even though the blacks' concerns were not a major consideration in the UAW's bitter power struggle, they were raised at the two conventions which the rival caucuses held in March 1939. Homer Martin's supporters, who met first, took the unprecedented step of creating an at-large seat for blacks on their International Executive Board and electing Frank Evans to that position. [74] This action as well as the appointment of a black as regional director-at-large, encouraged blacks in the opposing caucus to press their demands. Yet even though the majority of the union's leading blacks had sided with the anti-Martin Unity Caucus, they found that its convention gave scant attention to their concerns.

The small group of eight black delegates to this convention introduced several resolutions, but most of them got buried in committee. The proposal occasioning the most serious debate was the one calling for a black member-at-large on the Board. But as Tracy Doll, the president of the Hudson local and member of the International Executive Board, had informed the Detroit NNC shortly before the UAW convention, a black could not be added until an intensive educational campaign had been conducted among the large body of prejudiced whites in the union. Oscar Noble tried to bring the subject to the floor, but the new UAW president, R. J. Thomas, as convention chairman, personally intervened to block discussion. He wanted all to know that a black would be welcome on the board, but he could no more support a specifically designated black seat than a Polish or an Italian seat. Categorically rejecting the blacks' argument that a black seat should be created because the discredited enemy Homer Martin had set up one, he avowed his consistent opposition to segregation—a position he had taken in his votes against retaining the Negro Department. "I don't believe," he said to the applause of the delegates, "that the majority of the Negro people themselves want a 'Jim Crow' car attached to the International Union." Another resolution, aiming to guarantee that all future contracts with auto companies should include an anti-discrimination clause for apprenticeships and promotions, never even reached the floor. On the other hand, with Thomas and his associates recognizing the need for black organizers, especially in any new drive against Ford, the convention readily recommended their employment on the "permanent" organizing staff and their representation on the Ford Organizing Committee.[75]

In the bitter aftermath of these two conventions, Frank Evans, as the leading black in Homer Martin's group, sought to exploit the disappointment of the blacks in the Unity Caucus convention, by reminding them of the white delegates' hearty applause for Thomas as he ruled the discussion of the black seat out of order. However the blacks in the Unity Caucus, which was of course recognized by John L. Lewis and his colleagues as the official CIO union, judiciously refused to make any public criticism. Henry Clark, the man who had introduced the resolution for a black board member, denied that the convention's rejection was proof of any race prejudice; rather he preferred to charge that the continuing job discrimination in the auto factories was due to Homer Martin's failure to act.[76] For their part the white UAW-CIO leaders soon took a few steps to cement ties with the black auto workers and the Negro community spokesmen. R. J. Thomas quickly brought Hardin back to the staff as "General Negro Organizer," and shortly afterwards the two men along with Secretary-Treasurer George Addes hosted a luncheon for black leaders. Those assembled, who included not only UAW supporters such as Diggs and Louis Martin but also conservatives like Wilbur C. Woodson as well (although the NAACP's McClendon was conspicuous by his absence from the list), heard the unionists plead for support, while conceding the existence of discrimination in the plants and admitting that the union faced an important task in educating its white members.[77]

With the split between the two factions irreconcilable, and Martin having taken his supporters into the AFL, a period of competition ensued between the two UAW's, with each side struggling to win NLRB elections and to undermine strikes called by the other.[78] In the most dramatic of these conflicts—the Chrysler lockout and strike of 1939—the role of black workers became crucial when management encouraged a back-to-work movement among its Negro employees at Dodge Main. Yet the strategy failed to defeat the union, and in fact as a result of Chrysler's effort to capitalize on racial antagonisms, the UAW-CIO actually emerged from the struggle with more support in black Detroit than ever before. Significantly in all these ways the course of events in the Chrysler-Dodge strike of 1939 proved to be a dress rehearsal for the far more important Ford strike of 1941.

The labor dispute began when management locked 24,000 workers out of the Dodge Main plant, including its black work force of 1700. The union then struck all of Chrysler's factories in retaliation.[79] With production having thus been completely halted for several weeks, the company finally resorted to desperate tactics. Seeking to capitalize on black alienation from the union, Chrysler officials developed their strategy of a back-to-work movement. The company, as the second largest employer of Negroes in Detroit, had long had a relatively favorable image among blacks, although those working there were of course fully aware of Chrysler's shortcomings. As a prominent black journalist had put it, while a small number of the company's Negro employees were skilled workers, "the diversity of employment there does not at all compare with that given Negroes at Ford's." There was resentment of the narrow range of job opportunities open to blacks, and of how young white foundry workers were rapidly moved up while "the Negro stays right where he is." As one Negro put it, "The company's Jim Crow policy has kept the workers divided for years." The blacks also resented their white fellow-workers and the fact that the union did nothing about the situation. Accordingly the black workers were for the most part cool toward the strike, and a few hundred, motivated by economic need and by what they perceived as union indifference rather than by any illusions about the company's concern for their welfare, participated in the back-to-work movement.[80]

With black workers alone clearly in no position to resume production by themselves, the Chrysler strategy was evidently calculated to break the strike by producing interracial violence and the calling out of the National Guard. In this gambit the corporation's officials apparently operated through various channels. Black leaders in Detroit sympathetic to the UAW-CIO suspected that the Urban League's John Dancy may have played a key role behind the scenes. More sinister was the activity of an all-black "labor union," the National Association of American Workers, organized just a few days before the work stoppage began by an ex-convict and an obscure Baptist preacher, the two of whom, it was charged, actually recruited strikebreakers.[81] Most important, aid for management came from Homer Martin's rump UAW-AFL. Finally Chrysler's officials themselves directly encouraged the strike-breaking.

The back-to-work movement was precipitated on Friday morning, November 24, when sixty blacks, seeking to pick up their paychecks, forced their way through the picket line at Dodge Main. They were met by a barrage of bricks and stones, and in the melee two policemen and six blacks were injured. But most entered the plant, where the foundry superintendent promised to put them to work if they reported again when the weekend was over.[82] That same night, as if synchronizing their activities with Chrysler's, Homer Martin and his associates held what R. J. Thomas denounced as a "Jim Crow Back To Work Meeting," at which Frank Evans was one of those urging the audience to return to the Dodge plant. Convinced of the opposition's hypocrisy, Evans denounced the CIO leaders for "preying on the Negro."[83]

Yet by then Chrysler's strategy was already backfiring. The UAW-CIO was able to charge management with blatantly and callously using blacks to deliberately stir up the explosive racial issue, and Detroit's black leadership, even more than the union, became alarmed at the potential for widespread rioting. The local

at once appealed to Senator Diggs, who promised his full cooperation in discouraging blacks from returning to work.[84] More important, Horace White called together twenty-five prominent local
black spokesmen "in a last minute effort" to prevent the anticipated racial confrontation Monday morning. The participants in the
conference ranged from unionists like Hardin and Key and long-
standing UAW supporters like Louis Martin, to conservatives like
William Peck, Wilbur Woodson, and the attorney and Republican
politician, State Labor Commissioner Charles H. Mahoney.
Present also were two ministers who now became new recruits to
the ranks of militant black supporters of the union—Malcolm
Dade, a recent arrival in Detroit and rector at St. Cyprian's Episcopal Church, and, especially important, Rev. Charles Hill, who
had started his career as Bradby's assistant pastor and had long
served as minister of the popular Hartford Avenue Baptist
Church.[85] Taking the lead, Senator Diggs and Rev. Horace White
voiced "strong resentment" against a corporation so exploitively
callous as to risk the lives of its black employees; since a handful of
Negro workers could not by themselves reopen a large industrial
plant, their presence could only be intended to "invite physical violence and bloodshed." So great was the apprehension of a possible riot that the highly diverse individuals present easily united
behind a public statement announcing their opposition to using
blacks as strikebreakers. Next morning thousands of black church-
goers received leaflets signed by White, Diggs, Louis Martin, and
Hill urging them to shun the back-to-work movement whose high
riot potential would "spell doom to Negro workers in the factories."[86]

Despite these efforts by the union's friends, Chrysler and its
allies were able to recruit a couple hundred blacks, who along with
half a dozen whites gathered several blocks from Dodge Main early
Monday morning. Awaiting them, massed at the entrance to the
plant, were 6000 pickets—virtually all whites—while 1000 policemen sent by apprehensive city authorities formed "a solid wall for
blocks leading to the main gate." Horace White, intercepting the

strikebreakers before they reached the plant, futilely pleaded with them to disperse. He then joined Richard Frankensteen, head of the UAW's Chrysler Division; Samuel Fanroy of Chrysler Local 7, one of the few black workers among the demonstrators; and the leaders of the Dodge Main Local 3, in urging the pickets to refrain from attacking the strikebreakers. Their counsel reenforced the arguments contained in leaflets distributed by the local: the company "is trying to trick us into violence as an excuse to call the State Troops and National Guard to . . . break our strike. . . . Today and tomorrow it may bring a few Negro workers into the plant. Let them through the line. There will be company agents planted in our ranks to provoke us into a battle which might develop into a race riot. . . . DO NOT BE PROVOKED." Catcalls greeted the strikebreakers as they walked into the plant, but the pickets, undoubtedly as much restrained by the presence of the police as by the advice of Frankensteen and White, made no other attempt to intervene. That night Homer Martin, seeking to augment the back-to-work movement, held another mass meeting, and the following morning about 430 blacks with a sprinkling of whites again marched in a body into Dodge Main, amidst the jeers of thousands of pickets.[87]

To the relief of both the union and the black leaders, violence had been averted again, and late in the day James F. Dewey, federal labor conciliator, was able to arrange a pact that ended the strike.[88] How much the failure of the strikebreaking effort had encouraged the company to compromise at the bargaining table is unknown. But if, as the UAW charged, management's aim had been to trigger a race riot to break the strike, clearly the union officials, aided by black community leaders, had forestalled such a denouement. Even the pro-industry Detroit *Tribune* refused to throw its weight behind the back-to-work movement, while anti-union spokesmen such as Rev. Robert Bradby were completely silent. Indeed, for its part, the UAW was deeply appreciative of the support of the black leaders. Even though only a small number of blacks were willing to walk the picket line, and a few hundred actually crossed it, the role of the black leaders was symbolically significant. Leading black unionists publicly thanked not only the UAW's sympathizers but also people like Woodson, Mahoney, and even James McClendon of the NAACP. And the *United Automobile Worker* singled out for special praise the four signers of the leaflet and particularly Horace White for "invaluable work" in defeating the AFL back-to-work movement.[89]

In fact, although the strike did not mark the inauguration of an intensified effort to recruit blacks under the UAW's banner, it had long-range significance precisely because it marked an important advance in the growing ties between the UAW and black community leadership. The two influential ministers, Dade and Hill, were valuable additions to the ranks of the union's supporters. More important, foreshadowing developments in the Ford strike of 1941, the labor dispute at Dodge Main indicated that the UAW-AFL still posed a serious threat which an employer could dangerously exploit, but it also revealed that, with the possibility of massive interracial violence always simmering not far beneath the surface, the UAW-CIO could mobilize support even from conservative elements in the black community.

### 4

UAW-CIO leaders knew that the union's place in the auto industry would be insecure until Ford was forced to sign a collective bargaining agreement, and they believed that this could not be accomplished without substantial support from the company's black employees. Yet in the year following the Chrysler strike, despite all the apprehension that the black strikebreakers had generated at Dodge Main, and despite the help rendered on that occasion by black civic leaders, the UAW had done little about the grievances of the black workers. Discrimination on the job remained essentially unchanged; much was left undone on the touchy issue of black participation in union social functions; and only slight improvement was registered in the number of blacks holding elective and staff positions in the UAW.

Two things, however, had been accomplished since the victory of the Unity Caucus in the spring of 1939. Complaints ceased about wage differentials between whites and blacks doing the same work—a practice that had existed in some plants.[90] Secondly, in some of its new contracts the UAW obtained clauses barring racial discrimination in seniority and promotion. Thus the contract signed with Chrysler after the 1939 strike provided that "Rank on the seniority list shall not be affected by the race . . . of the employee." Certain smaller foundries had contracts that even more specifically stated, "When new jobs are created or vacancies occur, the oldest employee in point of service regardless of race, creed or color shall be given preference in filling such new job or vacancy so far as practical and consistent with proper ability to perform the service required." Yet most UAW contracts—including the new one signed with General Motors in 1940—failed to include this protective clause.[91] Moreover, regardless of the contract's language, the union still felt unable to correct managerial discrimination in hiring new workers, and companies continued to pass over high-seniority blacks for promotions on the claim of "insufficient" skill or ability. Even the clause in the Chrysler agreement was not followed by noticeable improvement in opportunities open to blacks—a fact that would fuel Negro workers' continued dissatisfaction with the union there.[92] Early in 1941 certain influential East Side locals, who were at the time actively assisting recruiting efforts in the Ford drive, made demands for the inclusion of a nondiscrimination clause in the new contracts about to be negotiated with GM. Secretary-treasurer George Addes publicly noted the validity of the blacks' complaints: "This discrimination does exist as a [GM] company policy. It is time, I believe, that we should begin to educate corporations in the spirit of the UAW's constitutional guarantee against discrimination. . . . We should also commence to educate our membership."[93] Unfortunately remedial action did not follow.*

Given GM's past history, the clause's omission was scarcely surprising. Yet the UAW's inability to require its inclusion only reenforced the skepticism of Ford's black workers about the union's intentions. The fact was that, although UAW leaders still blamed the industrialists, as Addes had conceded the union faced such serious problems with its white members that it was unwilling or unable to press the issue forcefully in most of its contractual negotiations. Moreover, at the 1940 UAW convention, a resolution calling for guarantees of black inclusion in training programs for skilled jobs received scant attention. As a well-informed observer stated about this time: "The matter of promotions for Negro workers is the toughest problem the union is facing. There is a very strong feeling among the white workers whenever this issue comes up. I've heard them talk about it and I know. White workers have told me, 'I'll be g-damned if I'll work with a g-damned nigger.' Even union officials who would like to see Negroes get the promotions they deserve are afraid to handle the issue. . . . Most union officials want to organize the Negro because they know he is a potential scab as long as he is unorganized, but many officials who sincerely think the Negro should get an even break are afraid to take a stand on promotions. The union isn't strong enough yet."[94]

By 1940 the situation in respect to black participation in social

---

* It is likely that this interest on the part of Addes and his allies in the Communist-oriented locals mentioned represented in part an attempt to embarrass Walter Reuther. The *Daily Worker*, in reporting the meeting of GM union leaders at which Addes made his remarks, noted the total lack of black delegates at the gathering. (*Daily Worker*, Feb. 10, 1941.) The hostility between the two groups was so marked at this point that there were complaints of the Communists circulating a disruptive leaflet at the Rouge plant attacking Thomas and Reuther at the height of the Ford Organizing Drive. (*Michigan Labor Leader*, March 14, 1941, and *ibid.*, August 1, 1941, saying Eddie Levinson had been forced out of the editorship of the *United Automobile Worker* because he had editorially attacked the leaflet.) Interestingly enough, the Packard local, where Addes had his base, was deeply infected with anti-black sentiment, as events during the war would show.

affairs was improving to some extent, and several locals with large black memberships conducted fully integrated dances and other social functions which Negroes attended freely. In the case of Briggs Local 212, for example, which had been compelled in the early years to cancel several social affairs because of discrimination by white proprietors and the resentment of white members of the locals, large numbers of blacks now freely attended the social functions. Yet, among the workers in most factories, particularly those with a large proportion of southern whites, the subject continued to be a delicate matter, and "full Negro participation is found in relatively few locals." In some locals with a substantial number of Negro workers, their presence had actually postponed the adoption of a well-rounded social program. The continued reluctance of many hotels, dance halls, and restaurants to accept black patronage did not, of course, help matters. Some of the eateries near the auto factories, heavily patronized by the white rank and file, refused to serve blacks; and even after winning the Ford strike in 1941, Local 600 had to cancel its "Victory Boat Ride" because the steamship company would not allow Negroes on board. The problem of public accommodations also arose at the UAW's 1940 convention in St. Louis, where black delegates found themselves barred from eating and sleeping at the hotels. The local arrangements committee had provided for separate accommodations in the black ghetto, and only after intensive protests from the blacks were they finally accorded service at the headquarters' hotel dining room. Their protests also received a vigorous airing on the convention floor, which passed a resolution promising that in the future, black delegates would receive the same treatment as whites.[95]

The situation regarding black representation in union offices was comparable. Thus the number of elective positions held by blacks in the locals gradually rose, not only as stewards in majority black departments, but in higher offices for which white workers were the majority constituency as well. Yet the blacks' representation in office remained tiny in proportion to their numbers in the UAW. By 1940 Negroes were serving as presidents of three locals (although all of them were outside of Detroit): William Neal, president of Local 429, New Haven, Michigan; Albert Shed, president of Local 490, Grand Rapids; and William Sneed, still head of Local 543, Chicago. At the same time at least three blacks were vice-presidents of Detroit locals—Luke Fennell at the Budd Wheel Local 306; Hodges Mason at Bohn Aluminum Local 208, and Nelson Merrill, elected to that position in Midland Steel Local 410 early in the year.[96] Occasionally also a black would be elected as secretary of a local—in 1939 Mauley Jefferson was financial secretary of Local 338, Jamestown, New York; and Paul Kirk, recording secretary of Local 281, Detroit; two years later union leaders boasted of secretary William Powell in the local serving the GM transmission plant at Saginaw, where there were only a handful of blacks employed.[97] There were cases, too, where Negroes were elected to the executive board of overwhelmingly white locals—such as William Slaughter in Local 235 in Detroit, and Percy Key, a worker at Cadillac in West Side Local 174, where Alex Hatcher, also of Cadillac, had been elected to the bargaining committee in 1938. Pontiac Local 653, with Oscar Noble and Isaac Smart on the bargaining committee, and Angelo White, a member of the publicity committee, remained something of a model of black participation. Oscar Oden continued to serve on the bargaining committee of Local 410; and the victorious CIO faction swept into office in that local early in 1940 included a black vice-president. Most outstanding of all was Bohn Aluminum and Brass Local 208, where as early as 1938, James Landfair had been elected chairman of the plant committee of Plant No. 3. Two years later not only was Hodges Mason the local's vice-president, but from the seven Bohn plants in Detroit were elected two black plant chairmen, two trustees, and five of the thirty plant stewards. Such participation was, of course, feasible only when Negroes formed a very high proportion of the work force—as they did at Bohn and Midland, where they constituted a quarter or more of the employees at the time. Elsewhere, even at a company like Briggs, where over one-tenth of the workers were Negro, and where the local was regarded as unusually responsive to their aspirations, black office-holding remained low. Other than several black stewards at the largely black Mack Avenue plant, the one Negro official was Leonard Newman, who served on the 26-man executive board beginning in 1939.[98]

The growing number of black officeholders in a few locals notwithstanding, overall the UAW did not convey to blacks the impression that it was aggressively encouraging black membership and participation. This may have stemmed in part at least from a feeling that "A Negro program publicized as such would serve to strengthen rather than weaken the barrier between the races." Whatever the reason, the International leadership itself proved hesitant in its response to reiterated urgings from black unionists that the number of black organizers be raised and that the "Negro Department" be reconstituted. During this period there were only three full-time black organizers—Hardin, Billups, and Key.[99]* Blacks in fact complained about the flouting of the 1939 convention resolution calling for expansion of the black organizing staff, as well as resolutions of the 1940 convention reaffirming this and mandating explicitly the formation of a Negro Department.[100]

This situation regarding the number of black officials only reinforced the alienation stemming from discrimination in jobs and social affairs. Accordingly for their part blacks were still proving to be reluctant joiners. A 1940 survey revealed that in plants organized by the UAW about three-fourths of the white workers were members, but only slightly more than half of the blacks—a record scarcely, if any, better than three years earlier. Blacks were more likely to be delinquent in paying their dues and less faithful than rank-and-file whites about coming to union meetings. In February 1940 R. J. Thomas publicly complained of the unsatisfactory black attendance in his old Chrysler local.[101] Similarly, blacks not feeling fully accepted proved harder than whites to mobilize for service to the union. Although on occasion black pickets were prominent, as

---

* William Bowman was one of two part-time organizers.

during the 1939 strikes at Briggs and General Motors, as Bailer observed: "Though colored members rarely refuse to obey orders to strike, it is more difficult to persuade them to engage in picketing, participate in flying squadrons, work in soup kitchens, collect union contributions, and to shoulder the numerous other responsibilities placed upon members in times of crisis."[102]

Negro union officials, like their white counterparts, were very disturbed at what they regarded as their fellow blacks' defeatist attitude, even where justified by the insensitive actions of white unionists. Hardin confided to one researcher, "I can't understand why Negroes are hesitant about going in when the doors to unions are open to them for the first time in 30 years." Convinced that this attitude had been largely responsible for the UAW's failure to push the battle against job discrimination, believing that black participation in union affairs would bring far-reaching changes in UAW policies, and fearful that blacks might lose out in the long run if they remained lukewarm or indifferent to the union, Hardin criticized black leaders who discouraged union activity on the part of Negro workers. Similarly, a year earlier Percy Key had warned that "hard as it might be for the Negro auto worker to maintain his worker's economic equilibrium in the union, it would be much harder for him to be sure of a decent job if he should persist in staying out." As Luke Fennell and Hodges Mason explained: "You can't expect that the enmities and discrimination of generations can be overcome in four years. But they are being lived down . . . in the true spirit of democracy."[103]

On the other hand, where blacks formed a high proportion of the work force and where the UAW local's leadership was characterized by skill and foresight, spirited black participation resulted. Thus at the Bohn Company, James Landfair was chosen to run for the Plant No. 3 chairmanship and for membership on the bargaining committee, in a deliberate effort to increase black involvement. Although in this case virtually all the blacks in the plant were union members, only a dozen came out to the meeting at which the election was held. His victory, however, encouraged

Negro participation, and the following year nearly half the blacks in the plant voted when he ran successfully for reelection.[104] Subsequently, once the Ford strike had been won, astute white leaders at the River Rouge Local 600 took care that blacks were significantly represented in the inner circle of the local's leadership.

In the end all these ambiguities reenforced the skepticism toward the union that was so pervasive among Ford's black workers, who were in any event reluctant to antagonize a management that had afforded them unusual job opportunities. A small minority of the blacks working at the Rouge plant were devoted and active UAW members, but basically, as the union put its new Ford drive into high gear late in 1940, it faced a difficult uphill fight for black support.

## 5

Following the 1939 Chrysler strike, the union appeared no more aggressive in reenforcing its appeal to black community leaders than in remedying the grievances of the black workers. Perhaps there was little practical that they could do until a new crisis galvanized labor and blacks alike into action and forced a realignment. Yet beneath the surface significant changes were occurring, even though these were being generated by stirrings within the black community itself rather than by any action that the union took. With both Senator Diggs and the more progressive members of the black professional class already the UAW-CIO's firm supporters, the NAACP, broadly based as it was across a wide spectrum of the black community, now became the major arena for further changes in sentiment among Detroit Negroes.

The low profile that the Detroit NAACP had maintained in the crisis surrounding the Chrysler strike was in keeping with the pro-company sympathies of many of its most active members and with its general posture of ignoring industrial employment issues. Now the largest and wealthiest NAACP affiliate in the country, and thereby the branch that was the most substantial contributor to the Association's national office, the Detroit NAACP achieved a membership of 2400 in the spring of 1937, nearly 3300 the following year, and over 6000 by the end of 1939.[105] The prominent physician James J. McClendon, a native Georgian who had graduated from Atlanta University and Meharry Medical College, was the most successful recruiter in the 1937 membership drive, and was rewarded with the branch presidency at the end of the year.[106] In an organization where the local unit's most important single function was to conduct annual membership drives to finance the national program, influence accrued to those most effective in securing members. Thus the conservative couple, Dr. and Mrs. W. A. Thompson, who headed the winning team in the 1939 drive, were numbered among the most powerful of the inner circle of leaders.[107]

McClendon, who was to preside over the branch for several years, announced a militant program at the start of his first term in office, but his only allusion to employment problems was a promise to press for jobs in the city government. The Detroit NAACP tackled discrimination in public welfare and the WPA, police brutality, exclusion from hotels, theaters, and restaurants.[108] But the one occasion when the Detroit NAACP concerned itself with labor unions, it "bitterly assailed" the CIO-affiliated Dairy Workers Union for failing to protect a black milk-driver fired by his employer. Essentially it continued to ignore the UAW. Epitomizing McClendon's indifference if not hostility toward labor unions was his role as chairman of a committee that investigated the dubious activities of the pro-Chrysler "labor union," the National Association of American Workers. This inquiry was sponsored by the Booker T. Washington Trade Association, then headed by Carlton Gaines, the realtor and NAACP board member. The NAAW, organizing workers in the taverns and eating places in the black ghetto, had challenged a bona fide trade union, the interracial Hotel and Restaurant Employees Alliance. The McClendon group, which included several other prominent NAACP leaders, issued a report declaring the NAAW a legitimate labor organization, amidst a chorus of criticism from black trade unionists, who charged that it actually signed sweetheart contracts with employers.[109]

On the other hand, the astute McClendon consciously sought a broad base for the NAACP branch in the black community. In 1937 the executive board included not only people like the Thompsons (Mrs. Mamie Thompson being treasurer), conservative businessmen Louis Blount and Carlton Gaines, and YMCA Secretary Wilbur Woodson but also the Reverends Malcolm Dade and Horace White, and one black UAW member, Prince Clark. Moreover, attorney Robert Evans, elected branch secretary in 1938, was a prominent member of the local NNC, in whose founding he had played a leading role.[110] Quite naturally the presence of a few pro-labor people on the Board helped the branch in membership campaigns, despite the conservative tilt of its policies. Thus the UAW's ally, the Michigan *Chronicle,* while giving warm support to the branch's 1939 membership drive, simultaneously complained that unfortunately the Detroit NAACP had often acted as "a mere club of the so-called upper crust of the town, and the dispossessed masses among us have been made to feel ill at ease in the presence of 'superior' ex-slaves. In industrial Detroit . . . the NAACP is a mass organization which should be as quick to defend a jim-crowed ditch-digger as a jim-crowed doctor."[111]

Moreover the branch's youth councils, operating with some independence of the adults, were already displaying a concern in labor matters and a sympathetic attitude toward interracial unionism. Since 1936, when the national office had undertaken a vigorous program of expanding its work among young blacks, the Detroit youth councils had become the most active in the country. By 1938 the Motor City boasted a half-dozen such units in as many black neighborhoods, coordinated under a Central Youth Committee by the dynamic Gloster Current, future NAACP national director of branches. They consisted of college students and workers in their early twenties, as well as some high school youths; their most outstanding leader was West Side Council president Horace Sheffield, who had followed his father into the Ford River Rouge foundry while attending college part-time.[112]

At first the principal activity of these youth councils was to conduct public forums, where a wide range of issues were debated. As early as the spring of 1938 an interest in unionism was evident; one public debate was on the topic "Resolved That Negroes Should Join Labor Unions." In the summer they were launching a "Job Opportunities Campaign," picketing and boycotting several white-owned ghetto stores that refused to hire blacks. By the next spring they had secured thirty-four jobs in this way.[113] In mounting their programs the youths chose projects and displayed an autonomy that rankled a number of the influential adult leaders. Undoubtedly a person like Horace Sheffield was irritating to some adults because of his vigorous support for organized labor, as when he and other youth council members helped a union organize a Neisner variety store.[114]

As Gloster Current reported in the official magazine of the NAACP, "The Detroit senior branch for a while looked askance at youth council activity. Ofttimes the attitudes of the seniors was 'quell and control the youth councils lest they wreck the association.'" McClendon, the skillful leader who always retained the youths' respect, appointed a special committee of inquiry in 1939 which recommended that the adult branch give the councils official representation on the executive board. Although the suggestion was accepted, the problem was by no means settled, and tensions would explode again less than two years later. Complaining to the NAACP's National Youth Director in February 1941, council leaders noted that on several occasions the senior branch either forbade outright or refused to assist projects involving picketing, petition-signing, or other militant forms of protest. "Are we expected," inquired one youth, "to be merely an agency through which money can be collected for the National office, or can we actually do something about the problems which face us daily?"[115] Given the youths' spirit and the challenge that the councils posed for the more conservative elders, they provided an important thrust that eventually pushed the adult branch into cooperation with the UAW during the Ford strike of 1941.

# 6

The effort to organize Ford was renewed in earnest in September 1940 when John L. Lewis sent in CIO official Michael Widman to head the drive. Appeals to blacks, while not entirely neglected during the pervious months,[116] were stepped up at year's end. Certain locals were particularly active in helping recruit Rouge workers: Briggs Local 212 and especially three influential Communist-oriented East Side locals—Plymouth Local 51, Bohn Aluminum Local 208, and the Amalgamated Tool and Die Workers Local 155—which established a joint Negro organizing committee headed by Paul Kirk.[117] More important were the seven salaried black organizers that by March had been added to Widman's staff. Two were Ford foundry workers, Joseph Billups and plant committeeman Veal Clough, who had earlier been fired for their union activity. From Briggs Local 212 came steward Leon Bates and from Chrysler Local 7 came one of its early black members, John Conyers; while William Bowman, who had been working as part-time organizer, was dispatched from Saginaw to work among Detroit's Negro ministers.[118]*

Directing this operation, however, was a white man, the former president of Briggs Local 212, Emil Mazey. Having first achieved prominence for his brilliant organizational work at Briggs during the sit-down strikes, the youthful Mazey, supported by the company's numerous black workers, had by the end of 1937 ousted the prejudiced white Southerner who was the local's first president. Thereafter under his leadership Local 212 developed an unusually favorable reputation among black workers. It had not only eliminated discrimination at social functions and from the very begin-

---

* In addition Johnson Buchanan and James Allen came from local 599 in Flint. Bates would become a long-time member of the salaried staff. (See *UAW*, Dec. 16, 1944, and *Chronicle*, Feb. 23, 1957.)

ning included a black man on its board of trustees, but also been the first to employ a Negro office secretary (appointed over the opposition of the white secretaries) and successfully fought to abolish racial pay differentials for equal work. In the view of Mazey, a Socialist, it was important for blacks, exploited by employers in the same way as white workers, to join and participate actively in the union; but equally essential was the reeducation of the biased white workers and the abolition of racial discrimination.[119] Thus Mazey, assigned to the Ford drive following his unsuccessful bid for reelection to the Briggs Local's presidency, was from the UAW leaders' perspective a logical choice to direct the organizing efforts among the Ford company's Negro employees. However, the black organizers, resentful that a Negro had not been placed in charge, complained to the International Executive Board. Mazey was retained as "coordinator," but Walter Hardin was hurriedly transferred from a Chicago assignment and installed as the new director of Negro organizational activities at Ford.[120] Finally Widman hired two black secretaries and secured from the CIO the services of Christopher C. Alston to edit the special Negro edition of *Ford Facts.*[121] Alston, a young radical with warm contacts in the old Auto Workers Union, who had worked at Briggs in his youth had subsequently spent some time in the South as an organizer for the CIO steel and tobacco workers organizing committees. His recently published pamphlet, *Henry Ford and the Negro People,* denounced the auto magnate as a hypocritical racist operating behind a façade of benevolent philanthropy.[122]

The black UAW-CIO organizers made innumerable personal contacts with Rouge employees; because of the harassment by Ford's Service Department, these were conducted mostly in workers' homes rather than around the plant. Both the UAW-CIO and the rival UAW-AFL, which had mounted its own drive, found organizing the company's Negro employees particularly difficult. The fact was that the combination of Ford philanthropy, company intimidation, and historic black skepticism of white-dominated unions continued to inhibit the recruitment of black workers, and only a small number were willing to identify with either labor organization. As Hodges Mason put it, amidst the protests over the failure to include an anti-discrimination clause in the new GM contract, "The Negro has a long history of discrimination by the AFL, and he is not yet convinced that such discrimination will not be continued by the CIO." For its part the company, fully aware that blacks were more resistant toward union overtures than any other ethnic group, recruited perhaps as many as two thousand unemployed Negroes, including some boxers and street-fighters, for use as strikebreakers. Thus by the end of March Ford had the largest black work force in its history, numbering some 14,000—about one-sixth of the Rouge plant's employees—and the foundry became so overcrowded that many workers did little more than loll about.[123]

Some black Ford employees, it is true, did militantly back the UAW-CIO. Besides organizers Billups and Clough, the list included NAACP youth council leader, Horace Sheffield, who worked in the foundry; Tanner Perry, chief steward in the Pressed Steel Department, where blacks, though numerous, formed only ten percent of the work force; Al Johnson, a crane operator who was elected chairman of the glass plant bargaining committee by an overwhelming white majority shortly before the strike; and Shelton Tappes, chairman of the Foundry Building bargaining committee, who in addition served on the negotiating committee during the strike.[124] A somewhat larger group vigorously backed Henry Ford. But most of the company's black employees held themselves aloof from what looked like another white man's battle. All in all the union faced an uphill struggle in recruiting blacks. NAACP assistant secretary, Roy Wilkins, reported that on the eve of the Ford strike informed estimates indicated that about one-half of the white workers had joined the UAW-CIO but only one-fourth of the blacks.[125]

Both sides simultaneously sought to strengthen their ties among black leaders and spokesmen. Predictably pro-Ford sentiment remained strongest at the Urban League (which in recent years had been referring some workers to the company) and among the ministers. Father Daniel had died in 1939, but men like Bradby were still vigorously behind Ford. Donald Marshall left no stones unturned to hold the preachers in line. In December 1940 he fruitlessly advised Charles Hill against allowing a UAW-sponsored meeting at his church, and even threatened to "fire every Negro in the neighborhood" if it were held. A month later three hundred civic and religious leaders, including nearly every black minister in the city, attended a banquet hosted by Donald Marshall and Willis Ward. Marshall contrasted Henry Ford's benevolences with the animosities of "foreign-born" workers who purportedly dominated the union and excluded blacks from skilled jobs, and he bluntly informed the ministers that their future depended on the company's victory. Other speakers included John Dancy and Rev. Robert Bradby, who declared, "If Henry Ford hires one colored for every ten whites, I am for him first, last, and always. It will be a sad day for us if the Ford Company changes its policy." Not surprisingly such efforts paid off. Two days before the Ford walkout began, the Interdenominational Ministers Alliance publicly endorsed Henry Ford's position.[126]

The UAW also renewed its campaign in the black community. Of course, old union friends like Louis Martin, Charles Diggs, Horace White, and the National Negro Congress maintained their staunch backing. Indeed early in 1941 the NNC's influence in the black community was strengthened by the election of Charles Hill as president of the Congress's Michigan Division[127]—an indication of the radicalization undergone by Bradby's former assistant pastor since joining the ranks of the UAW supporters in the Chrysler strike of 1939. In a widely published friendly exchange with Father Malcolm Dade, both R. J. Thomas and Michael Widman tried to discredit widespread rumors that blacks would lose their skilled jobs if the UAW won recognition from Ford. Using the columns of the Michigan *Chronicle* and Detroit *Tribune*, the two denounced Marshall's propaganda and promised that black interests would be protected. Thomas conceded that "The officers of this International union realize full well the education task they face" among the white workers, but he pledged that the UAW would "establish equality on jobs between the Negroes and the whites."[128]

Such assurances, combined with the growing likelihood of a UAW victory, had their effect. As the union issue became more hotly debated, increasing numbers of the black bourgeoisie began wavering in their loyalty to the company. Some were now arguing that it was "foolish to feel that Negro workers were sufficiently indebted to Henry Ford to fight white labor for him." James J. McClendon, himself uncommitted on the matter, now presided over a highly divided NAACP board, in which sentiment was tilting away from Ford and toward the UAW. At one extreme on the branch executive board was the school administrator Ernest Marshall, who—espousing the viewpoint of conservatives like the Thompsons—was a featured speaker at the banquet hosted by Donald Marshall and Willis Ward. At the other extreme was the branch secretary, Robert Evans, who, not unexpectedly in view of his long connection with the NNC, announced when the strike broke out that, since labor was bound to triumph, the failure to back the UAW would "plague us for twenty years." But what was really significant was that McClendon's predecessor as NAACP president, insurance company executive Louis Blount, had so far departed from his former anti-labor position that he was now "unequivocal on behalf of organizing by the Union." Blount's close associate in the Booker T. Washington Trade Association, the group's president, Carlton Gaines, was "on the fence," and the Detroit *Tribune* studiously avoided taking sides. Certain preachers, above all else fearful that a major riot might erupt, began counseling neutrality in the Ford conflict.[129]

Even in the Detroit Urban League two black board members had become supporters of the UAW—Geraldine Bledsoe and Beulah Whitby. Both, members of Horace White's Plymouth Congregational Church, were prominent in the black community's white-collar elite. Mrs. Bledsoe, a graduate of Howard University and wife of attorney Harold Bledsoe, a prominent Negro Democratic leader and political ally of Diggs ever since the election of 1932, was a placement officer in the Michigan Unemployment Commission and would become state supervisor of Negro placement in October 1941. Mrs. Whitby, wife of a leading dentist, graduate of Oberlin College and the University of Chicago School of Social Work, was the top-ranking black social worker in the city's welfare department. Given the prestige of their jobs, and the active role they played in black Detroit's civic life, their voice at the Urban League, though that of a distinct minority, was significant.[130]

Thus on the eve of the strike, the UAW-CIO had made a degree of progress in swinging sentiment among both black workers and community spokesmen over to its side. Yet the bulk of Detroit Negroes remained skeptical of the union, and to a considerable extent what it had achieved was a prudent neutrality and an erosion of the traditional loyalty toward Ford, rather than genuine support for the United Automobile Workers.

When the strike began spontaneously on the night of April 1, union leaders were justifiably worried about what the black Ford employees would do. Nearly all of the Negro workers did leave the factory with the whites, and most refused to cross the picket line; yet some men did remain in the foundry, and early the next morning before the UAW had cordoned off the area, hundreds more bypassed the barricades and made their way inside the gates. Throughout the morning the company broadcast radio appeals that the factory was open to those wishing to work, while inside the plant foremen held out promises of generous pay to those who remained. All told, along with the approximately 300 whites, mainly members of the Service Department, it would appear that between 1500 and 2500 blacks remained in the Rouge.* Since

* The estimates of the number of men inside the plant varied considerably for several reasons: sketchy information available to reporters, contradictory statements of the union and management, and changes over time as the strike progressed. Thus after hundreds of blacks withdrew later in the afternoon of April 2, the number

many of these men had only recently been hired loyalty to Ford probably played little part in their decision to work. Rather they were lured by promises of high pay, and by indifference, if not hostility, to the white unionists. Thus one man telephoned Rev. Horace White to say, "I know I am doing the wrong thing but I haven't had a job for a long time. I'm getting $15 a day and something to eat." The head usher in White's church, a cook at the plant, called him to explain: "I know you're mad at me. But I'm getting $25 a day. Mr. Bennett has promised the colored boys he's going to take care of them—union or no union."[131] Besides such inducements, the Service Department exploited the strikebreakers' fears of the white unionists, warning that angry pickets would beat up anybody who left the plant.[132]

As the national NAACP charged, Ford had deliberately injected the race issue by utilizing blacks as strikebreakers. The union and its sympathizers believed that the company's strategy—like Chrysler's in the 1939 back-to-work movement—was to provoke interracial violence and thus force the governor to break the strike with state troops.[133] The corporation's tactics on that first morning, April 2, lent credence to these suspicions when the strikebreakers were sent out twice to smash the picket lines. According to a local daily, "Iron bolts and nuts flew through the air in a wholesale barrage from the factory roof, while several hundred Negroes with steel bars and knives charged out of the main gate, No. 4 at the Rouge plant. . . . The men poured out of the gates both at ground level and on the overpass and began pelting the strikers, who picked up the missiles and threw them back. As a result of the wild melee, more than a score of pickets were treated at the union's

remaining in the Rouge declined to somewhere between 800 and 1500, while thereafter the figure dropped slightly as individuals trickled out from day to day. It should also be noted that at all times there were some UAW members in the plant sent by the union for necessary maintenance work such as keeping the furnaces going. Contemporary sources all noted that most of the strikebreakers were Negroes. (*Free Press*, April 3, 4, 9, 1941; *News*, April 5, 6, 7, 9, 1941; *Tribune*, April 5, 1941; Walter White's handwritten notes, April 7, 1941, NAACP Ford Strike File; Dancy to Eugene Kinckle Jones, April 9, 1941, DUL Box 4.)

field hospital. Both times the attackers, mainly black, were re-
pulsed by the pickets."[134] Organizer John Conyers was among the
unionists seriously injured in the violence, yet the fact that at this
stage only small numbers of blacks were among the thousands on
the picket line[135]* reenforced the tendency to perceive these
clashes as racial conflicts which might erupt into a race riot.

The company's plans to encourage a back-to-work movement
through the UAW-AFL only heightened the racial tensions.
Homer Martin had been hurriedly hired as an AFL national representative, Frank Evans was recalled to Detroit, and a black
foundry worker was installed as assistant director of organization in
the AFL Ford drive. At a mass meeting on the night of April 2,
around 3,000 Ford workers, mostly blacks, heard Donald Marshall
and Homer Martin urge them to return to their jobs. This movement collapsed largely because Martin's reputation as a tool of
Ford officials made him such an embarrassment that within forty-
eight hours the Wayne County AFL Council forced Federation
president, William Green, to dismiss him. But at first the UAW-
AFL's agitation intensified the fears of serious racial polarization.
The liberal and unabashedly pro-UAW New York daily, *PM*, observed that the predominance of blacks at Martin's mass meeting
revealed "one of the most ugly overtones of the strike. . . . It is
perfectly clear that Ford officials hope to accentuate the breach
now [between black and whites], and CIO leaders are desperately
trying to stem it before it reaches perilous heights."[136]

UAW-CIO leaders were deeply concerned about the racial animosity engendered by the black strikebreakers, although Walter
White perceptively observed that they "were less disturbed by the
number of Negroes who distrusted the union rather than by fear
that rioting would force the governor to call out the troops."[137] Indeed, getting the blacks out of the Rouge was a major objective of

---

* The *Daily Worker*, which gave low estimates of the number of strikebreakers, was
the only contemporary source to maintain that there were always large numbers of
blacks on the picket lines, and to picture the black workers at Ford as wholeheartedly supporting the strike. (*Daily Worker*, April 3, 5, 6, 7, 1941).

the union throughout the strike. To this end the UAW promptly
appealed directly to the strikebreakers; mounted a propaganda
campaign aimed at Ford workers and their families; and cooperating closely with the union's Negro friends, mobilized black community leadership to back its efforts.

Louis Martin was quickly prevailed upon to invite a large cross-
section of the city's Negro leadership to a luncheon to be held the
next day to hear the UAW's plea for help. Then during the afternoon of the 2nd, when the neutral state police were replacing the
anti-union Dearborn law officers outside the plant gates, the UAW
was able to take advantage of the situation to get many of the
blacks to leave. To the strikebreakers peering through the fence at
the scene, Widman shouted: " 'Come on, you fellows. You haven't
anything to be afraid of.' After some hesitation some 800 to 1,000
of the men, mostly Negroes, marched out. . . . 'That's the spirit,'
Widman called after them."[138] About the same time UAW secretary-treasurer George Addes was conferring with Charles Hill,
Horace White, and a few other black clergymen, and afterwards
the union issued a press release designed to reassure the Negro
community. Making it clear that the UAW held the Ford Motor
Company, not the blacks, responsible for the "crime" of strikebreaking, the statement expressed appreciation for the "overwhelming majority of Negroes" who had left the plant, and announced that the UAW-CIO "permits no racial discrimination
within its ranks." Not only were blacks on the UAW staff, but also
"Every Negro knows that by the principle of seniority the job of
every worker is safeguarded regardless of any discrimination the
management may try to exercise." Meanwhile the union's publicity
department circulated similar skillfully worded handouts addressed
"To All Negro Ford Workers." Emphasizing the concrete benefits
the union had brought Negro workers in the form of equal pay for
equal work, higher wages, and better job security, and pointing to
the examples of black participation as officers in the locals, the leaflets denounced Ford's collaboration with the AFL. "The Negro
people *must not* allow the company to use them as strikebreakers.

They must demonstrate to the world that they recognize the fact that the interests of Negro workers are the same as the interests of white workers." [139]

Even though a large body of strikebreakers had responded to Widman's appeals and left the Rouge, a thousand or more still remained in the plant, and with Homer Martin and the UAW-AFL encouraging others to return to work, the situation on the night of April 2 was exceedingly volatile. At this juncture Horace Sheffield brought the NAACP Detroit youth councils into action, providing dramatic support of the union's efforts to empty the Rouge and defuse the mounting racial hostility.

Sheffield, without consulting McClendon or the adult branch's executive board, had secured a UAW-CIO sound car, and at a meeting at midnight April 2 the youths ratified his plan to broadcast appeals in the name of the NAACP urging the black strikebreakers to leave the plant. [140]* This decision came none too soon. Early the following morning (April 3), four hundred strikebreakers, mostly black, "armed with five pound tractor tie rods, heavy iron pipe, and hammers," again charged out of the factory in "another serious battle." Several pickets were injured before the attackers were forced back into the plant. Then somewhat later another dozen men were wounded when angry pickets attacked a group of

---

*Though the national NAACP press release later stated that this was a project of both the adult branch and the youth groups, such was almost certainly not the case. (See NAACP press release, April 5, 1941, NAACP Ford Strike File.) Sheffield in his interview firmly stated that the youth initiated the project and carried it out without prior consultation with the adults, and this fits what we know of the relations between the youth and adults at that time. Interestingly, however, Walter White reported in a memorandum written a few days afterward, "Det. Br. paid $6.04 for sound truck." (Walter White, untitled handwritten memorandum [April 7, 1941] marked "Filed 6-3-41," NAACP Ford Strike File.) Very likely he had punctiliously insisted that the Detroit NAACP pay for the use of the sound truck to allay any possible criticism that the NAACP was acting as the UAW's agent. Afterwards in the *Crisis* it was reported that both the youth groups and senior branch "operated sound trucks urging Negro workers not to be strikebreakers." (*Crisis* 48 (May 1941):171), but the picture of the sound truck in the same issue clearly bore the sign "Youth Council National Association for the Advancement of Colored People." (*Ibid.*, p. 161.)

blacks who had driven by, taunting the strikers.[141] It was shortly after this incident that the NAACP youth councils' sound truck, driven by Sheffield, appeared. Circling the Rouge plant several times and then driving through black residential and business neighborhoods, the youths urged Negroes not to "fall for that Homer Martin–A.F. of L. stuff," and let themselves "be used to foment trouble that will affect every colored person in Detroit." While the appeal failed to persuade the strikebreakers to leave the factory, the youth councils undoubtedly helped to undermine Homer Martin's back-to-work campaign, and must have done much to deflect the rising antagonism among the white workers. The UAW quickly publicized the event in order to advance its cause among Detroit's blacks, at the same time reiterating the claim that racial discrimination was not tolerated by the union, and urging "all Negro Ford workers and all members of the Negro community not to permit any of their race to be made the catspaw of a conscienceless company" that was deliberately "inciting racial hatred . . . to break the ranks of its striking employees."[142]

The youth councils' action marked an important step in the Detroit NAACP's shift to a pro-union position, but more important in winning over the black community was the UAW's return to the strategy that had worked so well in the 1939 Chrysler strike— exploiting the Negro leaders' fears of a race riot and prevailing upon the apprehensive black spokesmen "to appeal to the Negro workers . . . to evacuate the plant."[143] Responding to Louis Martin's invitation, a hundred black Detroit leaders gathered for luncheon at the black YWCA on April 3 while the NAACP sound truck was still circling the Rouge. Although most of the ministers were conspicuously absent, otherwise the group provided an impressive cross section of black Detroit spokesmen and organizations. Leaders present ranged from Charles Hill and LeBron Simmons through Senator Diggs to James J. McClendon, Wilbur Woodson, and Carlton Gaines, and among the organizations represented were the AKA sorority, the Michigan Federated Demo-

cratic Clubs, and even the Detroit Urban League.* The gathering,
approving a statement drawn up by a small committee whose
members included both Simmons and Woodson,† not only condemned Ford's use of strikebreakers and the AFL back-to-work
movement, but more surprisingly actually endorsed the UAW-
CIO position that the Negro worker in the Ford plant would lose
no privileges because of union membership, and "stands to gain
additional privileges in the way of better jobs through the union's
promotion policy based on seniority, regardless of race. . . ."[144]

The unanimity exhibited by those present for this unprecedentedly vigorous expression of support was undoubtedly a product of several considerations. The statement, of course, reflected
the fear that the Ford-AFL strategy was heading toward violence.
It also revealed the growing conviction that the UAW-CIO was
bound to win; as the Pittsburgh *Courier* reporter put it, Detroit
black leaders "who lean toward the CIO point out that the day of
open shops has passed and that the Negro must line up with organized labor."[145] Finally, adumbrating future relations between the
union and the city's Negro protest leaders, the statement's word-
ing almost certainly reflected pledges that the black spokesmen
had obtained from UAW officials that they would protect the black

* Although the names of their representatives were not indicated, the AKA sorority
and the Urban League were undoubtedly represented by Beulah Whitby and
Geraldine Bledsoe, respectively. (The following year Whitby became national president of the sorority.)

† Woodson's conservative position on labor questions seems to have been to some
extent at least based upon very pragmatic considerations. The Conference of Negro
Trade Unionists met regularly in a clubroom at the Y, but when they sought per-
mission to hold a public meeting featuring R. J. Thomas as speaker early in 1940,
Woodson turned them down. He privately explained, "I'm in favor of unions but I
couldn't let them hold that meeting here. If I had, the next day Ward and Marshall
would have been down here to know why. That would have meant I couldn't recommend any more men to Ford's. I've got to be an opportunist. I've got to do what
is best for the largest number." The meeting was held at the YWCA branch instead,
apparently because the YWCA was not dependent upon any connection with the
Rouge personnel department. (Lloyd H. Bailer, "Negro Labor in the Automobile
Industry" [Ph.D. dissertation, University of Michigan, 1943], 167–68.)

workers' status at Ford and act aggressively against the pervasive discrimination in the industry.

In any event, delighted union officials triumphantly trumpeted the news with a banner headline in *Ford Facts:* "Negro Leaders Denounce Strikebreaking." Indeed the UAW could not have hoped for more. True, a substantial number of community leaders, including a majority of the ministers, remained as opposed to the UAW-CIO as ever, and indeed four days later the Interdenominational Ministers Alliance condemned as "erroneous" the UAW's claims of support among black clergymen. Yet a *Courier* reporter observed that while "sharp lines of cleavage" remained, even many former supporters of Henry Ford were upset because the company callously pitted blacks against the unionists.[146] Thus Horace White, Charles Hill, and Malcolm Dade were now joined by a few other pastors in openly endorsing the union, while even Robert Bradby failed to deliver his customary public defense of Ford and maintained an uncharacteristic silence. Nor was the Detroit *Tribune* any longer siding with Ford, though it did not adopt the *Chronicle's* pro-CIO stance. Instead, taking refuge behind the American flag, it declared: "the patriotic thing to do is to keep the wheels of our defense factories humming . . . while organized labor and industrial leaders iron out their difficulties at conference tables." As Horace Cayton, the widely read columnist, observed, "There is no doubt that the so-called Negro upper class believed in the great white father of Dearborn, but I personally was surprised at the number of individuals and organizations which came out for the union."[147]

Most significant was the changed attitude of the NAACP branch, Hardin happily concluding that the luncheon conference had resulted "in the NAACP taking its first stand with labor." McClendon himself was motivated chiefly by the fear of racial violence, but he was also responding to pressure from Sheffield and the youth councils. Moreover the pro–UAW-CIO position adopted by a man like Woodson must have strengthened McClendon's hand in dealing with the remaining anti-union members of his board, as

did encouragement he received from the Association's national office, Walter White wiring him to have the branch "take unequivocal position urging Negroes refrain from strikebreaking . . . and
cooperate fully with union."[148] Finally, even the Detroit Urban
League failed to endorse Ford in this crisis. With the NUL backing the UAW-CIO*, Dancy and his Board were effectively neutralized. When Lester Granger wired Dancy urging public support
for the UAW-CIO, the local league executive could not bring himself to present the request at the board meeting but instead asked
Geraldine Bledsoe to do it. The Board failed to take an official
stand, but among those present the "general discussion" indicated
agreement that the strikebreakers had placed the Negro worker in
"an unhealthy position," with blacks standing to be the losers
when the conflict was finally settled. By the time of this meeting,
Dancy himself, while remaining publicly silent, seems to have
warmed toward the UAW-CIO. Writing to colleagues at the
League's national headquarters, he criticized the Ford Company
for using blacks as scabs, and even conceded that the UAW leadership was sound on the race issue. While he still could not let himself forget that "the white man in the plant is the same fellow who

* The lacunae in the records of both the Detroit and National Urban League make
it impossible to ascertain fully the NUL's role. After the strike was over, Widman
wrote Lester Granger thanking him fulsomely for the "helping hand in the Ford
strike" (Michael Widman to Lester Granger, April 29, 1941, DUL Box 4), but precisely what Granger or other officials at the national office did is unclear. The only
contemporary evidence we uncovered on this is a telegram from NUL executive
secretary Eugene Kinckle Jones to the Michigan governor expressing alarm at the
possibility of racial violence, and placing his organization squarely behind the
UAW: "We know by experience that the Negro worker has no fundamental interest
different from the interest of his fellow workers. . . . We feel that the Negro worker must not permit himself to be used to break strikes nor to sabotage the efforts of
other workers to obtain living wages . . . , nor must those Negroes now employed
in industry be blind to current developments which demand that they become a
part of the organized labor movement" (Eugene Kinckle Jones telegram to Governor M. D. Van Wagoner, April 8, 1941, DUL Box 4). Subsequently Granger, seeking to highlight the League's role, went so far as to engage in a bit of hyperbole,
describing the Detroit League as one of the organizations that "sponsored" the
April 3 luncheon meeting called by Louis Martin. (Granger to Executive Secretaries of Affiliated Organizations, May 8, 1941, DUL Box 4.)

has been giving us h--- all these years," he claimed that privately he was now telling blacks "to connect with the C.I.O., for we know full well that the C.I.O. will eventually organize the factory and we want Negroes to be in on the ground floor."[149]

The favorable outcome of the luncheon conference had marked an important forward step for the UAW-CIO, but the situation remained exceedingly tense. Amid increasingly chaotic conditions inside the Ford plant, and with occasional violence continuing at the gates, union leaders, black spokesmen, and federal mediator James Dewey redoubled their efforts to remove the black strike-breakers. On April 4, Dewey personally piloted three hundred men through the picket lines, as UAW-CIO members cheered. Again that afternoon appealing over the sound car loudspeakers, Emil Mazey succeeded in persuading another twenty-seven to leave, but other strikebreakers stood behind lines of state troopers booing and yelling, "Down with the union." Yet reports circulated by Harry Bennett's staff that pickets would attack anybody daring to leave undercut both further pleas from the union sound trucks and an additional appeal made by Dewey inside the factory later that day. Consequently only a trickle of men came out. At the same time even though many blacks were now on the picket line, small incidents of interracial violence still occurred outside the gates. Thus on April 5, pickets beat up three black foundry work-ers who drove up hoping to collect their paychecks.[150]

Nor did the union neglect its campaign to convince the skeptics in the larger Afro-American community and among the black work-ers who had not joined the strikebreakers. The UAW publicity staff beamed radio broadcasts at the blacks and published special Negro issues of *Ford Facts*.[151] Senator Diggs was featured among the speakers at a mass rally April 4, where he told an enthusiastic crowd of thousands, "We shall prove that there are no Negro workers or white workers. We are just American workers willing to live or die together."[152] Over the weekend, responding to strong pressures from black leaders, the UAW purchased advertisements in the local newspapers, reiterating the union leaders' promise that under a UAW-CIO contract the Rouge's Negro employees "will not lose any privileges or position that they have enjoyed in the Ford Motor Company. On the contrary, they will enjoy greater privileges, more job security, and more promotions on the basis of the seniority system."[153]* And on Sunday afternoon UAW president R. J. Thomas personally walked the picket line and broadcast an appeal to the black workers in the plant. When one man responded by walking out of the gate and shaking Thomas's hand, the crowd of demonstrators cheered.[154]

As this minuscule response to Thomas's appearance indicated, the situation was still critical, since the remaining hard core of strikebreakers refused to vacate the Rouge. Nor had the threat of an AFL back-to-work effort, with all its potential for bloodshed, disappeared; on April 5 the UAW-AFL had held its own mass meeting where hundreds listened to speakers intone, "We are loyal to the man who gave us a chance, Henry Ford."[155] Accordingly the CIO supporters—old and new—in the black community spent Sunday April 6, in intense activity. The local NAACP adult branch and youth council distributed 10,000 leaflets at churches in the morning. Papering over differences within the organization, and seeking a positive response from as broad a segment of black workers as possible, the handbill announced: "We of the Detroit branch . . . are impartial toward your view of the Union. . . . Our only purpose in this matter is to avoid race riots and bloodshed. DO NOT BE USED AS STRIKEBREAKERS." Simultaneously several pastors read similar NAACP messages from their

* In his autobiography Walter White recalled that the union placed these advertisements at his urging during his visit to Detroit April 7–10. (White, *A Man Called White* [New York, 1948], 214.) Yet actually the union had arranged for them by April 6. Moreover White in a letter written at the time indicated that the advertisements were placed "at the urging of ourselves and others." (White to Harry Davis, April 17, 1941, NAACP Ford Strike File.) It is likely that at least some of this pressure came from the NAACP branch. McClendon, in the days following the luncheon meeting, was in frequent phone communication with White, who urged him to press the UAW leaders to make firm commitments in regard to the interests of the black workers. (White, telegram to McClendon, April 5, 1941, NAACP Ford Strike File.)

pulpits.[156] And that night there were mass meetings at Charles Hill's and Horace White's churches. At the latter, where McClendon and UAW-CIO organizer Leon Bates were among the speakers, the audience engaged in a spirited debate over whether the remaining strikebreakers at the Rouge were staying in because they were so loyal to Ford or because they were just frightened of the pickets. Moved by the discussion, White volunteered to go to the plant and use his persuasive skills to convince the Negroes that they could leave in peace.[157] Next morning White appeared at Gate No. 4, and using a union loudspeaker promised the men inside—a number of whom he knew personally—safe passage if they would come out. He must have been very disappointed when only a handful emerged.[158]

Federal mediator Dewey was increasingly disturbed at the strikebreakers' refusal to leave the plant. So also was NAACP Secretary Walter White, who flew in from New York on the afternoon of the 7th.[159] The NAACP official had been closely following events in Detroit since April 4 when McClendon, importuned by Sheffield, had telephoned White warning that a "disastrous" riot might erupt and asking the NAACP executive to personally help get the strikebreakers out of the Rouge. Although the national civil rights leader urged McClendon to have the branch unequivocally back the UAW-CIO, he himself did not rush to the Motor City.[160] Walter White, at the time himself engaged in a protracted controversy with General Motors over its discriminatory employment practices,[161] fully recognized of course that the UAW-CIO had not aggressively addressed itself to the problems of the blacks and to the prejudiced attitudes of the white members. Accordingly he pressed McClendon not only to align the branch publicly in support of the strikers but also to get R. J. Thomas both to commit the union to protecting the status of Negroes at Ford and to "pledge more aggressive action on behalf of Negro workers" in GM and other plants. At the same time, his reservations notwithstanding, White threw the weight of the national NAACP to the union's side. In telegrams to the news services he criticized their reports that equated blacks with strikebreaking, "which sharpens feeling against the whole Negro race and may lead to interracial violence." He maintained that many blacks were "working shoulder to shoulder with their white fellow members to win the strike." At the same time he issued a press release, publicizing the aid given the union by the NAACP youth in the sound truck. Over the weekend he kept in constant touch with Detroit by telephone. Like McClendon, union officials were also importuning White to appear personally at the Rouge,* and by Monday he decided that a flight to Detroit was imperative.[162]

Met at the airport by Dr. McClendon and an old acquaintance, UAW-CIO publicity director Edward Levinson, White was driven immediately to a downtown hotel where Thomas, Addes, and Widman were waiting. They told of the growing racial animosity among white strikers and "how the strike was threatened with failure because of the Negro workers" and the black preachers. Pressed by White, they conceded that Ford had given blacks "a better break" than any other employer, and that the union had been slow to move beyond rhetoric in correcting the black workers' grievances. But the UAW leaders assured the NAACP Secretary that they now planned to work aggressively for the promotion of blacks to all job categories and that they asked only for the opportunity to show that the union would do more for blacks than Ford. Armed with these pledges, White met that evening with the local NAACP executive board. To the dismayed skeptics he dwelt on the assurances the union leaders had just given, and explained

---

* The precise role of union officials in bringing White to Detroit is difficult to ascertain. Shelton Tappes recalls that Richard Frankensteen telephoned White, but Frankensteen had no recollection of the call. (Interview with Tappes, Aug. 15, 1976; interview with Frankensteen, Nov. 10, 1976.) Tappes also commented that the union paid for White's trip. But the only contemporary evidence for this is very slight—Donald Marshall spreading a rumor that the UAW-CIO picked up White's Detroit hotel bill. (*Courier*, April 26, 1941.) Surviving evidence on who actually financed the trip does not exist either in the UAW and NAACP files, and if the union actually did pay White's expenses it undoubtedly would have done so in the form of a later financial contribution to the NAACP rather than as a direct reimbursement.

that with unionization at Ford inevitable it would be dangerous for blacks to remain in the opposition. After McClendon spoke up in support of White, the board voted to work with the UAW leaders and give them a chance to fulfill the promises they had made.[163]

With the UAW's critics in the local branch thus neutralized, the NAACP chief next personally went to the Rouge plant, and accompanied by McClendon and Horace White, circled the factory in a union sound car, urging the strikebreakers to leave. Three or four came out, to the cheers of union men, but "the rest of them turned quietly away from the windows when White finished speaking." On Wednesday, April 9, the NAACP executive addressed the foundry workers at the Dearborn Arena, and later that evening returned in a sound car to Gate No. 4, where he had no greater success than on the previous day. In short, Walter White's efforts were no more helpful in evacuating the plant than anyone else's.[164]*

Meanwhile the NAACP Secretary conferred further with key black spokesmen and union leaders. He spoke at length with Hardin, who described the black organizers' resentment that Mazey

---

*In his autobiography White consistently overdramatized his role in the Ford strike. Although by the time he spoke with NAACP branch leaders, key figures on its board had already swung over to the union—as his own notes at the time made clear—White later recollected the situation differently: "I sensed the moment I entered the room that I was in an atmosphere so definitely anti-union as would have been that of a meeting of the board of directors of the Ford Motor Company," and he pictured himself as single-handedly turning McClendon and the board around. Similarly he phrased his description of the sound truck incident in such a way as to imply that large numbers of strikebreakers responded to his appeal and left the plant. A local newspaper, however, reported, "Speaking from a union sound car in front of Gate 4 . . . White declared that the men would be permitted to leave safely, and that they would best serve their own cause and that of democracy, by doing so. About 100 men lined up . . . near the gate to hear the talk, but only one followed White's advice. . . ." White's recollection that he turned down the union offer to supply the sound car because "Our judgment was against incurring obligations of any character to either side," was also at variance with contemporary press reports which stated that he spoke from a union vehicle. (White, *A Man Called White* [New York, 1948], 215–16; *News*, April 9, 1941; *Free Press*, April 10, 1941.)

was still directing their activities, and the blacks' intense dissatisfaction because the UAW-CIO had made such negligible efforts to
destroy discrimination at companies like GM.[165] At the same time
the top UAW officials were urging the NAACP executive to issue a
strong public statement supporting their position. Favorably dis-
posed toward industrial unionism, White had no doubt that the
UAW-CIO would win. Yet he was deeply disturbed by the gap between the union's professions of non-discrimination and the realities in the industry, and he must have known that most of the
Negroes had walked out of the Rouge not because they supported
the union but because they wanted to avoid being caught in the
middle between the UAW and management. Accordingly White
thought his tactics through carefully.[166] Finally on the 9th he publicly endorsed the UAW-CIO yet simultaneously prodded the
union to take forthright action on black grievances by serving notice that he shared the reservations of Ford's Negro workers.

Noting that Ford was the one automobile manufacturer who had
given blacks any opportunity—a fact "which contrasts sharply with
Knudsen's General Motors,"*—White nonetheless counseled the
Rouge's black employees "that they cannot afford to rely on the
personal kindness of any individual when what the workers want is
'justice.' " He warned that "The attempt to use Negroes as a club
over the heads of those who wish to organize themselves in unions
in the Ford plants" was dangerous; the few Negroes who "in their
desperation for jobs" had stayed in the Rouge plant, "are not helping themselves, the cause of the Negro, nor labor relations generally." The NAACP executive pointedly contrasted the favorable
policies of the CIO with those of the AFL, which was bent on trying to "dupe" Negro automobile workers, while its lily-white affiliates barred them in other industries. Glossing over the UAW-
CIO's past lack of performance, he pressed the union to live up to

---

* William S. Knudsen, formerly president of GM, was at the time head of the Office
of Production Management; in both capacities he had ignored NAACP protests
about GM job discrimination.

its democratic claims: "The UAW-CIO has conducted itself admirably in trying to remove the color line in this strike. It needs to do much more to wipe out [black] distrust based on sad experiences of the past with union labor," but "if the UAW-CIO wins the right to represent the Ford workers, as now seems inevitable," he was "confident" that it would take advantage of the "golden opportunity to demonstrate to Negro workers everywhere in the country that some labor unions are straight on the race question."[167]

This carefully balanced statement, endorsing the UAW-CIO while holding it accountable for adhering to its principles, was warmly approved by the Detroit NAACP Executive Board. White flew back to New York just before the strike ended in a union victory on the 11th, with the company's agreement to an NLRB election. The NAACP Secretary had not fulfilled his original hope of bringing the strikebreakers out of the factory, but he had put the Detroit branch forcefully behind the union. He was actually quite pleased with his role in consolidating sentiment on the UAW's behalf in the black community and especially in the NAACP.[168] Most important in long-range terms, his activities in the Motor City set the stage for the subsequent alliance between the NAACP—both nationally and in Detroit—and the UAW-CIO. At the time he was well aware that in endorsing the UAW he had placed the Association and himself out on a limb, but as he explained to a skeptical national board member, "the Negro worker had the grim choice of casting his lot with the union or having its hostility after they organized Ford. The union, at the urging of ourselves and others, made an unequivocal pledge" to fight aggressively on behalf of the black workers.[169]

It is probably not too much to say, as two students of the union's history have put it, that the UAW had "won the hesitant neutrality of the Ford Negro workers, which was enough to ensure the success of the strike." This "hesitant neutrality" was based in no small part on the endorsement of so many prominent and respected black spokesmen. A pleased president R. J. Thomas, singling out not only dependable supporters like Louis Martin, Horace White,

Malcolm Dade, Charles Hill,* and Charles Diggs, but James Mc-
Clendon and Walter White as well, informed the UAW annual
convention that the union owed all of these black leaders a "great
debt" for swinging the Negro community behind the strike and
helping to smash the back-to-work movement.[170] Yet, even though
Walter White left Detroit convinced that the union's victory in the
strike "will open the eyes of the colored people in Detroit to the
new order of things,"[171] not surprisingly there still existed among
black workers and community leaders alike considerable loyalty to
Ford and much skepticism toward the CIO—a fact that became
abundantly clear in the National Labor Relations Board (NLRB)
election held six weeks after the strike's end.

In preparation for this election both the UAW-CIO and the
Ford-backed UAW-AFL worked feverishly to attract blacks. The
two rivals each established East Side and West Side offices specifically to woo Ford's Negro workers. With Mazey's departure as
coordinator, Hardin assumed full responsibility for supervising the
expanded CIO operation. The two CIO offices, headed by organizers John Conyers and Leon Bates, were each staffed with a black
clerk, while two Negro secretaries were employed at the Rouge
local's main headquarters; a Ford foundry worker was added to the
staff to handle transportation. Organizers Johnson Buchanan,
Oscar Noble, and Joseph Billups spread the word by sound car in
the black neighborhoods; Bowman and Leonard Newman were assigned to work with the churches. Miriam Lee, Hardin's former
secretary, undertook "the difficult job of organizing the wives of

---

* The National Negro Congress's activity seems chiefly to have been in the form of
propaganda. Its role in urging the strikebreakers to leave the factory was less
publicized, and quite clearly less substantial. Hill later recalled that he had spoken
from a union sound car urging the workers to come out, but contemporary sources,
including the *Daily Worker*, do not mention it. John P. Davis, like Walter White,
flew into Detroit and similarly spoke from a union sound car, but his efforts received little notice. (Oral History interview with Charles Hill, May 8, 1967,
Reuther Library; Louis Martin, "The Ford Contract: An Opportunity," *Crisis* 48
[Sept. 1941]: 285.) On the other hand, the youthful Coleman Young, recently
named secretary of the Michigan NNC, worked closely with the Ford Organizing
Committee. (*Tribune*, March 15, 1941; *Daily Worker*, April 7, 1941.)

Ford workers;" and Christopher Alston continued to produce more black editions of *Ford Facts*. These efforts were reinforced within the factory by black union activists like Horace Sheffield, Veal Clough, Al Johnson, Tanner Perry (whom the stewards in the Press Building elected chairman of their bargaining committee shortly after the strike), and Shelton Tappes.[172]

For its part, the Ford Motor Company people were far from idle. Many of the blacks who had remained in the Rouge plant during the strike were soliciting members for the AFL group. Taking the offensive against the spokesmen who supported the UAW-CIO, Donald Marshall publicly denounced as traitors "the various doctors, ministers, dentists, and other near-professional men of the race who are ranting over the radio and riding in union sound cars to exhort the Negro to follow them." Hinting that for money the NAACP had "made deals with the CIO," he added a swipe at Senator Diggs and at the newly elected state representative, Horace White: "It would also be interesting to know how campaign expenses for certain individuals are paid." To this the NAACP national office retorted, "Donald Marshall has been on the Ford payroll so long that, of course, he speaks only as the mouthpiece of the Ford Company."[173] At the same time, outbreaks of violence were erupting inside the Rouge plant, especially in the foundry, where blacks greatly outnumbered whites and where the UAW-CIO was weak. Fistfights, beatings, even stabbings occurred, as AFL or non-union Negroes, chiefly men who had stayed in the factory during the strike, attacked CIO members with the encouragement of the Service Department. While some of those assaulted were Negroes, white unionists were especially singled out, and the struggle again assumed the dimensions of a racial conflict. Repeatedly UAW-CIO leaders urged their members not to allow themselves to be manipulated by people trying to hurt the union through fomenting a race riot, while alarmed civic and business leaders in the black community worriedly held meetings to consider how to prevent such a catastrophe. McClendon, for example, seeking to defuse racial tensions, issued a statement placing the blame on the Ford management, while from New York Walter White hurriedly wired Michigan's governor M. D. Van Wagoner demanding that he "ascertain who is instigating such attacks and who may be paying these men to assault union members." Although the governor had already dispatched state troops, these attacks continued until the end of the month.[174]

Serious cleavages still existed in Detroit's black leadership, and, as Roy Wilkins observed, certain local Negroes "are still bowing down to Massa Ford." As usual such sentiment was strongest among some of the clergy. The Baptist Ministers Conference actually twice went on record endorsing not only Ford but also the AFL as "a truly American organization . . . that . . . has acted in the best interest of the Negro in the United States." Though Bradby's name was conspicuously absent, forty preachers signed the statement.[175] On the other hand, right after the Ford strike, McClendon had joined leaders of the National Negro Congress in a Citizens Committee to generate more support for the UAW-CIO*. The NNC sponsored an open letter, whose signers included Senator Diggs, NAACP Secretary Robert Evans, and several prominent black unionists, urging black workers to reject the advice of "Henry Ford, King of the open shop," and the blandishments of the "hypocritical" AFL: "Vote CIO . . . in defense of America and for complete equality for black men upon the labor front."[176] The union itself sponsored radio programs featuring its close allies among the clergy, hosted a luncheon for a hundred leading clubwomen at which Widman, Rev. Malcolm Dade and Hardin spoke, and gave a testimonial dinner for the four black newspapers that circulated in the Detroit area.[177] The celebrated Paul Robeson arrived in Detroit to lend his support, and on the eve of the voting, Diggs joined his fellow state senator, Stanley Novak, in a stirring appeal to the Ford workers to cast their ballots for the CIO.[178]

---

* McClendon, knowing of Walter White's anti-communism and hostility toward the NNC, assured the NAACP secretary that he was aware of the problem and explained, "Personally, I have kept our Association away from them except on specific issues." (McClendon to Walter White, May 7, 1941. NAACP Ford Strike File.)

At the May 21 NLRB election the UAW-CIO won a sweeping victory, securing at Rouge about seventy percent of the votes. Ironically, however, the CIO succeeded without the support of the majority of black workers. While no exact statistics are available, contemporaries all indicated that most blacks, following the Ford Company's new-found enthusiasm for the AFL, displayed a preference for that union.[179]

A hasty assessment of the vote might suggest that the UAW-CIO's intensive efforts and the growing support it enjoyed among the black community's leaders had gone for naught. Yet longer-range developments indicated that the opposite was true, for the Rouge's black employees quickly transferred their allegiance to the union. In large part this occurred because the retaliation from the UAW-CIO and the loss of skilled jobs that many blacks had feared did not materialize; but the intensive campaign which the union had mounted and the fundamental change of opinion that occurred in the black community during the Ford drive and strike were also of critical importance.

One black Ford employee who had staunchly backed the AFL happily noted: "There wasn't any trouble. The AFL fellows shook hands with the CIO boys and they all said 'Let's let bygones be bygones.' I told the CIO boys I could be just as much for the CIO as I was for the AFL." Another reported that, following the NLRB election, while a substantial number of white workers regarded blacks as scabs or viewed them with a watchful skepticism, most others "completely accept the Negro." For their part, only a small number of blacks remained hostile, while most were soon "falling in line with the union." They were impressed that Shelton Tappes was a member of the sixteen-man committee that hammered out the first Ford contract and secured the inclusion of an anti-discrimination clause.[180] Most significantly there developed "a definitely large increase in active participation" by "conservative rank and file" blacks, and black involvement in union activities as shop stewards, and on grievance, department and building committees, was sustained.[181] Nearly all these positions were in the foundry, but Tappes, who had become president of the foundry unit, was chosen late in 1941 to fill the post of Ford Local 600's Recording Secretary. Quite naturally the presidency of the majority black foundry unit remained in black hands, while in 1942 Tanner Perry became vice-president of the overwhelmingly white Pressed Steel Building.[182]

On the other hand it should be emphasized that the higher status of many blacks in the Rouge work force and their participation in Local 600's affairs was still a unique situation. Far more typical throughout the industry were the ambiguities in black-UAW relations that had characterized all the organizing campaigns and the role of Negroes in the Ford strike itself. As has been repeatedly observed, the behavior of the black workers at the Rouge had reflected not only appreciation of Henry Ford's policies but also continuing skepticism of the UAW-CIO's promises. The very visible participation of some blacks in the organizing drives and in union affairs at Ford, the fact that during the struggle at the Rouge a significant number of Negroes did join picket lines and did vote for the UAW-CIO, and the well-publicized role of Walter White, Dr. McClendon, and other black leaders all served to counteract among whites the negative image that the black vote produced. In the final analysis, both the black skepticism toward rank-and-file white workers and the UAW's alliance with important elements among the Negro leadership—especially the national officials of the NAACP—would each prove to be part of the enduring legacy of the Ford strike of 1941.

# III

*Black Protest, Union Principles,*
*and Federal Intervention:*
*The Struggle Against Job Discrimination,*
*1941–1943*

## 1

In the aftermath of the Ford strike there came a rearrangement in the pattern of black Detroit's alliances. The Ford Company retreated from its concern with black philanthropy, and blacks began looking to the UAW for help in achieving better job opportunities and in redressing other grievances as well. At the beginning this shift in the outlook of Detroit's Negroes was to a considerable extent pragmatic, and criticism of the UAW largely collapsed because, as one contemporary student observed, "It is now realized that organized labor holds a powerful position and the major misgiving at the present time is that by refusing to cooperate, Negroes may find themselves frozen out of employment by the unions."[1] As had been true previously of Henry Ford and his enterprise, the UAW was far from a perfect friend; yet like the company in earlier years, the union was an organization whose top leadership was far in advance of other sectors of the white community in its racial attitudes. The note of white paternalism and black hero worship that had characterized Negro relations with Henry Ford was absent from the new tie with UAW leaders, but, like the motor corporation's management during the 1920's and 1930's, UAW officials recognized black labor's importance and the value of working with the city's Negro spokesmen. Given the combination of Ford's loss of interest in black welfare, the newly achieved power of the UAW, and its leaders' belief in the desirability of interracial working-class solidarity, the union relatively easily replaced the auto magnate as black Detroit's closest ally.

Significantly this alliance developed in the face of serious limitations in the ability of union leaders to deliver on the promises they had made during the Ford strike to eliminate racism in the auto plants. The old problem of company bias both in hiring and promotion of course remained. And in grappling with the difficulty posed by management policies, the UAW-CIO operated under two contradictory acts of restraints. Given the International leaders' belief in interracial unionism, the promises to black workers, and the bridges so carefully constructed to influential sectors in the black community, the union was clearly under pressure to battle aggressively against the discriminatory practices that abounded. Yet on the other hand, to advance the interests of black auto workers meant arousing the fears and prejudices of rank-and-file white members, and often of officers in the locals as well.

The posture of the locals varied considerably, ranging from the relatively supportive policies of Local 600 at River Rouge (where, given their numerical strength and their long-held beachhead on assembly lines and in highly skilled jobs, the Negroes' position was unchallenged by the white workers)[2] to the highly racist actions that typified so many members and officers of Packard Local 190. There were even alarming reports of Ku Klux Klan infiltration of the union, especially at the Packard plant.* Beyond such organized

---

* In 1940 and 1941 the Ku Klux Klan openly engaged in a serious effort to recruit auto workers in Detroit and to infiltrate UAW locals, alleging that it aimed to drive Communists from the union. Imperial Wizard James M. Colescott journeyed from Atlanta on more than one occasion personally to aid the campaign. The extent of his success is unknown. (See very good article in St. Louis *Post-Dispatch*, March 22, 1942, and following in the Catholic labor journal, *Michigan Labor Leader:* April 12, 26, Aug. 30, 1940, June 6, Oct. 10, 24, 1941.) There were charges that perhaps as

hate groups lay the generalized racial tensions in Detroit and the specter of massive interracial violence. Incidents of racial conflict were endemic in the city,* erupting into serious conflagrations in the 1942 Sojourner Truth housing controversy and in the major riot of 1943. The union did not—and in view of its main constituency perhaps could not—deliver on the rosy promises made during the Ford strike, and instead it handled black grievances ambiguously and contradictorily.

The Detroit blacks' struggle against job discrimination in the automobile factories after the Ford strike and the improvements that followed both came in the context of the labor dislocations caused by the Second World War. Conversion from civilian to war production produced at first a temporary worker surplus that by 1942

---

many as 200 delegates at the 1941 UAW convention were Klansmen, that nearly half of the Packard delegation were in the organization, and that in the delegations of two Chevrolet locals, Klan members constituted the majority. (*Chronicle*, Oct. 4, 1941, clipping NAACP Ford Strike File; Louis Martin to Walter White, Oct. 2, 1941, NAACP Ford Strike File.) Shortly afterwards, R. J. Thomas personally took time out from the CIO convention to make a forceful statement against this infiltration, and a couple of months later nearly an entire issue of the Packard local's edition of the *United Automobile Worker* was devoted to denunciation of the Klan and its attempt to infiltrate the local. (*Ford Facts*, Nov. 5, 1941; *Tribune*, Nov. 22, 1941; *UAW, Local 190 Edition*, Feb. 15, 1942.) At this point the Klan was helping incite the opposition to black occupancy of the Sojourner Truth Public Housing Project, with its denouement in the riot at the end of February 1942. (See Chapter IV.) There was also much talk in union circles about the Klan promoting the later hate strikes at Packard and the race riot of 1943, but the actual degree of such influence was undoubtedly greatly overestimated by worried UAW leaders. (C. E. Rhett, "Memorandum for the Attorney General: Re Detroit Race Riot—June 20 and 21," July 12, 1943, attached to Francis Biddle to C. Gill, July 24, 1943, NA RG 212.) In any event the Klan was clearly not responsible for the existence of serious racial tensions in Detroit.

* In the fall of 1941 Louis Martin observed that the dislocation and the unemployment crisis associated with conversion to war manufacturing was the source of "numerous racial disturbances. . . . The economic pinch has led a lot of whites to seek scapegoats. Negroes are more belligerent and the whites see jobless days ahead. . . . This general tension is evident in the acute school situation here. Student race riots are growing and this week a serious racial situation has developed in Ferndale, a Detroit suburb." (Louis Martin to Walter White, Oct. 2, 1941, NAACP Ford Strike File.)

was replaced by a serious labor shortage; and simultaneously there was a sharp decline in the kinds of foundry jobs in which blacks were customarily employed. Not surprisingly, the Motor City's blacks—and union officials as well—looked to Washington's new federal manpower agencies to help end the race discrimination rooted in the policies of management and the prejudices of rank-and-file white workers.

The situation in the nation's capital was certainly not fully satisfactory from the standpoint of those battling for racial justice in the job market. The succession of war manpower agencies—the Office of Production Management (OPM) during 1941, the War Production Board (WPB) during the first part of 1942, and thereafter the War Manpower Commission(WMC)—were of course concerned with mobilizing scarce labor resources, not with promoting equal economic opportunity. Moreover the Committee on Fair Employment Practices, created by President Roosevelt's Executive Order 8802 in June 1941, was limited in its budget and authority. At first, responsibility for increasing black labor utilization was assigned to the well-known black New Deal official Robert C. Weaver,* who served as chief of the Negro Employment and Training Branch in OPM and WPB, and then as chief of the Negro Manpower Service in WMC until the autumn of 1942. FEPC, the product of the kind of persistent black agitation that had prompted Weaver's appointment in the first place, was theoretically an independent body responsible directly to President Roosevelt. Actually it was supervised by the successive war manpower agencies, and operated with such slender finances that at first it depended heavily for investigative assistance upon Weaver and his field representatives.

Both of these government bureaus lacked enforcement powers, but they employed their highly limited leverage in contrasting ways. Weaver and his staff made careful investigations, tactfully

---

* Weaver, a prominent member of the group of Negro officials in the Roosevelt administration known informally as the "black cabinet," had been Advisor on Negro Affairs in the Department of Interior and later a Special Assistant to the Administration in charge of race relations in the U.S. Housing Authority.

negotiated with management and unions, and politely prodded high officials in the manpower agencies and in the War and Navy Departments. On the other hand, FEPC relied chiefly on public hearings that sought to expose and embarrass recalcitrant corporations and labor organizations.[3] Inevitably tensions and rivalries arose between the two, but even after FEPC had won the bureaucratic battle, forcing the dismantling of Weaver's setup in the autumn of 1942,[4] it became evident that WMC chairman Paul V. McNutt had no intention of encouraging a serious effort to fight racial inequities. Reneging on his promise to transfer Weaver's field representatives to FEPC, McNutt made them responsible instead to the less sympathetic WMC regional directors, and, more important, he thoroughly demoralized the FEPC in January 1943 by canceling eagerly anticipated public hearings on discrimination in the railroad industry. Only angry protests from blacks and sympathetic whites finally led Roosevelt to revive the agency five months later, with expanded staff and responsibilities.[5]

Essentially the tactics of the black advancement organizations were rooted in the serious wartime labor shortages, and it can be argued that these shortages made possible the improvements in job opportunities for Negroes that occurred during World War II. But as black Detroiters well knew, most war manpower officials would move only slowly and reluctantly at best. Blacks also realized that neither Weaver nor the FEPC possessed leverage beyond their personal persuasive skills or their ability to garner a modest amount of newspaper publicity. Yet the Negro civic and labor leaders in the Motor City, seeking to exploit the possibilities presented by the labor scarcity, grasped that fact that if any progress was to be made, federal intervention would be absolutely essential, and from the beginning they skillfully exploited the shifting bureaucratic arrangements in Washington. From time to time they also received effective support from the armed forces contract compliance officers stationed in Detroit—Captain A. S. Wotherspoon for the Navy and most notably Colonel George Strong for the Army Air Corps. Throughout, the protesters had the extraordi-

narily helpful services of a skillful black civil servant, J. Lawrence
Duncan. A long-time Detroit resident and director of Negro placement in the Michigan Unemployment Commission, Duncan joined
Weaver's staff in May 1941,[6] and subsequently spent considerable
time in the Motor City as a regional field representative first for
Weaver and later for the WMC, including a stint as an investigator
on loan to the FEPC.

The form taken by the struggle to achieve job equality was
strongly affected not only by the mushrooming and influential wartime federal bureaucracy but was also bound up with changes in
black Detroit's leadership structure that occurred in the wake of
the UAW victory over Ford. The NAACP branch easily remained
the most important race organization in the city. Still possessing
the largest membership of any branch in the nation, it continued
to grow rapidly during the war, reaching 20,000 members in
1943.[7] In the summer of 1941 it had become the first NAACP
branch to employ a full-time executive secretary, the popular mu-
sician and activist Gloster Current. Deeply interested in labor
problems, and working closely with black trade union leaders,
Current devoted a considerable portion of his energies to fighting
job bias in the city's war industry and did much to advance the cooperative relationship now developing between the Detroit
NAACP and the UAW. Bradby and other conservative ministers
found their role considerably diminished, while the *Tribune* displayed a new openness toward the CIO, and J. C. Dancy was
quietly turning into a UAW ally. Ironically the politically ambi-
tious Horace White came to occupy an increasingly marginal position, but the militant, pro-labor Charles Hill became a major
spokesman. The latter's base was the Michigan Division of the
NNC, restructured with himself as president and the youthful
Coleman Young as executive secretary; but given the weakness of
what was essentially a paper organization, Hill operated principally
through forming broader coalitions which he served as chairman.
At the same time black union leaders such as Hardin, Sheffield,
and Tappes emerged as important community spokesmen in their

own right. Thus there was a marked shift to the left, with well-es-
tablished race advancement organizations such as the Urban
League and NAACP now becoming aligned with organized labor,
while individuals like Current, Hill, and the Negro unionists
emerged as prominent figures.

At first, as the issue of bias in defense industry became increasingly salient during the year before American entry into the war,
the local NNC and the NAACP branch each agitated on the problem. This episodic protest increased in forcefulness, especially on
the part of the NAACP, following President Roosevelt's promulga-
tion of Executive Order 8802.[8] After Pearl Harbor a stronger and
more unified agitation emerged with the development of two coalitions—the interracial Metropolitan Detroit Council on Fair Employment Practices and the overwhelmingly black Citizens Committee for Jobs in War Industry. The former, organized early in
1942, was a federation of more than seventy civic groups, social organizations, and labor unions chaired by Edward McFarland, a
white Wayne University economics professor. Prominently involved were black unionists like Hardin (who had headed the original provisional committee), Prince Clark, Tappes, and Noble;
Negro civic leaders like Current, Hill, Dade, and Geraldine Bledsoe; and sympathetic whites like the attorney and leading feminist
Zaio Woodford, the civil liberties leader Jack Raskin (executive
secretary of the Civil Rights Federation), and representatives of
the Protestant, Catholic, and Jewish faiths.[9] Then, with the encouragement of black union leaders in Local 600, Rev. Charles Hill
established the Citizens Committee for Jobs in War Industry. The
composition of this umbrella group, which emerged as an important force in the fall of 1942, closely paralleled the Negro membership of the Metropolitan Council, including as it did individuals
from LeBron Simmons through Malcolm Dade to representatives
of the Urban League and the NAACP. Black UAW officials such as
Sheffield, Tappes, and Hardin played highly visible roles; and
NAACP's Gloster Current served as secretary. The activities and
tactics of the two coalitions overlapped to some extent; but while

the Metropolitan Council confined itself to assisting the national
FEPC's Detroit investigations and propagandizing for the latter's
proposed public hearings in the Motor City, the Citizens Committee operated as a militant protest group. "Embracing the whole
Negro community," it became, in the words of a federal investigator, "the main instrument for exerting . . . pressure" upon government, union and plant management.[10]

Given the salience of the job issue, the NAACP considered it essential to support the Citizens Committee generously, although
McClendon and many of his colleagues were skeptical about Hill
and the NNC, and McClendon himself gave little time to the
Committee's work. Not only did Gloster Current become the coalition's secretary, but NAACP branch treasurer Mamie Thompson
handled its finances, while the NAACP office was virtually the new
group's headquarters. Yet there was open opposition on the
NAACP board to these arrangements. The critics were worried by
the NNC's Communist connections and also feared that the
NAACP branch, by submerging itself in the coalition, would be
denied proper credit for its contributions.[11]

Such fears soon proved justified. Although the coalition's vigor
owed much to the NAACP, the NNC people, including left-wing
unionists like Shelton Tappes,* openly criticized what they
deemed the branch's indifference to labor problems, and in December 1942 Hill challenged McClendon for the presidency.
Charging that McClendon catered chiefly to the black elite and ignored the working masses, Hill ran a strong campaign, with Le-

---

* Tappes had participated in Communist-inspired activities since the early 1930's,
was an important leader in Local 600's left wing, and achieved election to important
offices in the local owing largely to carefully organized Communist support. Yet he
never joined the party. His persistent refusal to do so eventually earned him the
enmity of the Communists and cost him his high position in the local. (See statement of Shelton Tappes, March 12, 1952, in U.S. Congress, House, 82nd Congress, 2nd Session, Hearings Before the Committee on Un-American Activities,
*Communism in the Detroit Area—Part 2* [Washington, 1952], 3117–45, *passim*.) For
Tappes's participation in the activities of Communist-front organizations see also
Herbert Hill, transcript of Oral History interview with Tappes, Oct. 27, 1967,
Reuther Library.

Bron Simmons and Shelton Tappes acting very visibly on his behalf. Current, unhappy because, despite his effectiveness as
NAACP executive secretary, the fiscally cautious president had
refused to increase his minimal salary, also backed Hill, who promised to rectify the situation. Many of McClendon's supporters were
indeed of the old guard. The Draft McClendon Committee,
though astutely enough headed by the UAW member and former
branch labor committee chairman, Prince Clark, included Beulah
Whitby and Horace White, but was peopled chiefly by individuals
like Bradby, Mamie Thompson, and Booker T. Washington Trade
Association leaders Rev. William Peck and Carlton Gaines. In the
hotly contested election Hill was overwhelmingly defeated, with
McClendon's well-organized majority consisting largely of people
drawn from Bradby's Second Baptist Church, acting under instructions from their pastor. A frustrated Tappes angrily denounced the
vote as a "farce" managed by "the so-called Negro Chamber of
Commerce" to keep the NAACP from helping the black masses.[12]

Afterwards McClendon astutely consolidated the branch's position. He ended one source of divisiveness by effecting a rap-
prochement with Gloster Current, eliminated another by drawing
the UAW more directly into NAACP activities, and effectively
isolated Hill and the Citizens Committee. With lack of labor representation on the Association's board during the preceding year
having been an issue in the campaign, McClendon now brought
both Prince Clark and Walter Hardin on the Board by making
them co-chairmen of a revived labor committee, which soon became the most active and largest in the branch.[13] McClendon's
canny appointment of Hardin and the branch's now highly visible
involvement in the job issue undoubtedly did much to undermine
the effectiveness of Hill's Committee. Moreover, the branch executive board, by denying Hill's group further use of the NAACP office, and by refusing to have anything more to do with its finances,
in effect delegitimized the Citizens Committee's operations among
the mainstream of the black community. Thereafter the Committee virtually ceased to function.[14] Yet for a few brief months it had

brilliantly articulated black protest against race bias in Detroit's war plants, and Hill himself remained a figure to be reckoned with.

Detroit's race advancement organizations and coalitions, in battling job discrimination in war industries, worked closely with black union leaders. Some were men like Walter Hardin, who held paid staff positions as International representatives. Others were prominent in their locals; especially notable in this category were Horace Sheffield and Shelton Tappes of Local 600, who represented the largest body of black workers in the UAW and functioned in one of its most militant locals. For its part, the International union during the war's early years had two main agencies with jurisdiction over job discrimination. At the demand of black unionists, the International Executive Board established an Inter-Racial Committee headed by Hardin with general responsibility to help in combatting race bias. In addition, specific cases often came within the purview of the union's War Policy Division, where they were handled by the division's assistant director, Victor Reuther, with the help of Oscar Noble.* On the whole the black staff members tended to function primarily in the solution of specific complaints brought by black workers and to help in crisis situations, while Sheffield and Tappes were more likely to be in the forefront of the agitation mounted in Detroit and Washington by the black civic organizations. Over time the Inter-Racial Committee declined markedly in influence, until it was dissolved by R. J. Thomas in June 1943, while throughout Victor Reuther's office was the principal troubleshooter.† Finally, at the very highest union

* For a brief period in mid-1942 the International employed a special co-ordinator to help the locals' Fair Employment Practice Committees solve black complaints (see references in Duncan to Weaver, June 12, 1942, Duncan, field report n.d. (p. 1 missing) [Oct. 1942], both in FEPC Archives Reel 58 FR), but the post was soon eliminated, evidently because its responsibilities simply duplicated the work of Hardin and Victor Reuther.

† The incomplete nature of the UAW Archives makes it impossible to determine the full extent of the activities of the two units or the degree to which they coordinated their activities. Discussion of specific cases in which each was active, as well

levels, International officials, particularly Thomas, operated on an ad hoc basis, intervening when serious crises compelled them to do so.

Like the blacks both inside and outside of the union who were pressing the UAW to take more aggressive action, the union's International leaders frequently looked to federal agencies for help. As a government investigator privately reported, these union officials welcomed government pressure, and not infrequently sought to obtain federal intervention on behalf of the blacks. Robert Weaver and J. Lawrence Duncan understood this very well; bringing to bear upon reluctant managements as much pressure as the attitudes of higher officials in the manpower and military agencies would permit, they simultaneously kept in close touch with union leaders. Thus when Weaver, acting upon black protests, had succeeded in getting a company to inaugurate a change, he was often obliged to seek help from the UAW International to diffuse the frequently open resistance of the white workers. Weaver and Duncan in fact recollect that they "worked hand-in-glove" with top union officials like Thomas, Addes, and Victor Reuther, who privately encouraged them to take firm action which they could then openly support. In the view of the two black war manpower officials, International UAW leaders were sympathetic to the blacks' demands, but preferred to have federal officials take responsibility for forcing both management and hostile white workers to accept blacks in new job categories.[15]* Unfortunately, with high WPB

as details on the formation of the Inter-Racial Committee will be presented in the course of the historical narrative that follows. The Inter-Racial Committee in the final analysis, however, does not seem to have proved to be a very useful mechanism, and gradually Hardin and the other black International representatives on it found their function pretty much limited to organizing among the black workers. (Interviews with Oscar Noble, Nov. 10, 1977, and March 16, 1978; with William Bowman, Nov. 3, 1977; and with Shelton Tappes, Oct. 22, 1977.)

* Duncan even recalls that there were certain occasions when he and Hardin felt that they had to "protect" Thomas, "times when we had to avoid putting him on the spot . . . when we discouraged him from being out front for blacks. We protected him and told him that he shouldn't speak out on a particular issue . . . because if Thomas, who was a lovable guy . . . was out front too often, his head would have

and WMC bureaucrats themselves indifferent or reluctant, the UAW officials found that they could not consistently depend on a forceful federal stand which they could then back up, and this fact greatly accentuated the ambiguity and inconsistency in the International leadership's own actions. Yet on critical occasions the union was able to appeal successfully for federal intervention; R. J. Thomas himself went at least once to Washington to secure such assistance.

Thus progress on the job front in Detroit war industry came only gradually and through a tangled web of interaction among Negro advancement groups, black workers, officers in union locals, International UAW leaders, corporate managements, and the various concerned federal agencies. As the months passed, in the changed milieu following the Ford strike, the adversary quality that characterized the relationships between the black groups and the union's highest leadership on this issue would disappear, to be replaced by united efforts to secure forceful action from the war manpower agencies and the FEPC. In the end, pressed by the black workers and leaders and encouraged periodically by interested personnel in the federal agencies, the UAW's International leaders played a key role in broadening black industrial opportunities. All this became abundantly clear in the two years between the Ford strike of 1941 and the race riot of 1943.

## 2

As Gloster Current, the Detroit NAACP's new executive secretary, pointedly observed in July 1941, President Roosevelt's re-

been chopped off and who knows who would have become president then? . . . R. J. Thomas would come through for blacks all the time if you just showed him how he should do it—but we wouldn't let him kill himself." (Interview with Duncan, April 9, 1977.) Noble, in more restrained fashion, recollects Thomas as a man "who wanted to do something on race equality—but who felt that he did not have too much power. He would do things that did not cause too much flak." But sometimes he was pressed into taking a vigorous stand, and when he finally took a position backing the upgrading of blacks, "he usually stuck it through." (Interview with Noble, Nov. 3, 1977.)

cently issued executive order on fair employment was doing nothing for the Motor City's black workers, whose jobs were being sacrificed as the automobile industry converted to war production. Military production involved far less foundry work, and so for blacks the mass layoffs that accompanied the cutbacks in civilian work were not followed by the anticipated large-scale rehiring as defense jobs opened up. By October Louis Martin was informing Walter White: "We are in a hell of a spot out here as a result of the curtailment in auto production. Our boys are being laid off and they are not getting transferred to defense work."[16] Although seniority and ability were supposed to determine rehiring and job advancement, as earlier, "ability" was in effect still defined to mean acceptability to management and white workers. Even after the Office of Production Management had negotiated a joint management-UAW "Six Point Transfer Program" in October, providing for rehiring employees for defense work on a strict seniority basis, blacks discovered that this guiding principle was repeatedly flouted. For its part, the UAW preferred to avoid the problem, continuing its past failure to challenge the existing pattern of concentrating blacks in unskilled and foundry work. Thus when companies refused to consider black employees for wartime assembly-line jobs that began opening up, the UAW locals were reluctant to do anything about it.[17]

The most dramatic instances of black worker discontent with transfer practices during the summer of 1941 occurred at Chrysler's Dodge Division, where on at least three occasions they staged angry walkouts to protest the discrimination. At Dodge Truck, where since 1937 only whites had been hired and the small number of blacks were nearly all janitors, the issue of promotions to better jobs had actually long been simmering. Negroes had acquired substantial seniority, yet, despite the non-discrimination clause in the 1939 contract, only whites were upgraded and admitted to training programs. After repeated complaints, the local's indifferent officers did finally confer fruitlessly with an unsympathetic management. Nothing further was attempted until a year later when the local's leaders, prodded by a black walkout in July 1941, requested that the men be transferred to the assembly line. Although the local compromised the blacks' rights by proposing a jim crow unit, management would not even accept that. NAACP protests to the company were unavailing, and even Dancy's old friend, Chrysler personnel director Charles Winegar, was singularly unresponsive. The following month black employees at Dodge Main twice walked out because only whites were being transferred to defense jobs at the Chrysler Tank Arsenal. Although in this instance the local lodged a vigorous complaint, management again remained obdurate. Gloster Current, after appealing to FEPC for several weeks, angrily concluded that blacks were simply "getting a grand runaround by management, government and the union."[18]

Supplementing the workers' angry demonstrations was the more sustained pressure on the UAW's leadership coming from prominent black union leaders and community spokesmen. In July, about the time of the first Chrysler walkout, Current wired R. J. Thomas for help in securing enforcement of Roosevelt's FEPC order. As the crisis deepened, Louis Martin found himself "arguing with the union heads" that they had a duty "to tackle the discrimination in job transfers." At the UAW convention in August the twenty-nine black delegates were openly critical of the abstract anti-discrimination resolutions of previous years and demanded more potent measures this time. When the conclave responded by calling for equal opportunity in hiring, promoting, and training for all job categories, and for transfers "solely on seniority" of men displaced by cutbacks in civilian auto production, the blacks were still dissatisfied because of the failure to specify concrete enforcement procedures. A few weeks later a delegation of black union leaders from Chrysler Local 7 and Rouge Local 600 protested to the UAW's International Executive Board about the many violations of seniority in transfers to war production, and the failure of UAW local officers and regional directors to do anything about it. In response the Board decided to act and, voting unanimously to notify companies and union locals alike that such racial discrimination would no longer be tolerated, created an Inter-Racial Committee, responsible to R. J. Thomas, to monitor unequal treatment. The latter promptly appointed a body consisting of four prominent white officials and six black International staff members, chaired by Walter Hardin.[19]*

Maintaining the pressure, the NAACP branch immediately scheduled an Emergency Labor Conference for early October to generate "Negro pressure blocks" inside UAW locals, and later in the same month the Negro International staff members sponsored their own conference on transfer problems. The latter gathering, which also included NAACP leaders like McClendon and Current, excoriated the International union for its weaknesses "on the Negro Question." Addes, who was present and later reported the matter to the UAW Board, pointedly assured the blacks that "now is the time to put into practice what the UAW-CIO Constitution says." Robert Weaver, who was also there, promised to help the new Inter-Racial Committee try to settle the long-simmering dispute over Chrysler's anti-black employment policies.[20]

As these two conferences revealed, black union leaders and Negro civic spokesmen not only were working in close cooperation, but also were fully aware that they would get nowhere without government help. As early as September in fact, Current's protest about problems at the Dodge Main had elicited action from Washington. When FEPC turned this complaint over to Weaver's office for investigation, J. Lawrence Duncan met with Winegar and the UAW regional director, who both conceded that discrimination existed. The union conferees even frankly "admitted the need for firmer control over the locals," and Duncan departed with a commitment that, if the local's grievance machinery did not

---

* The delegation of black unionists consisted of Conyers and Fanroy from Chrysler, and Sheffield and two obscure individuals from Local 600. The members of the Inter-Racial Committee were Melvin Bishop, director of region 1 in Detroit; Frankensteen; Leonard; Walter Reuther; Hardin; Al Johnson, William Bowman, Leon Bates, Oscar Noble, and Conyers.

come up with a solution, the International would step in, and if
necessary refer the case to Weaver and the FEPC. Members of
Hardin's Inter-Racial Committee did indeed assist by conferring
with Weaver and Chrysler officials, and early in the year the local's
leadership vigorously backed the black workers with a strongly
worded resolution denouncing the Chrysler company. In a couple
of months 225 black janitors were transferred from Dodge Main,
many of them to better jobs.[21]

By the beginning of 1942, significant accomplishments had been
achieved at three smaller companies employing relatively large
proportions of blacks in certain job categories—Briggs, Kelsey-
Hayes Wheel Company, and Murray Body.[22] At Kelsey Hayes,
where management had promised the NNC in June 1941 that
black workers would be used at its new defense plant, white employee opposition had vitiated the agreement, so the Negro workers had appealed to the FEPC and Weaver. Duncan, given responsibility for the case, successfully negotiated with the local's
leaders and management on the basis of the Six Point Transfer Program, and in November they agreed to shift 150 eligible men. To
avert further trouble, Duncan astutely arranged to have Victor
Reuther meet with the unhappy white workers, who thereupon
voted to approve the transfer, and soon nearly a third of the company's Negro employees had been moved to semi-skilled jobs.[23]
Meanwhile Duncan was resolving black complaints at Briggs. Originally assigned to the case after Gloster Current had protested to
the FEPC back in August, he found that without a categorical government order the company intended to maintain the job ceiling in
its aircraft division. Moreover the union local's new president,
though sympathetic, was able to be of little help. With both sides
evidently preferring to have forceful action from federal officials
end the impasse, Weaver and his field representative pressed
management and the United States Employment Service, and over
the following months Duncan reported considerable progress was
being made under the Six Point Transfer Program. By July 1942,
some 400, or about one-third of the company's Negroes, had been

transferred from auto production, with 200 of these engaged as riveters or in assembling planes for the army and navy. Training was being accelerated, further transfers were taking place daily, and in other Briggs divisions which were retooling, a few Negroes were moving into skilled operations. Undoubtedly the tradition of black participation in Local 212 affairs that had earlier developed under Mazey's direction was largely responsible for the smoothness of the transition, even in the face of some white complaints. Duncan reported that white walkouts were prevented "because of the progressive leadership of the union, and the fact that some Negroes are members of the executive board and shop committees of the various Briggs plants."[24]

In certain General Motors plants Duncan succeeded in opening up new positions by deftly developing strategies jointly with union staff people or sympathetic local leaders. Ironically, although GM still had the worst employment record of any of the "Big Three,"[25] it did not experience numerous black worker protests. On the other hand, when Negro employees at both Chevrolet Gear and Axle in Detroit and at the corporation's Flint plants did raise the issue, union staff worked closely with Weaver's office successfully to redress their grievances. At the Chevrolet Flint plant in November 1941 the 240 blacks classified as "janitors" (although many of them actually worked as machine cleaners and electric-truck drivers) were threatened with layoffs; they appealed to the UAW's Inter-Racial Committee and FEPC because their seniority made them eligible for transfer to defense production. Again Washington assigned the case to Duncan, who investigated the situation with Hardin. Finding Local 659's president Terrell Thompson and UAW regional director Carl Swanson both unsympathetic, they enlisted the help of Victor Reuther and Oscar Noble in developing a strategy to force the reluctant local into line. Encouraged by Noble, the black workers sponsored protest rallies to publicize their complaints, while Hardin, Reuther, and Noble warned the foot-dragging union functionaries of an impending visitation from

OPM's Duncan. Placed in an awkward situation, Swanson and Thompson forestalled further government intervention by inviting these men from the Inter-Racial Committee and War Policy Division to Flint, where the transfers were thereupon negotiated.[26]

Meanwhile during the winter and spring of 1941–42 the intervention of Hardin and Duncan at Chevrolet Gear and Axle expedited the promotion of some black workers of long seniority.[27] Finally in June 1942, assisting the sympathetic leadership in Local 599, Duncan resolved a troublesome situation in the Buick Division in Flint. Investigating at the request of Colonel Strong, Duncan found that the efforts of the local's officials to end company discrimination were being undermined by former officers, who were exploiting the race issue in a factional fight. Heightening the tension was white resentment that fully 70 percent of the black workers, skeptical of the union, had stopped paying dues. Duncan's persuasive talents quickly brought the rehiring of nearly all the 600 black foundry workers and their integration throughout the entire plant as oilers, drill press operators, welders, lathe operators, and milling machine operators. In the wake of these changes there were minor disturbances, but, with the help of the local's leaders and Colonel Strong, serious trouble was averted.[28]

The changes described in the preceding pages had not been accomplished without some grumbling from white workers. Dissatisfaction with the transfer and upgrading of blacks to wartime production jobs took a far more serious form in the series of wildcat "hate strikes" that began late in 1941. Erupting over the following months at Packard, Chrysler-Dodge, Hudson Naval Ordnance, and Timken Axle, these confrontations reached their climax in the renewed Packard walkouts of the spring of 1943. Although wildcat walkouts over numerous issues posed a serious challenge to union leadership during the war,* the hate strikes, in addition,

---

* We are thankful to Ray Boryczka and to Nelson Lichtenstein for calling our attention to the connection between the hate strikes and the other kinds of wildcat strikes during the war.

epitomized the dilemma of the International officials who wished to promote the utilization and integration of black workers yet were fearful of antagonizing the white rank and file.

Top union leaders were caught off guard in the earliest and nearly simultaneous hate strikes at Packard in Detroit and Curtiss-Wright in Columbus, Ohio, during the fall of 1941. The sharp contrast in the way in which UAW officers handled these two walkouts not only reflected their sensitivity to the varying attitudes of workers and employers in different settings but also foreshadowed the inconsistency with which the union would meet such challenges in the months that followed. Much also depended on the erratic responses of the relevant federal agencies. Yet in the end the union would emerge with a nationwide reputation as a champion of the blacks in their battle for opportunity in war industry.

In the Curtiss-Wright aircraft case, management was receptive to government requests for upgrading blacks, a prejudiced union organizer was actually largely responsible for the walkout, and UAW president Thomas intervened decisively. He removed the staff member and even negotiated an agreement that extended black employment to all departments and in a wide range of semi-skilled and skilled positions.[29]* On the other hand the Packard hate strikes occurred in a stronghold of virulent anti-black hostility that characterized not only the workers but high levels of management as well. They thus presented the union's leadership with a thorny problem that defied easy solution.†

---

* In this case War Department officials also intervened, and Thomas personally went to Columbus to talk with the strikers. By March 1942, four months after that walkout, the scores of blacks working in the plant included women in production jobs and even a few men in the tool-and-die department. Over the next couple of years the company added thousands of blacks to its work force, a number in skilled jobs.

† Packard was known at the time for its substantial proportion of Southern whites in its work force, although the largest single component was Polish-American. Anti-black hostility was prevalent in both groups, and in fact some union members of Polish extraction reportedly participated in the 1942 Sojourner Truth rioting. (See Richard Deverall to Clarence Glick, June 7, 1943, Richard Deverall Notebooks, copy courtesy of Nelson Lichtenstein. For recollections of attitudes of white work-

Actually at first Packard Local 190's leadership, pressed by Christopher Alston and his fellow black activists, had persuaded company officials to transfer blacks on the same basis as whites. But in October 1941 when, in line with this agreement, two black metal polishers were moved from automobile to defense work, 250 white metal polishers conducted a brief sit-down strike, and the union steward returned the two men to their old jobs. Thus began a six-month controversy that *Fortune* wryly called "a wrestling match" between the Government, the union, and the company, "over two American citizens' rights to contribute their skill to the production of Tanks." The local's leadership first supported the Negroes, but when the white metal polishers threatened another strike it backed down again. Even the white members of the local's interracial committee were afraid to recommend that the problem be referred to Hardin's office. Alston and his fellow blacks on the committee thereupon turned to Duncan, and with him jointly mounted a campaign to enlist the International's help. But even

ers by Local 190's treasurer at the time, see Oral History interview with Adam Poplawski, May 2, 1960, Reuther Library.)

The Packard local was a George Addes stronghold, and some of its leadership—considered in certain quarters to be closely aligned with the Communists—was undoubtedly sympathetic to the blacks' aspirations. (For connections of the local's leaders with Addes and the Communists see, *e.g.*, Jack Skeels, "The Development of Political Stability Within the United Auto Workers Union" [Ph.D. dissertation, University of Wisconsin, 1957], 234; press release, "Negro Defense Workers in Detroit Area To Move Out Unless CIO Stamps Out Klan Membership," Nov. 26, 1941, ANP Archives; and Deverall to Clarence Glick, June 7, 1943, Deverall Notebooks, copy courtesy Nelson Lichtenstein.) Yet the intense prejudices among the rank-and-file whites—epitomized by the reports of Klan infiltration, and exploited by the company's racist officials—immobilized the local's leaders. Accordingly, the series of Packard hate strikes during the war provide a classic study of the weakness of a union local's officials in the face of their white constituency's prejudices, and of the challenge which this situation posed for national union leaders interested in fostering interracial working-class solidarity.

Unfortunately the surviving archives, both the local and the International, are not helpful in illuminating the union's internal dynamics. On the other hand the Packard confrontations offer an unusually full picture of the interplay between government, industry, and union, because of the rich quality of the surviving documentary records from the federal agencies involved.

then a whole month elapsed before Hardin's committee finally took up the issue.[30] Duncan and Hardin, now working closely together, pressed the UAW's highest officers, Addes and Thomas. Thomas, responding to their requests, first asked the local's president, Curt Murdock, to enforce the upgrading under the Six Point Transfer Program; and then, when the two Negroes complained that Murdock had presented the request to his stewards in an equivocal manner and that the local was still dragging its feet, Thomas summoned the Packard union leaders to International headquarters. At this unusually high-level conference—which involved Victor Reuther and Noble of the War Policy Division, Hardin and Bates speaking for the Inter-Racial Committee, and Duncan representing the federal government—Addes and Thomas backed the blacks in no uncertain terms. Chastened, Local 190's officers informed the company's industrial relations manager, C. E. Weiss, that they wanted the two black metal polishers transferred the very next day, but the Packard official refused, truculently remarking that "the next step" was up to Thomas.[31]

Thomas now embarked upon a three-pronged strategy. He simultaneously continued to ask the local to "put every possible pressure on the management," while seeking "a firm stand" from his International Executive Board. Yet obviously he was not sanguine about the effectiveness of any unilateral action; as he privately informed Murdock, "Perhaps we can get the Government to step in and force the company to make these transfers." Duncan, seeking to firm up Thomas's hand with his Board, arranged for Weaver to send the UAW president a strong telegram. Duncan, who was in close contact with both Hardin and Noble and knew what was going on, had good reason to be concerned, for the Board meeting in mid-December double-talked around the issue, merely reaffirming its anti-discrimination stand but "ducking responsibility on the Packard case." Now Thomas was left only with his third alternative—he authorized Hardin and Noble to submit the case to Duncan for intervention from Washington. Every attempt "to solve this problem with the machinery of our union has failed," they declared, and the UAW president was determined to have the Packard transfers made.[32]

Duncan now entered upon some highly delicate negotiations with Packard personnel director Weiss and union leaders. The prejudiced Packard executive, who kept insisting that metal polishing was "a white man's job," claimed he required absolute guarantees from the union that the white workers would create no trouble if the transfers were made. Duncan patiently arranged a settlement under which he would have Washington forcefully push the company, while the International union itself agreed to bear complete responsibility if resistance arose. Addes and Thomas lived up to their end of the arrangement, not only committing the union in writing to this position, but forcing the reluctant regional director, Melvin Bishop, to join them and Hardin in further discussions with Packard officials. But to Duncan's utter disappointment, Weaver's boss Sidney Hillman would only send Packard president M. M. Gilman an innocuous note, which the latter answered in kind, blandly denying any discrimination.[33]

Hillman's failure to act decisively left R. J. Thomas out on a limb and caused angry division in the UAW. The white local leaders, having reluctantly committed themselves to risking the wrath of the white rank and file, now castigated OPM, while the black workers, doubting the sincerity of these local officials, denounced them for foot-dragging. Although a few top leaders like Walter Reuther wanted to resolve the impasse by having the International forthrightly warn that the union would not defend workers fired for engaging in hate strikes, the Executive Board meeting late in January again confined itself to pious words. Black civic leaders were becoming impatient with all the delay, Louis Martin lashing out in the *Chronicle* at this "stupid buck-passing and political trickery. The management, the union and the government agencies all must share blame for the injustice." But the International leaders' hesitancy at this point could only have been reenforced by fears of an epidemic of violence arising from the anti-black riot at the Sojourner Truth Housing Project in February, and the fact that Local

190 was in the midst of an election campaign that had serious racial overtones, with the incumbent president and one of his challengers accusing each other of being Ku Klux Klan members. After Murdock's reelection he had his opponent suspended for instigating racial troubles but did nothing about the black metal polishers.[34]

Nevertheless Weaver and Duncan kept pressing, and in mid-March finally got Weiss to promise the transfers if Local 190 requested them in writing. Weaver, now seeking to put stronger pressure on Murdock, sent his best-known staff member, the black journalist Ted Poston, to make a personal appeal before the UAW's International Executive Board. With that body vigorously reaffirming its anti-discrimination policy, Duncan prevailed upon Murdock to accede to Weiss's demand that the local guararantee to discipline any union members trying to prevent the transfers. Clearly the firm commitment from the union had finally made it impossible for the company to duck the issue any longer, and within days the two black metal polishers were back at their new jobs, six months after the controversy first began.[35]

During the first half of 1942 hate strikes broke out irregularly—at Hudson in January, at Dodge in February, and then in a group of serious crises during the early summer—at Dodge and Hudson again in June, and at Timken in July. As the months passed, the union, aided by an increasingly vigorous federal response, became firmer and more decisive in dealing with these challenges and disciplining the ringleaders.

At Dodge Main, white worker opposition to black transfers continued to fester amidst the reassignments that had been occuring since the beginning of the year. When company executives decided to shift Negro "loaders" to Highland Park on a strict seniority basis, whites threatened to walk off the job, and with the local seemingly impotent, the International sent vice-president Richard Frankensteen to handle expected trouble. Three brief stoppages accompanied the transfers in February, but they subsided after sharp warnings from Colonel Strong, the company, and the union;

even the local's representatives joined Frankensteen in advising management to fire anyone refusing to return. Duncan continued to prod company officials and the union on resolving the blacks' promotion and seniority grievances at various Chrysler plants, and in early June his persistence at Dodge Truck resulted in a transfer that precipitated the most serious hate strike thus far.[36]

For months Duncan had been vainly trying to convince Robert Condor, Chrysler's director of labor relations, to order the shift at Dodge Truck, and finally turned for help to Robert Weaver. The Negro manpower chief arranged to have his WPB colleague, the prominent southern white liberal Will Alexander, contact certain Wall Street financiers who were influential in Chrysler affairs. Alexander argued the case so persuasively that Condor received instructions to arrange the transfers. On June 2, when a small group of 26 blacks arrived at their new jobs, a walkout of 350 whites forced a plant shutdown, and 3,000 workers were sent home. Once again the local's officials proved impotent, and only firmness by R. J. Thomas, the WPB, and the company forced a reluctant acquiescence. Thomas at once sent in Morris Field, assistant director of UAW's Chrysler Division, who bluntly announced that "the local will have to accept the Negroes." With Chrysler likewise standing resolute, two whites who had agitated the walkout were fired, and production resumed within several hours. As Weaver reported to his superiors, this was a "notable instance" of labor-management cooperation achieved by his office. Especially significant was the fact that for the first time, punitive sanctions, with the UAW's active support, had been taken against the hate strike leaders.[37]

Detroit blacks were delighted with the International's toughness in the Dodge Truck case. Walter Hardin saw the prompt ultimatum as the beginning of a new day. Similarly Louis Martin editorialized favorably in the *Chronicle*, though he warned that with racism rife among the white rank and file the International must now "pursue a more vigorous campaign of education . . . it is the responsibility of the UAW-CIO to shatter this anti-democratic prejudice in as determined a manner as is humanly possible."[38] Significantly, in assigning credit to the union, neither man noted that the UAW's firmness was predicated upon government pressure and the company's responsiveness to it. But over the next few weeks the importance of federal intervention was again seen, even more dramatically, in the confrontations at Hudson Naval Ordnance and Timken Axle, involving as they did officials in the highest levels of the Navy and War Departments.

Hudson was actually more amenable to expanding job opportunities for blacks than most other companies, but as usual racism among white employees made progress difficult. As early as December 1941 management had been training a few black janitors for machine jobs, and had conferred with OPM and the UAW to forestall a walkout. Such groundwork notwithstanding, when two blacks were assigned in January, 200 whites promptly walked off. The company returned the pair to their old janitorial jobs and refused to do anything further. Moreover, Local 154's president disclaimed any power to require the rank and file to obey the union's constitution, and any possibility of change seemed foreclosed indefinitely when the Sojourner Truth riot erupted. But neither the UAW International, operating through its War Policy Division, nor Duncan allowed the matter to drop. Repeating the tactic he used in the Chevrolet-Flint case earlier, Oscar Noble, meeting with Hudson's black stewards and rank-and-file workers, organized them to become more active in union affairs. By April results were evident. Local 154's executive board now included two blacks, and the local leaders backed the transfer wholeheartedly. Meanwhile Duncan, working hand in glove with Noble, conferred repeatedly with Hudson executives. The latter, facing increasing problems in recruiting machine operators, were now finally prepared to act, and in May arranged a coordinated strategy with the leaders of Local 154 to prepare whites for the impending promotions. The company placed large posters throughout the plant backing Executive Order 8802, while the union issued circulars invoking the authority of "President Roosevelt, the Army, the

Navy, the War Production Board and our own UAW-CIO Constitution—all of which forbid discrimination against anyone because of race or color," and warning that "Violators cannot expect to get the support of Hudson Local 154, UAW-CIO in any discipline they may suffer" for defying the transfer.[39]

Everyone concerned—management, union, and government officials—anticipated that a major hate strike was still likely at Hudson, but all these agencies were now prepared for such an eventuality. On June 18 when a handful of blacks were assigned to machines, about 10,000 whites stopped work. Thomas, who was in Washington, dispatched regional director Melvin Bishop to the scene, and immediately wired Local 154's president that, because the strikers' "display of vicious race prejudice" violated the UAW constitution, "they face expulsion from the union unless they return to work at once." Moreover, he warned that the International would not intercede for the reinstatement of any who were discharged for staying off the job. At the same time Secretary of the Navy Frank Knox sent an equally tough telegram denouncing the strikers for disloyalty and threatening wholesale firings. Within an hour after this wire arrived, most of the men were back on the job. Next day, however, a minor walkout occurred when the company placed several more black trainees on machines, and Frankensteen immediately flew in from Washington. The UAW and the company now cooperated in disciplining the demonstrations' ringleaders, four being fired with the wholehearted approval of Frankensteen. Thus the largest hate strike yet had been crushed by the concerted stand of management, government, and the UAW.[40]

Black leaders, concerned about the proliferation of such wildcat strikes, were alarmed at the intensity and size of this one at Hudson. Hurriedly convened meetings sponsored by the NAACP, NNC, Detroit Urban League, and the UAW Inter-Racial Committee lavishly praised R. J. Thomas but called for a Department of Justice investigation of the whole affair. For their part, the International leaders made it clear that they had every intention of maintaining a firm posture. The *United Automobile Worker* complimented Frankensteen and Melvin Bishop, who bore the brunt of exhorting the strikers to return, and publicized Thomas's denunciation of the "small minority" who had engineered the walkout. He accused them of having "sabotage[d] the national war effort" by their "flagrant violation of the union's constitution," and of having "disgrace[d] the name of the UAW-CIO." [41]

Hardly had these sentiments been expressed when the promotion of a single Negro helper to hammer machine operator precipitated a new hate strike at Timken Axle on July 7. Once more the International office, the company, and the highest levels of the federal bureaucracy jointly took a firm stand. From Washington, Undersecretary of War Robert Patterson, backing the efforts of Colonel George E. Strong in Detroit, demanded obedience to Executive Order 8802. Again the International sanctioned the firing of those who had agitated for the hate strike. Victor Reuther arrived on the scene to shore up wavering Local 174 officials, and at a meeting of the rank and file he secured a pledge to refrain from further stoppages. Just days later, negotiating under the watchful eye of a representative from the UAW's headquarters, Timken's management and the local agreed "that all Negroes who were eligible should be upgraded." And when, soon after, a second black was placed on a hammer machine, hardly any whites walked off. [42]

Thomas's toughness at Chrysler, Hudson Naval Ordnance, and Timken heightened the expectations and the militance of black unionists and their leaders. Black UAW members appreciated the International Executive Board's reaffirmation of the organization's anti-discrimination stance, and the top officials' intervention. Yet they contended that all these crises only demonstrated how much more needed to be done. Thus the seventy-five Negro delegates at the union's August convention*—the largest black representation at any UAW convention thus far—pressed for stronger action, threatening to lead a floor fight for more effective penalties against the strikers. [43]

---

* At least two served on important convention committees—Tappes on Resolutions and Sheffield on the Education Committee. (*Tribune*, Aug. 15, 1942.)

The white International leaders still faced the ticklish problem of remedying black grievances without simultaneously alienating the white members. Highlighting this dilemma was the UAW's recent defeat in a collective bargaining election at Vickers, where management had exploited the union's anti-discrimination policy.[44] Accordingly the convention's Resolutions Committee proposed to sidestep the hate strike problem but placate the blacks by urging a stronger national FEPC and assigning the UAW Education Department responsibility for promoting "interracial cooperation" among the members. Thomas wanted black support for this resolution, and while he publicly excoriated weak-kneed local leaders, who in previous conventions had voted for equal rights and then countenanced racism in the plants, he reminded the Negro delegates of his steadfast past support and how it had offended many whites in the union. He failed, however, to turn the blacks from their demands for a resolution that would punish violators of the UAW's constitutional ban against discrimination. In response the Committee submitted a new draft, admitting now that "many backward" members in plants like Hudson, Dodge, and Packard had fomented hate strikes, conceding that in most unionized factories blacks were relegated to the worst jobs regardless of qualifications, and calling for the creation both at the International level and in every local of "Power-to-Act Committee[s] on Discrimination in Employment" that could enforce union policy. This effort to satisfy black demands produced a furor on the convention floor, and after a Packard delegate angrily denied that race prejudice caused the walkout there, Resolutions Committee chairman Victor Reuther, with Thomas's backing, deleted both references to specific locals and the confession that rampant discrimination still existed in most plants under union contract.[45]

Although the resolution was thus emasculated by deletion of its strongest language when it finally was approved by the convention, it nevertheless represented an important symbolic victory for the blacks. On the other hand, even though Thomas enlarged and restructured the Inter-Racial Committee in the autumn, the union's new anti-discrimination machinery did not become operative. Because black Detroiters recognized the political reality within the UAW, they still operated on the assumption that federal agencies were the most effective lever for changing employment patterns. This was dramatically shown, for example, in the long campaign initiated by trade union leaders in Ford Local 600 to lower the barriers against the employment of black women.

## 3

The Ford Motor Company remained one of the nation's largest employers of blacks. But in a striking reversal, its hiring policies became the most discriminatory among Detroit's large corporations. By the end of 1942 Ford managers virtually ceased recruiting black males; and when turning to female labor to staff the assembly lines at their new Willow Run bomber plant, they fought hard to keep the work force there lily-white. Ford's policy toward Negro women paralleled the practices of other corporations in the Detroit defense industries, but black agitation quite naturally focused on the Willow Run problem both because of Ford's past importance as an employer of black labor and because of the enormous size of the factory, which was designed to employ thousands of female workers. Black civic leaders and trade unionists fought a sustained and energetic battle to open Detroit war production to black women, but because government manpower officials gave discrimination against Negro females low priority, the gains were negligible when compared with those achieved by the city's black male workers. And for its part, the Ford Company continued its successful resistance to recruiting Negro workers of either sex, making only token concessions to the demands of both FEPC and Detroit's black citizens.

Even before the Willow Run plant opened in the spring of 1942, UAW officials raised the question of recruiting black women during contract talks with Ford management,* going so far as to pro-

* Those involved in these negotiations included Richard T. Leonard, director of the Ford Division; Emil Mazey, research director of the Ford Department; Interna-

pose that Negroes constitute a quota of at least 7 percent of the women hired. But with the company adamant in its opposition, the union negotiators felt obliged to accept only vague assurances of non-discrimination. This arrangement at once became embroiled in the Rouge local's factional struggles. Building committeeman Otis Eaton and others among the black foundry leaders who were critical of Shelton Tappes's performance as president of the foundry unit, charged that Ford was even refusing to accept job applications from Negro females, denounced the evasive agreement as worthless, and led a demonstration of 200 black women at Willis Ward's personnel office. In an obvious slap at Tappes, who participated in the local's highest councils, Eaton explained that blacks themselves had to deal directly with the company because "they lacked proper representation" on Local 600's executive committee.

Sensitive to the charge that black interests had been ignored, Sheffield, Tappes, and Richard T. Leonard, director of UAW's Ford Division, rebuked those involved in the demonstration. But the company reneged even on its modest commitment, informing the union in March that the time was not propitious for carrying out the non-discrimination pledge. J. Lawrence Duncan, to whom Sheffield turned at this juncture, made some discrete approaches to his friends Willis Ward and Donald Marshall, but despite their reassurances, the Ford management openly announced in April that no black women would be hired because integration would create "disturbances." To disprove this prediction, Leonard, Noble, Sheffield, and other representatives from the local met with Willow Run's white female employees, and in the presence of Ford personnel officers actually secured from the workers involved an overwhelming expression of support for the UAW's view that integration at Willow Run would produce no problem.[46]

Meanwhile, to the considerable irritation of Ford executives, Detroit's angry black leaders became more and more aggressive. A committee headed by Senator Diggs sponsored a mass meeting of

tional representatives John Conyers and Oscar Noble; and Horace Sheffield of Local 600's Defense Employment Committee.

500 black women in April sharply criticizing the corporation; another women's group led by Beulah Whitby pointedly sent Henry Ford and Harry Bennett a resolution calling the company's attitude toward black females "unpatriotic" and "indefensible"; while black leaders like Horace White and Dr. McClendon added their own condemnations of the corporation. They all received as little satisfaction as the union bargaining committee did. Refused access to influential white executives, they were usually relegated to dealing with Willis Ward, who at first declared that the Sojourner Truth rioting showed "the time was not right" to hire black women, and then announced that the black leaders' own antagonism toward Ford was keeping the women out of Willow Run. Ward suggested that they apologize to Henry Ford for their "vicious unjustified attacks," since "committees, letters, and the sending of government investigators and agitators" would never move the company. Shortly afterward ministers Bradby and Peck and several others in an interracial delegation from the Detroit FEPC Council obtained a rare audience with Harry Bennett. Patronizingly praising Bradby for his early "constructive influence" on Rouge's Negro workers, Bennett noted that now the company "didn't have near as many knifings as they used to." Excoriating "communistically controlled" UAW officials and ungrateful black civic leaders, he declared that Henry Ford, far from permitting discrimination, had always been "very kind and generous to the colored people." Moreover, since Ford had employed black men at Rouge when other companies maintained a white-only policy, it was unjust to make the auto magnate "a guinea pig" in hiring black women for assembly line jobs.[47]

J. Lawrence Duncan, who preferred to work quietly behind the scenes, at first regarded the black leaders' agitation as counterproductive, making the company more intransigent. The son of a long-time foreman at the Rouge, he had married a woman whose parents had warm ties with the Ford family (his father-in-law being head of the garage used by the highest rung of Ford management, while his mother-in-law was an Episcopal church social worker

Battle of Overpass at Ford's River Rouge plant, May 26, 1937: a black and
a white employee of Bennett's Service Department chasing a UAW
leafleteer. (Courtesy, Archives of Labor and Urban Affairs, Wayne State
University.)

Ford Drive Organizers, 1941. Seated: Joe Billups, Walter Hardin, Veal Clough, Leon Bates, and John Conyers. Standing: Christopher C. Alston and William Bowman. (From collection of Rev. William Bowman, copy supplied courtesy of Oscar Noble and UAW.)

Ford strikers in battle with strikebreakers at gate of River Rouge plant, April 1941. (Courtesy, Archives of Labor and Urban Affairs, Wayne State University.)

Sound car driven by Horace Sheffield, NAACP Youth Council leader, during Ford strike, 1941. (Courtesy, Archives of Labor and Urban Affairs, Wayne State University.)

Ford Strike, 1941. Horace White, center, talking with white automobile worker. On the right is organizer Leon Bates. (From collection of Rev. William Bowman, copy supplied courtesy of Oscar Noble and UAW.)

UAW men at Ford contract negotiations, 1941. Seated in center of first row is Shelton Tappes. To Tappes's right is CIO president Philip Murray. Other prominent UAW leaders seated are Richard Frankensteen, 2nd from left; George Addes, 3rd from left; R. J. Thomas, 3rd from right; Richard Leonard, 2nd from right; and director of Ford organizing drive, Michael Widman, at extreme right. (Courtesy, Archives of Labor and Urban Affairs, Wayne State University.)

Sojourner Truth Housing Riot, 1942: van attempting to move in a black family's possessions. (Courtesy, Archives of Labor and Urban Affairs, Wayne State University.)

Scene during the Sojourner Truth Housing Riot, 1942. (Courtesy, Archives of Labor and Urban Affairs, Wayne State University.)

Sojourner Truth Housing Controversy, 1942: flyer distributed by white "improvement association." (Courtesy, Archives of Labor and Urban Affairs, Wayne State University.)

UAW president R. J. Thomas and black staff, late 1944. From left to right, Horace Sheffield, William Bowman, Walter Hardin, Leon Bates, Arto Johnson, Oscar Noble, William Lattimore, George Crockett (shaking hands with Thomas), William Fowler, Wesley Thompson, and John Conyers. (From collection of Rev. William Bowman, copy supplied courtesy of Oscar Noble and Archives of Labor and Urban Affairs, Wayne State University.)

who conferred regularly with Mrs. Edsel Ford). Duncan, who knew Harry Bennett personally, initially believed that this influential executive would have begun hiring black females if the civic leaders had left him alone. To Weaver the WPB field representative confided: "Because of these charges and counter-charges of the union, Negro organizations, and the company, I have purposely remained aloof from the controversy except to keep in touch with each of these groups in order to know what progress is being made."[48] Then at the end of May, acting upon Ward's suggestion, he wrote Bennett, expressing "alarm about the present campaign being waged by certain Negro elements," and offering to work with Ward and Marshall to produce "a workable formula whereby the employment of qualified Negro women can be effected." But all he received was Bennett's assurance, transmitted indirectly through the Rouge's employment manager, that Negro females would be hired "as soon as Negro groups, whose sole interests are political, stop their agitation."[49]

Of course the criticism continued, and in fact was a leading issue in the Local 600 elections held in early June. Tappes, running for his first full term as Recording Secretary (a post to which he had been appointed six months before), stepped down as president of the foundry unit. The two leading contenders for the latter position were his ally, Horace Sheffield, and his vocal critic, Otis Eaton. With Sheffield on the defensive because of his involvement in the Willow Run negotiations, Eaton exploited the issue and won an overwhelming victory.[50] Ironically the agitation against Ford now died down for more than a month, but this did not encourage Bennett to change his position. Duncan now decided upon a direct approach to Edsel Ford, who had largely taken over his father's responsibilities in running the company, but this only produced a reply denying any discrimination whatsoever. Duncan found a little consolation in the fact that almost immediately afterwards some black males had been hired at Willow Run "in the skills for which they had been trained," but of course nothing at all had been done about the black women.[51]

Actually the initiative was being taken mainly by black union leaders. Acting on behalf of Local 600 and the International, Sheffield, Conyers, and Noble sought a conference with Harry Bennett late in July. The latter did not even deign to respond. When the UAW annual convention met, shortly afterwards, the three men reported to the delegates that there was still not one black among the 3000 women then working at Willow Run. Clearly nothing was going to be done without Washington's direct intervention. Consequently, responding to the appeals of Negro unionists, both the national UAW conclave and Local 600's General Council passed resolutions demanding federal action.[52] A few days later Walter Reuther in Washington, and his brother Victor from Detroit, followed up this mandate by pressing War Manpower Commission officials, while the NAACP branch similarly cooperated by sending bitter complaints to FEPC executive secretary Lawrence Cramer and WMC chairman Paul V. McNutt.[53] At the same time Local 600's black leaders, aided by various civic organizations, dramatized the issue with an interracial picket line outside the employment office at River Rouge on August 20. Duncan hoped that this demonstration would strengthen his own efforts, and gearing his actions as usual to those of the Negro unionists and race advancement organizations, conferred with Ward and other Rouge officials, who told him firmly that Harry Bennett had decided to hire the first twenty-five black women for Willow Run within the next few days. Weaver, convinced that this was a genuine breakthrough, persuaded FEPC to "withhold action" on the NAACP's request for intervention.[54]

Detroit's blacks were, however, less impressed by Bennett's word and felt that Weaver had in effect pulled out the rug from under them. Gloster Current, already unhappy with Weaver because the latter, on behalf of WMC chairman McNutt, had recently informed the NAACP branch that the black female issue was too "complicated" for rapid solution, lashed out at the WMC and insisted that the federal government publicly censure Ford for its racist hiring: "If the government will stop vacillating on this problem and kindred problems, effective solutions might be speedily effected. There had been too much 'hush hush,' 'tut tut,' about this whole matter." In addition, the NAACP joined with black union leaders at the Rouge—who were now united in their strategy—in scheduling further demonstrations. At a planning meeting on August 27 Gloster Current, Walter Hardin, Otis Eaton, Shelton Tappes, and Horace Sheffield all excoriated Bennett and demanded that Washington enforce the President's Executive Order, and, with neither Ford nor FEPC having acted, blacks held another mass demonstration at the Rouge in mid-September.[55]

A few weeks later the company finally hired twenty-five black female production workers—but not at Willow Run. Instead they were placed together as a segregated unit at Ford's small Ypsilanti plant. Rouge's foundry workers were enraged, but Bennett simply used their anger as a pretext for suspending any further hiring of black females. In an explosive mood, the foundry on October 11 unanimously resolved to give the company thirty days to settle the issue or face "STRIKE ACTION," and Local 600's General Council backed the blacks by threatening their own "plant-wide demonstration."[56]

Paralleling the growing bitterness in the Rouge was a rapidly escalating militance among black community leaders. Although here and there the Ford Company, its temporizing notwithstanding, could garner small amounts of public support in the black community,[57] most of the city's prominent Negroes now decided to band together in a united struggle to obtain FEPC intervention and public hearings in Detroit. The vehicle employed was Hill's Citizens Committee for Jobs in War Industry, which now became active for the first time. The Committee's viability clearly predicated on a decision by the NAACP branch that the issue could best be attacked through a broad coalition, its activities were carefully coordinated with those of Local 600's black leaders like Tappes and Sheffield, and also enjoyed the support of the UAW's War Policy Division and Hardin's Inter-Racial Committee.

The NAACP branch invited both Victor Reuther and Charles Hill to address its mid-October meeting, where the latter unveiled the Citizens Committee's plans to send a delegation to confer with Paul McNutt in Washington. The protest mushroomed. On October 25 the coalition, publicly excoriating federal inaction, scheduled a "gigantic rally" featuring R. J. Thomas as the principal speaker for the following Sunday. That same day it was announced that Horace Sheffield, representing the UAW and Zaio Woodford of the Detroit Fair Employment Council, would go to Washington. There the interracial team strongly urged FEPC executive secretary Lawrence Cramer to schedule public hearings for Detroit.[58]

From the perspective of the Detroit protesters, the delegation's trip occurred at an opportune juncture in the history of FEPC. Up to this point the agency had withheld its intervention in deference to Weaver's request; moreover during the early autumn Cramer's energies had been absorbed in negotiations over the Committee's status within the WMC. By late October, however, with the dismantling of Weaver's office and his transfer to the staff of WMC's director of operations General Frank J. McSherry, FEPC received jurisdiction over all race discrimination cases. It is true that McNutt denied FEPC an adequate staff and forbade any hearings without prior approval from his office, and that McSherry, although more sympathetic toward the blacks' demands than McNutt ("as long as the boat was not rocked too much"), like his boss considered public hearings detrimental to the war effort.[59] Nevertheless, now for the first time FEPC could take up Willow Run complaints. In fact, Cramer, right after seeing Sheffield and Woodford, and with his resolve reenforced by a phone call from the chairman of Local 600 War Activities Committee warning that the blacks at Rouge would almost surely carry out their threatened walkout unless some tangible intervention occurred quickly, obtained from McSherry approval to dispatch two FEPC investigators to Detroit at once.[60]

The FEPC representatives arrived in the Motor City on the heels of the Citizens Committee's November 1 mass meeting. Ex-

emplifying the unity of Detroit Negroes on this issue, Robert
Bradby had opened his church to Hill's coalition for the Sunday afternoon rally, where nearly a thousand heard Sheffield and Woodford recount their lobbying efforts in Washington, and listened to
R. J. Thomas publicly identify himself for the first time with the
Willow Run protest. Sounding as if he had been privately criticized for not speaking out earlier, the UAW president recalled the
numerous times prejudiced white union members had denounced
him as a "nigger lover," and he dwelt on the fact that the job
problem for black males was still far from settled. Warmly praising
the Citizens Committee for pressing the national government, he
also made quite clear his own strategy of encouraging federal intervention to help the union reduce discrimination: "You can tell
every Negro in Detroit" that if Washington would only implement
Executive Order 8802, nobody would "go farther to give you free-
dom than I."[61]

While the Citizens Committee firmed up its plans to send a
large delegation to see McNutt, the FEPC agents observed for
themselves the total absence of black female production workers at
Ford factories; learned from Geraldine Bledsoe at the USES how
her agency referred numerous black women with training certifi-
cation to the Ford Company, only to have them summarily rejected; and interviewed Harry Bennett, who both argued that he
would have already hired black women except for the Citizens
Committee's interference and yet insisted that he was unable to
because of the overwhelming white opposition. Moreover, as the
FEPC men must have anticipated, the local WMC staff was, as
Duncan had previously discovered, "reluctant to tackle the Ford
situation," and advised delaying any public hearing until more negotiations could be held.[62]

Given these negative responses from both the Ford Company
and the local war manpower people, it was wise that the Citizens
Committee was simultaneously carrying out its program of mass
meetings and direct-action demonstrations. The first week in November, 150 Committee members and friends braved a driving

rain in an interracial picket line at the Grand Boulevard offices of
the federal manpower agencies.[63] The Hill group then highlighted
the discrimination against black women at Ford's Highland Park
plant, where there was considerable opposition to their introduction, and where the handful of black employees had found the
local's officials indifferent. Now, however, its president was willing
to join Tappes, Horace White, and LeBron Simmons in addressing
a mass meeting of Highland Park workers, and soon unionists and
Citizens Committee members were picketing the plant, with Gloster Current and others passing out handbills explaining the reasons
for this wartime demonstration. Then at the end of the month
Local 600 lent further support to the struggle by carrying out its
earlier decision to picket the Rouge complex.[64]

At first neither all this militant activity nor the recommendation
for hearings made by the two FEPC investigators seemed to move
FEPC's bosses in the WMC. McSherry withheld approval, and
Victor Reuther proved no more persuasive when he went to Washington to enlist the general's support.[65] Finally on November 20
Hill arrived in Washington heading a large interracial delegation in
which the UAW black spokesmen were well represented—Tappes
on behalf of Local 600, Sheffield speaking for the UAW-CIO Ford
Department, and Oscar Noble representing the War Policy Division. Conferring with Undersecretary of War Patterson, Mc-
Sherry, and McNutt's deputy, Fowler V. Harper, the Detroiters,
without mincing words about the flagrant violations of Executive
Order 8802 in regard to black males, dwelt on the more obvious
discrimination against Negro women. Hill explained that not only
was Ford blatantly biased, but other Detroit companies were no
better: of 58,000 female war production workers, fewer than 100
were black.[66]

With Cramer enthusiastic and McSherry sounding sympathetic,
it seemed that the weeks of agitation were beginning to pay off,
and the delegation departed considerably encouraged. Within two
weeks McNutt had given his approval, and Cramer announced that
the hearings would be held in February.[67] Promptly on the heels

of this Citizens Committee victory over the foot-dragging men in the WMC, Ford began hiring black women. By mid-December there were sixty-six at the Rouge, with a few at Highland Park and Willow Run.[68]

Clearly the threat of hearings produced by the long, intensive struggle of Detroit's black union and civic leaders had finally moved Ford. UAW officials like the city's civil rights leaders were very proud of their accomplishment. Thomas, in his next annual report, even claimed for the UAW sole credit for the victory. And as one might have anticipated, during Local 600's 1943 elections, when the incumbent president Paul Ste. Marie was being challenged by Percy Llewellyn, who had held the post at the time of the Ford strike, both sides sought to capitalize on the issue. Tappes (running for reelection as Recording Secretary on what proved to be the victorious Llewellyn slate) and Sheffield both charged Ste. Marie with opposition to the demonstrations at the Ford employment office. But Otis Eaton, the man most responsible for those demonstrations, was running against Tappes and claimed that Ste. Marie had led the battle.[69] Actually neither Ste. Marie nor Llewellyn had played a really significant role, and the support they lent the protest came at the behest of the rival black leaders in the local. Undoubtedly this very divisiveness, by compelling both black factions to outdo each other in battling to open up the jobs for women, heightened the race militance that was ultimately responsible for bringing federal action. But in any event UAW support both in Local 600 and at the International headquarters came in response to black demands, and the real credit for the victory must go to the campaign conducted by Rouge's black foundry leaders in cooperation with the Citizens Committee.

In the end the victory turned out to be more the promise of FEPC public hearings in the Motor City rather than any substantial change on the part of the Ford Motor Company. For Ford's new policy toward black women amounted to tokenism. In March 1943 the Willow Run plant employed 25,000 women, but less than 200 were black. The number continued to rise only very slowly, and in the autumn poorly educated Southern white females were still being hired while qualified black women were being turned away by Ford interviewers, who unabashedly told them that they were being barred for racial reasons.[70] And constant complaints over the following months from union officials, FEPC and WMC investigators, and race organizations all continued to be exercises in futility.[71]

Actually Ford was not atypical in its policies regarding the hiring of Negro women. Black women remained a rarity in Detroit's war production, and most of those in the plants were matrons, janitors, and stock handlers. At the end of 1942 Packard and Hudson employed a mere half dozen each. Not one was working at Chrysler's huge Highland Park plant, at Dodge Main, or at GM's Cadillac plant.[72] From time to time government officials negotiated with various companies, yet it is evident that their efforts to alleviate labor shortages by recruiting females were confined almost entirely to whites. When representations were made, only token settlements resulted. Small but precedent-setting additions of black women to production or assembly line work were regarded as significant accomplishments, as when the Citizens Committee late in 1942 secured an agreement with Kelsey-Hayes to hire seventeen black women, and at Murray Body obtained jobs for fifteen women with the help of the UAW local there.[73] Easily the best results were achieved at Briggs, where following persistent pressure from Duncan on both the company and Locals 212 and 742, there were forty women in production jobs by the end of 1942.[74] As late as the summer of 1943 a government report termed the pool of 25,000 available black women the city's "largest neglected source of labor." Six more months passed and at a time when the district manpower director was practically begging women to take patriotic work in war plants, Walter Hardin grimly pointed to the thousands of black women, who having qualified themselves through training courses, still could not obtain production jobs.[75]

Ford's policy toward Negro women not only reflected an industry-wide problem but also was part of the drastic change in the corporation's relations with black Detroiters generally. A year after the strike, Ford unceremoniously ended all philanthropic interest in Inkster,[76] and by mid-1942 there was emerging an obvious pattern of discrimination in the employment of black males. In the last six months of that year, while about 30,000 whites were being added to the payroll, the number of black men employed remained stationary or even declined slightly.[77] Violating wartime regulations, Ford was actually recruiting white labor from other Michigan cities while turning away black applicants in Detroit. Alerted to this situation by J. Lawrence Duncan, Gloster Current arranged for Walter White to protest to the WMC in Washington, but even though the Michigan USES quickly obtained assurances from Ford's personnel department that the practice would cease, black males continued to be closed out.[78] A USES report revealed that during the spring of 1943 nearly half the whites whom it referred to Ford were hired, but only 1 percent of the blacks. As Geraldine Bledsoe reported in February 1943: "The company gives as its reason for restricting the use of non-white workers at its other plants the fact that it hires a disproportionately high percentage of non-whites at Rouge, but non-white workers are being constantly rejected at this plant when other workers are being hired."[79] Moreover in obvious violation of the anti-discrimination clause in the company's union contract, a high proportion of the relatively few men transferred from the Rouge to Willow Run were dismissed,[80] and at the Rouge itself the management instituted segregation in the new steel and aluminum foundries, while sharply limiting transfers to other departments. Tensions in these two foundries became so intense that in April 1943 three thousand blacks walked off the job in an angry three-day wildcat strike.[81]

In the wake of this protest, which the company blamed on black draft-dodgers, Bennett ordered an end to hiring any more blacks at the Rouge. With the departure from the scene of both Donald Marshall (due to illness) and Willis Ward (who had entered the army), whatever influence these men may have exerted was now gone; and in May the black personnel office was closed down entirely.[82] Union leaders like Tappes and black civil rights spokesmen like McClendon and Hill continued to attack Ford and periodically reiterate their request that FEPC publicize the company's record at a public hearing.[83] But because Ford was still one of the country's largest employers of Negroes and was now hiring a token number of black women, the Committee's staff reluctantly concluded that "a systematic policy" of discrimination could not be proven.[84] And when FEPC did attempt in September to press Harry Bennett directly, its three negotiators were treated contemptuously, with Bennett making them cool their heels in an outer office for three hours before deigning to see them, because the delegation included a black man, G. James Fleming, the agency's regional director.[85] While verbally agreeing to an anti-discrimination arrangement once he finally conferred with them, Bennett characteristically refused afterwards to confirm the commitment in writing. The situation did not improve significantly during the following months. For example, shortly before the war's end, blacks of both sexes at Willow Run still numbered only 735—a mere 3.5 percent of the total employment there.[86]

### 4

When in late 1942 Detroit's Negro leaders pressed FEPC to hold public hearings in the Motor City, Ford headed the long list of companies whose discriminatory policies they hoped to expose. After the Committee had scheduled the hearings for February, Cramer followed through with a systematic investigation of Detroit's industries. The arrival of the FEPC investigators and the piecemeal, limited improvements stimulated by their presence served to both heighten the expectations and militance of the black workers and simultaneously to accentuate the fears of the prejudiced whites. The result, given the volatile racial tensions in Detroit, was a series of wildcat walkouts by both whites and blacks, culminating in the most serious hate strike of the war—the one at Packard in June 1943.

At the start of the new year, Cramer dispatched the black staff member G. James Fleming to the Motor City to head the inquiry.[87] Formerly managing editor of the Philadelphia *Tribune*, Fleming would eventually spend more than a half year in Detroit, gathering proof for the oft-postponed hearings, and along the way resolving a number of specific complaints of discrimination. He assembled a staff that at its height between February and April 1943 numbered six professional workers, including Geraldine Bledsoe and J. Lawrence Duncan on loan respectively from the Michigan USES and the regional WMC office.[88] In securing evidence he benefited from the help of black and interracial civic organizations as well as knowledgeable trade unionists intimately familiar with "the hiring practices and policies from the inside."[89] Although in the end the FEPC's Detroit hearings were never held, Fleming and his staff, possessing this threat as their only real leverage, acted as a gadfly, prodding foot-dragging and sometimes hostile managements, navy department personnel,* and WMC regional and district officials.

The War Manpower representatives in the Motor City were in fact highly dubious about the value of hearings, unhappy with the Citizens Committee's requests for FEPC to come in, and desirous of veto power over FEPC's activities in Detroit. Regarding the latter as overly susceptible to pressure from minority groups that wanted a "shoulder to weep on," and believing that job integration in war industry could not come "overnight," least of all by threats or "executive fiat," local WMC people felt that without their prior approval, FEPC should schedule no investigations or hearings. Fortunately they received no such authority, but this did not prevent them from continuing to maneuver against a hearing.[90] For

---

* Despite Captain Wotherspoon's cooperative attitude, Fleming found that "next to industry, the navy was the hardest nut to crack." Thus, for example, he cited the inspector of naval aircraft at Briggs as being guilty not only of discrimination against Negroes in recruiting inspector-trainees, but of chiding an NAACP official for thinking that Executive Order 8802 had ever been intended to be enforced. (See Fleming to George M. Johnson, Jr., Jan. 23, 1943, FEPC Archives Reel 40. See also below for role of Navy Department in calling off Detroit hearings.)

example, in the spring of 1943 exaggerated accounts about the job progress of Detroit blacks were planted in the local press and the New York *Times*. The latter, completely misrepresenting an FEPC investigator's careful explanation of the "spotty improvement" and "the changing pattern from out-and-out refusal to hire Negro men . . . to employing them for the most part, in unskilled categories," distorted the data into a rosy version of wholesale job gains blacks had supposedly made.[91] Yet despite Fleming's reservations about the local WMC and about certain manpower people representing the armed forces as well, he cooperated with them as much as possible in trying to resolve the specific grievances he uncovered.[92] Actually, Fleming and his staff really possessed such circumscribed authority that their role became peripheral when hate strikes resulted from the upgrading of blacks that FEPC's presence had produced. Instead it was Colonel Strong, having the power to impose sanctions, who characteristically intervened and provided the force that sustained the expansion of Negro economic opportunity.

Fleming was no pussyfooter, and he boldly pushed his mandate to the limits, injecting his investigative staff into crisis situations far more than WMC superiors in Washington would have approved. Yet just days after he had arrived in Detroit, the weakness in FEPC's position—and in that of black Detroiters as well—was demonstrated when Paul McNutt peremptorily pulled the rug from under them. On January 11, the WMC chairman not only announced the indefinite postponement of the highly publicized inquiry into the railroad industry (set for January 25) but took steps to quash the Detroit hearings he had earlier approved. Information leaked to the press revealed that at the behest of Navy representatives in Detroit Assistant Secretary of the Navy Ralph Bard had prevailed upon McNutt to ask FEPC to "abandon" its plans for Detroit. Almost immediately a delegation of Detroit Negroes, headed by Hill—and including the UAW's Horace Sheffield—rushed to Washington to seek assurance from Lawrence Cramer that the hearings would not be dropped, but they found the FEPC executive secretary noncommittal.[93]

Black Detroiters were now desperate. Not only did they need the glare of publicity offered by FEPC hearings, but the reports about imminent cancellation were impeding Fleming's investigations.[94] Accordingly, leading Detroit Negroes and white civil right advocates joined a group of New York labor people—including representatives from the Red Caps, the National Maritime Union, and the Communist-dominated Negro Labor Victory Committee— in a conference with McNutt on January 20th. Headed by Charles Hill, the large delegation represented an impressive array of Detroit organizations, ranging from the Council of Churches, Jewish Community Council, and Catholic groups, through the NAACP and Urban League, to the Willow Run and Rouge locals of the UAW. Along with Hill, prominent roles at the meeting with the War Manpower chief were played by Louis Martin, Horace Shef- field (who earlier in the day had heatedly confronted Assistant Sec- retary Bard), and Shelton Tappes. Most of the discussion focused on the railroad issue that had aroused blacks to such a furor across the country, since, as the Detroiters were well aware, the fate of the railroad hearings would set a precedent for FEPC's course in their own city. When WMC deputy chairman Fowler Harper de- fended McNutt's bowing to railroad pressure, Tappes angrily re- torted: "You have the nerve to tell this body that the southern railroads are so powerful they can defy the government." McNutt not only offered no encouragement whatever, but also appeared arrogant toward the delegation, and when Hill politely tried to end the discouraging conference, several heatedly interrupted to con- demn the War Manpower chief for this "paternalistic and insulting reception."[95] Unfazed, McNutt not only shelved the railroad hear- ing but also carried out his resolve indefinitely to postpone the one in Detroit.

In this demoralizing crisis, with the uncertainties stemming from Washington having their counterpart in the coolness of the WMC locally, Fleming and his staff resolutely carried on their work. Paradoxically, their efforts also undermined preparations for the hearings by encouraging token compliance with Executive

Order 8802. Even when Fleming had first arrived in Detroit and observed the improvement brought about by Duncan and the Citizens Committee, he had advised FEPC officials in Washington that a Detroit public hearing would need to be "approached somewhat differently from past hearings." The problem was that, as Fleming observed, with few companies now openly refusing to hire blacks altogether, "Some of the firms we may call for a public hearing will be able to show statistically that they now have Negroes employed." FEPC's low standards of compliance reflected, of course, both the lack of sanctions in the Executive Order and the lack of broad legitimacy that the new principle of fair employment practices then enjoyed. Accordingly, over the months, the diligence of Fleming and his staff, aided by the threat of rescheduled hearings, ironically produced results that made it more and more difficult to assemble the kind of prima facie evidence needed to win WMC's approval for those hearings. Fleming worked hard to resolve well-authenticated complaints, only to be forced to accept token settlements. Thus, as he later reported, some of his "best cases" slated for public hearing evaporated, and by May most larger Detroit companies were adjudged in formal compliance. For example, Chrysler and Hudson Naval Ordnance had made significant progress, while others like Packard, which had recently placed a few Negro women as drill press operators "as a sign of . . . living up" to the Executive Order, thus "saved themselves from a hearing."[96] Packard in fact was not cited, even though its 2000 black employees were virtually confined to unskilled and semi-skilled work and still almost entirely concentrated in the foundry. Elsewhere in the plant almost none were operating machines, and newly employed whites were being trained for machine work, while blacks with years of service remained janitors.[97] Again, with Ford still ahead of all others both in numbers of black workers and in the range of skills in which they were utilized, and with a few hundred Negro women at Willow Run, "There seems no way in which this company may be called to a public hearing."[98]

By this time, with FEPC in Washington so thoroughly demoralized that staffers, Committee members, and even Chairman Malcolm MacLean had resigned in disillusion, a hearing seemed more remote than ever. Fleming, his staff now reduced to two professional workers, journeyed to Washington in a desperate effort to revive the inquiry and succeeded in persuading the Committee to reschedule it for May 24–25. McNutt, of course, was still unfavorable toward holding the Detroit hearing, but as Cramer soon discovered, there was another serious difficulty. Maceo Hubbard, the black staff attorney whom the FEPC executive secretary dispatched to Detroit to select carefully Fleming's strongest cases, found that unfortunately these were all minor manufacturers; by FEPC standards, complaints against major companies were all "satisfactorily adjusted."[99]

With the big corporations thus excluded from the projected hearing, the tactical question arose: should it be held at all? When the acting FEPC chairman and militant black Chicago attorney Earl Dickerson went to Detroit to consult with the city's Negro leaders in mid-May,* he found them agreed that a public hearing was still essential, but sharply divided over whether it should be delayed an additional month. People like the NAACP branch leaders, concerned about keeping the protest momentum alive, strongly favored proceeding at once. Others, particularly the black unionists from Packard and Ford, felt that the hearing would be a flop without "big name" companies, and that a brief postponement would allow time for gathering more evidence. Moreover, a delay would also act "as a big stick" over the heads of recalcitrant companies. Renewing previous assurances that they could supply adequate proof of discrimination, Alston and Tappes at once took a delegation of union and NNC people to Washington where they appealed to FEPC for postponement.[100] Ironically these representations dovetailed with the desires of Paul V. McNutt, who was

---

* Among those attending were the editors of both black papers—Martin and Ulysses Boykin—Current, Hill, Horace White, as well as the national NAACP's chief counsel, Thurgood Marshall.

still in no hurry for a hearing. Accordingly it was again put off until the end of June. [101] *

In the end, even though revitalized and strengthened, FEPC went ahead with the railroad hearings, the plans for a public inquiry in Detroit simply petered out. Undoubtedly because of concessions employers had made in the face of the combined pressures from blacks, key union leaders, and federal agencies, Francis J. Haas, the new chairman who personally visited the Motor City, must have concluded that the Committee's resources could be better used elsewhere. [102] Indeed the utilization and upgrading of black workers that accompanied Fleming's presence in Detroit had been substantial enough to rekindle the anxieties of prejudiced whites and produce a revival of the hate strikes that had subsided after the determined government and union actions in mid-1942. At the same time blacks, frustrated and angered by the persistence of flagrant discrimination, sometimes resorted to their own walkouts.

## 5

Easily the most serious of these confrontations occurred at Packard, but altogether there were about a dozen hate strikes during the first six months of 1943. Most of them were brief and involved small numbers of people, yet they clearly revealed the existence of underlying tensions with explosive possibilities, even at plants where earlier demonstrations of this sort had been resolved in the blacks' favor. [103] One of these erupted rather surprisingly at Briggs's Mack Avenue plant, when black women were placed on an assembly line. Mazey, recently reelected president of Local 212, was one of the few local officials to act promptly in terminat-

---

* The above discussion is written from the perspective of the black protestors in Detroit. For analysis of this decision from the perspective of the embattled FEPC itself, and of Dickerson's reasons for having scheduled the Detroit hearings even without McNutt's approval, see Louis Ruchames, *Race, Jobs, and Politics: The Story of FEPC* (New York, 1953), 55–56.

ing such a protest. He directed the UAW plant chairman to inform the strikers that the union would back the company one hundred percent in firing them, and within ten minutes everyone returned to work.[104]*

For their part, dissatisfied black workers, often finding their local union leaders unsympathetic, at times also walked off the job. Thus at Chevrolet Gear and Axle. Local 234 officials had told black sweepers, "We can't do anything," when the latter complained that even with seniority they were denied upgrading in favor of newly hired whites. At Timken, where the earlier arrangements to assure blacks fair treatment had broken down, leaders in the local turned their backs when the company refused to promote any more Negroes to machine jobs.[105] Similarly blacks at Chrysler's Highland Park plant found Local 490 slow in taking up their grievances. Here, during the first couple of months in 1943, management had upgraded seventy-five black janitors and had hired Negro women to replace them, but two hundred Negro custodians twice walked out, angrily charging that the women had been assigned to heavy common labor, while promotions for the remaining male janitors were virtually negligible. These workers, however, quickly responded to appeals from Addes and regional director Leo Lamotte, the Detroit Urban League and the FEPC to return and utilize the union's grievance machinery.[106] Then over the next days, other blacks at Chrysler's Jefferson plant staged additional work stoppages. Significant improvements at both factories followed, and indeed over the following weeks progress at

---

* One of the most serious of these early 1943 wildcat strikes erupted on March 25–26 in the non-union Vickers plant when 800 whites walked off because the company, at the persistent urging of Fleming and other interested Negroes, put two blacks in the lathe department. Given this firm's earlier exploitation of the race issue to defeat the UAW in a collective bargaining election, the whites' reaction should scarcely have been unexpected; but management, backed by government agencies, stood fast and subsequently recruited additional blacks. (*Chronicle*, April 3, 1943, and especially " 'Hate' Strikes in Which the Services of the President's Committee on Fair Employment Practice Have Been Requested," attached to Fleming to Jack Raskin, July 20, 1943, Michigan Civil Rights Congress Archives, Box 54.)

Chrysler would be such that Fleming, seeking to ascertain why he had not received complaints about the company, was informed by Walter Hardin that under the revamped upgrading policy the workers "have not been faring so badly."[107]

Yet these black protests had epitomized the Negro workers' unhappiness with both management and the UAW locals amidst the proliferating hate strikes. An exasperated Hardin told an NAACP Labor Committee that he would "quit my job with the UAW-CIO and go back into the shop unless some of the Negro's labor problems are solved."[108] Hardin was virtually powerless to fight individual grievances or resolve crisis situations; nor did he have the confidence of the UAW's regional directors.[109] Yet in April, serving both as secretary of the UAW's Inter-Racial Committee and co-chairman of the NAACP's Labor Committee, he was able to mobilize forces for an important symbolic protest—a parade and mass rally at Cadillac Square against the continuing discrimination in war plants. More than 5,000 marched down Woodward Avenue to the Square, where 10,000 blacks and whites listened to speeches from McClendon, Hill, Colonel Strong, and UAW vice-president, Walter Reuther. The last pledged that "the UAW-CIO would tell any worker that refused to work with a colored worker that he could leave the plant because he did not belong there." Completing the ritual on this occasion, the audience solemnly adopted "The Cadillac Charter," commiting themselves to combat discrimination.[110]

As this demonstration indicated, the UAW's top officials said the right things, even though they still often proved impotent against deep-seated white resentment. Although Hardin, hurt by sniping from old NAACP hands who felt that he had slighted them in staging the rally, abruptly resigned from his NAACP post,[111] leaders of the UAW and the branch continued to cooperate. Thus a few weeks later R. J. Thomas, meeting with NAACP officers planning for the Association's forthcoming National Emergency Wartime Conference, impressed them with his sincerity and steadfastness. Nonetheless, as Fleming observed, although top UAW leaders condemned hate strikes and "have been insisting that non-discrimination is the thing, this thinking has not yet altered to any real degree the attitudes of the individuals who make up the rank and file." [112]

Thomas's personal assurances to the NAACP notwithstanding, within days Fleming's more accurate assessment received dramatic confirmation when 25,000 whites walked out at Packard in one of the most serious hate strikes of the entire war. Packard had been among the slowest companies in modifying its employment policies, and its personnel director, C. E. Weiss, was probably the most unabashedly bigoted executive in the industry. When a white FEPC investigator once brought Fleming to a conference, Weiss's first comment was, "you ought to know better than to bring a Negro in here to settle this thing." Constantly mouthing racist clichés, Weiss portrayed blacks as given to irresponsibly high absenteeism and addicted to dice-playing on the job. On another occasion, boasting that while working for Chrysler back in 1917 he had been responsible for bringing the first "load of niggers" from the South, he told an FEPC field representative that Local 190's Inter-Racial Committee was "one of the most disruptive elements" in pitting black against white. [113] Actions of Packard officials like Weiss's made it quite evident that they were exploiting the racial prejudices of their workers in order to undermine the union, especially during the June walkout. The UAW quite accurately charged Packard management with encouraging white employee resistance to black upgrading and deliberately fostering hate strikes. Given the combination of management's policies and the virulent racism among so many rank-and-file whites, tensions at the plant naturally remained high after the work stoppages of 1941–42. [114] Therefore when Packard, like Chrysler and some other firms, responded to Fleming's presence in Detroit by occasionally upgrading a few black workers, it would have been difficult to avoid antagonizing the hostile whites, but the UAW charged that the company went about it in a way calculated to induce the hate strikes. [115] In this context the leadership of Local 190 remained timid and divided on how to handle the issue, with blacks charging that they received a "runaround" when they made complaints.[116]

A series of lesser work stoppages had erupted in February and March, precipitated by the addition of small numbers of black women to the work force. Even though the Packard chief stewards had recently gone on record in support of equal rights for Negro workers, on February 12 white women walked off the job when three newly trained black females were assigned to drill presses, and the local's representative sent them back to the training school, hoping that the whites would cool down. With Local 190 in the midst of annual elections, and all candidates fearful of getting "their necks . . . chopped off," Christopher Alston, co-chairman of its Inter-Racial Committee, was flatly turned down when he appealed to the executive board to overturn this decision.[117] After the election, prodded by the FEPC field staff in Detroit, Weiss and the local finally reassigned the black women to the drill presses, and one hundred white women quit work. But the local's new president Norman Matthews, supported by the firm position of Colonel Strong, acted decisively, and the women angrily complied with his order to resume their jobs.[118]

Three Negro women had now received the positions for which they had been trained. Packard management, however, openly exhibited its distaste by ordering the new drill-press operators to use a jim crow toilet—a practice that Fleming stopped by getting Local 190 officials to protest. Still, Packard officials, with the government looking over their shoulders, added four more black women drill-press operators on March 18, leading to two new walkouts involving about 3,000 whites. At first the union's International officers floundered helplessly, but when Fleming's assistant, alerted by a UAW staff member, contacted Strong and Addes, he found that the colonel with "characteristic forcefulness" was already working with UAW officials in getting the whites back.[119]

Thus far Colonel Strong, acting together with key local and International UAW officials, had avoided a major catastrophe. But the situation remained volatile, and the company continued to proceed very slowly in placing additional blacks in production work. Fleming, who was working through Alston to obtain the evidence needed to hail Packard before the forthcoming public hearing, concluded that Packard had hired the women "principally for token purposes" to avoid being summoned to the inquiry. Yet even these cosmetic gestures made most of the white workers increasingly apprehensive, and by late spring rumors were circulating among them that the company was prepared to make "extensive upgrading" if seriously pressed by the union or FEPC.[120] In this atmosphere it took only a few more promotions to trigger the series of white and black wildcat walkouts that reached a climax with the massive hate strike of early June.

First, several hundred whites put down their tools on May 24 when Packard upgraded three black males to the aircraft assembly line. For Local 190's highly divided leadership, the situation, involving as it did white males who were their chief constituency, was far more serious than the recent protests of the white females.[121] Efforts by the union local, management, and Colonel Strong to get the whites to return proved unavailing, until the local's leaders temporized by proposing to remove the blacks from the assembly line until a mass membership meeting could deal with the problem. No sooner had the whites resumed work than the majority of the blacks, angered by the union's indecisiveness, walked off under the leadership of men like Chief Steward Christopher Alston. The foundry, where most of the blacks were employed, completely closed down for three days. Now management, government, and union representatives had to direct their appeals to the blacks, and only Colonel Strong's promise to restore the three men to their new jobs brought the blacks back to the factory.[122]

However, the trouble had only begun. At the May 30 membership meeting, boos from all over the auditorium interrupted the vigorous defenses of black rights made by both Strong (who threatened to fire white strike leaders) and R. J. Thomas. Hundreds ostentatiously stalked out as the UAW president pledged to enforce the International constitution, declaring, "This problem must be settled or it will wreck our union."[123] That night when the three blacks returned to the assembly line, Weiss inflamed the situation further by informing them that their new jobs could be kept only with the white workers' approval. Then he and other Packard officials told the whites that they did not have to work with blacks. Moreover, according to a government observer, the factory superintendent worsened matters by "going through the plant telling the workers they have no union and that they might as well come back into the company union." Naturally the whites walked off again, and the company removed the blacks once more. Thomas and UAW regional director Leo Lamotte publicly denounced Weiss for inciting racial conflict and encouraging white resistance.[124] But the situation within Local 190 itself was so bad, with the faction defeated in the February elections undermining Matthews's mediating efforts, that he and secretary James Lindahl were the only officers supporting the stand taken by Thomas and the International.[125]

The first two days of June were filled with conferences among union people, management, and officials from the War Department and U.S. Labor Department Conciliation Service. Given the enormous and the painfully obvious difficulty of getting the whites to accept the upgrading, intervention from Washington seemed imperative, and UAW leaders debated the advisability of asking the War Labor Board (WLB) to step in. Thomas favored this course, but Lamotte and others sharply disagreed, fearing that this would establish an unfortunate precedent. Nevertheless with the situation so serious, Thomas went ahead and on June 1 asked the Labor Department to certify the dispute to the WLB. At the same time, leaving no stone unturned, he also requested the FEPC to enter the case officially, and appealed to the Army Air Corps' field representatives to have Weiss removed from his job. There was uncertainty at the WLB concerning its jurisdiction as well as fears by the FEPC that it might prejudice the case for the projected public hearing by getting involved at this point, and so there was no immediate help from Washington. But the lengthy discussions in Detroit finally produced an agreement on June 2 providing for the blacks' return to their production jobs. That night, however, when the company carried out the transfers, white employees promptly began walking off again, and by next day over 25,000 workers were on a wildcat strike, which virtually shut down the plant.[126]

Colonel Strong, who usually proved so helpful in settling this kind of confrontation, had been called out of town on another assignment, but Matthews and Thomas immediately took a firm position. They condemned the walkout and dispatched Local 190 stewards to the scene to persuade the morning shift to go back.[127] But as thousands milled around the gates listening to racist speakers, some of the stewards actually circulated among the strikers urging them to remain out. Matthews and those local officials who backed him were jeered as they circled the area in sound trucks. At one point it appeared that angry workers were going to wreck one of the vehicles, and minor functionaries in the local frankly admitted to the press that they had "lost all control over their members." By the next day, June 4, a small percentage of workers did heed the calls to return, but the overwhelming majority remained out, and "throughout the day crowds lingered at the factory gates, booing both the union officials who continued to speak from sound cars and the blacks who went through the gates to their jobs." Meanwhile a divided Local 190 executive board considered issuing "an ultimatum" threatening "discipline by the union," but the meeting broke up without reaching agreement.[128]

Thomas displayed no such uncertainty. Again publicly blaming Packard officials for this crisis,[129] he secretly flew to Washington to seek federal intervention. At the WLB Thomas urged officials to order the strikers back; at the War Department he pleaded with authorities to take over the plant or at least to return Colonel Strong to Detroit immediately. He also asked the FEPC's new chairman, Monsignor Francis Haas, to apply additional pressure with these agencies. As he explained to Haas, because of its forceful stand on behalf of blacks, the UAW International office was "out on a limb" with the rank and file and needed decisive government action.[130]*

Thomas's efforts in Washington were fruitful. The WLB's deputy executive director dispatched a strongly worded telegram telling Packard workers to "resume production of vitally needed war material at once." Simultaneously the Army ordered Strong back to Detroit, and at once he announced that anyone who persisted in encouraging the strike would be fired.[131] Thomas, returning on the 5th, armed with assurances from Washington—and with a new WLB directive signed by chairman William H. Davis himself—lost no time in laying down the law to the strikers, threatening expulsion from the union to those who would not return. As he told an approving conference of Ford union representatives that very evening, "I delivered the strongest ultimatum I have ever made in asking those Packard workers to go back, but I'm going to make it even stronger—even if it requires that large numbers of white workers out there lose their jobs. . . . That's the only point of view this union can take. . . . Some people in front of the Packard

* Given the sparse surviving evidence, it has been difficult to document in detail the deliberations of the UAW's International officials or the movements of R. J. Thomas during the critical two days of June 3 and 4. The Associated Press of June 3 reported that "A union official, who could not be quoted, said the U.A.W.-C.I.O. leaders had decided to ask Army authorities to take over the plant after several thousand workers crowding at the plant gates this afternoon ignored stewards' pleas to return to their jobs." (AP dispatch, June 3, in N.Y. *Times*, June 4, 1943.) References to Thomas were, we found, missing from reports in the press for events on June 4, and our reconstruction of what he did when he was in Washington is based largely on circumstantial evidence. We know he was in the nation's capital because an FEPC official logged a telephone call from the black civilian aide to the secretary of war, Truman K. Gibson, Jr., reporting that the UAW president had left Washington to return to Detroit. (E. Trimble, report of phone conversation with Truman K. Gibson, Jr., June 5, 1943, FEPC Archives Reel 55FR.) Although a search of Gibson's files in the National Archives produced no further evidence on Thomas's visit, Gibson has informed us that at John Dancy's request he arranged an appointment for Thomas with the head of the labor relations section in the War Department. He also has the impression that Thomas secured appointments with other War Department officials. (Interview with Truman K. Gibson, Jr., July 18, 1977.)

plant say that if they stay there on the street long enough the International union must retreat. We will not retreat. I say to you that if we take any other position our organization is lost."[132]

By then the growing signs of government and union firmness had begun to bear fruit, and indeed about one-third of the day-shift had already returned. Colonel Strong immediately inaugurated an investigation of the shutdown, and on June 6 nearly thirty "ringleaders" were suspended.* Thereafter resistance crumbled, and on June 7 nearly everyone had returned to work.[133]

Thomas's consistent strategy of pressing government agencies to take decisive, even punitive action, which he could then vigorously support had this time paid off even more dramatically than in the Hudson Naval Ordnance walkout a year earlier. Because government officials hesitated in the face of the complete shutdown of a major war plant by thousands of angry employees, and because the UAW Local 190's leadership was divided when the walkout began on June 3, Thomas's efforts had been an exceedingly delicate operation. A few days after the confrontation, addressing a UAW International Executive Board meeting that unanimously endorsed the position he had taken, he praised Colonel Strong and at the same time admitted "how very close the Union came to losing that Local." In fact, for some time afterward Thomas was attacked for his stand in the Packard strike, and Local 190 even sent a delegation to the 1943 UAW convention pledged to oppose his reelection.[134] Although it had been federal intervention that ended the strike, and few could have known the extent of Thomas's role in obtaining that intervention, his action enormously strengthened the UAW's standing in the black community. As a leading official of the National Urban League, for example, crediting the UAW president with breaking the Packard impasse, de-

---

* A few days later several were reinstated (*News*, June 10, 1943), but some lost their jobs permanently. In the group suspended were a few blacks who had led the earlier walkout. Their suspension reflected Strong's desire to appear even-handed toward both races. Among those losing their jobs was Christopher Alston, who although 31 years old and with dependents, lost his draft deferment and was hurriedly sent into the Army. (Interview with Alston, Oct. 30, 1977.)

clared: "The strike did not end until R. J. Thomas . . . announced
that the union would not countenance the action of the white
union members and threatened to expel members who refused to
comply with the order."[135]

What happened in the aftermath of the Packard confrontations
resembled the token changes in employment patterns that had
characteristically occurred following the earlier hate strikes. The
particular complaints that led to the hate strikes were resolved,
but fundamental changes in the deeply ingrained policy of job bias
did not automatically occur. Ultimately, relatively striking improvement did come about, but this was achieved only through the
determined and sustained efforts of the reorganized and rejuve-
nated FEPC.

This agency, which had played only a very peripheral role during the ten days of open conflict in May and June, now vigorously
asserted its jurisdiction only to find both Packard foremen and
union stewards alike dragging their feet and resisting any further
changes. Matthews in fact was so discouraged over the attitude of
the white workers that he had "given up." Fleming, until his departure from the Motor City in mid-summer, continued to press
forward in amassing the evidence of discrimination against Packard
as well as other major Detroit employers, and in early August the
FEPC officially submitted fresh allegations to both the company
and Local 190. In filing these charges the FEPC did not hesitate to
place much of the blame on the stewards and other union officials
as well as Packard management. At a meeting in Weiss's office one
representative from Local 190 had even referred to blacks as irre-
sponsible dice-players endlessly badgering the UAW: "If you give
them colored fellows an inch they'll take a mile."[136]

Yet over the next four months tortuous negotiations carried out
by tenacious FEPC field representatives—combined with an assist
from blacks who staged a work stoppage—eventually produced significant improvements. First, at the end of August, came an agreement between Weiss and the Union providing immediate promotions for eleven complainants, with a number of other cases to be

processed through the regular union-company grievance machinery. But even then, one black with excellent qualifications was denied upgrading simply because Packard and the union local jointly decided that a white walkout might follow in that particular department, and other blacks filed additional charges, blaming their problem on "politics within Local 190." Nevertheless the transfer of Negroes to better jobs was actually accelerated.[137] By the time of the UAW annual convention, Matthews proudly listed more than 300 semi-skilled jobs that blacks now held outside the Packard foundry—with practically every one constituting transfers in the past few months.* In fact Matthews wishfully asserted "that our problem at Packard is just about solved," but black foundry workers soon set him straight by staging another walkout on November 12 protesting the continuing difficulties in obtaining more transfers. This brief demonstration, by forcing Colonel Strong's intervention, produced unprecedentedly rapid gains. By Thanksgiving FEPC staffers reported that 200 had been upgraded in the preceding ten days.[138]

In both this black work stoppage and the much larger one the preceding May, the Negroes' militance was clearly rooted in heightened expectations stemming directly from FEPC pressure. In the spring it had been the threat of the agency's public hearings, and now it was FEPC's negotiated agreement with management and Local 190, but both times FEPC spurred the improvements which kindled the foundry workers' hopes and led to dramatic protests against the gradualism that relegated most of them to the least desirable jobs. In the final analysis other federal agencies—particularly the Army Air Corps—were required to resolve the crises, but the key roles played in the dynamics of social change both by FEPC and by black activism are clear.

---

* Matthews appears to have engaged in some hyperbole, by claiming that advances were made into skilled rather than semi-skilled jobs. In any event the non-foundry jobs included 5 on aircraft assembly; 200 on bench assembly and light machines; 50 wrappers and shippers; 11 precision polishers; 30 hand contour polishers on crankshafts; and 8 scrap supervisors. Interviews with Christopher Alston, Nov. 5, 13, 1977, were helpful in analyzing the data.

The spring series of confrontations were especially significant. The largest hate strike thus far in the war, it came at a time of extraordinary racial tension in the city. In fact the white wildcat strike which followed the black walkout had been scarcely settled when the Detroit race riot exploded in June. In the wake of this major civil disorder, just as in the Packard strike, the UAW-CIO International emerged as black Detroit's most helpful and outspoken ally. Taken together, the Packard strike and the riot were to prove a major milestone in the consolidation of the alliance between black Detroit and the UAW.

# IV

## The Forging of the Alliance
## Between Black Detroit and the UAW:
## 1941–1943

Just days after Thomas had so forcefully risen to the occasion and taken a stand supporting the black workers in the Packard strike there came the Detroit riot of 1943, one of the most serious racial conflicts in twentieth century America. Again Thomas and the UAW emerged from that conflagration as the one influential force in the Motor City willing to take an outspoken position on the blacks' behalf, thus further consolidating the emerging black-labor alliance which a few Negro civic leaders such as Louis Martin had long advocated.

The role played by the UAW's top leadership in the wake of the June riot was no isolated act. For even though the union's International officials could only begin to resolve black grievances in the job market, they lent Detroit blacks valued help in the succession of racial crises that beset the Motor City during the war years. At such critical junctures, the NAACP and other black advancement groups found in the UAW the one important organization willing to take a vigorous public stand in support of the black community. Thus, despite considerable criticism from prejudiced white members, the union's International leaders openly backed the blacks in a series of controversies stemming from Negro demands for public housing. Given the congestion created by the massive influx of war workers, housing rivaled jobs as a major source of conflict between whites and blacks, causing the Sojourner Truth riot of 1942 and contributing to the major outbreak of interracial violence in June 1943. Moreover, the latter confrontation brought to the foreground another long festering issue: police brutality against blacks. Here again union leaders—already concerned because of the problems that organizers and strikers had long experienced with the city's police department—championed the blacks' cause. Eventually the emerging alliance was consolidated in the Negro-labor political coalition that appeared during the bitterly contested municipal election of 1943. Even though racist appeals on the part of the victorious mayoralty candidate led many rank-and-file white auto workers to desert their union leadership at this point, the close cooperation between Negro civic groups and the union's top officials signaled the final crystallization of the black-UAW alliance. Thus out of the crucible of wartime conflict in the Motor City was forged the warm relationship with the union that would dominate the thinking of black Detroit for years to come.

## 1

To cope with the drastic wartime housing shortage that accompanied the influx of thousands of defense workers into the Detroit area, the federal government constructed several public housing projects, and the right of Negroes to live in them became an issue around which the period's heightened racial tensions crystallized. For Detroit's black citizens this was an especially important question because, with the expansion of Negro neighborhoods sharply limited by restrictive covenants blanketing white residential areas,[1] wartime conditions only exacerbated the already critical overcrowding in the black ghettos. First came the controversy over the Sojourner Truth Housing Project, located in a predominantly white area, but named for the celebrated black abolitionist and designed especially for black workers. Subsequently Detroit's race advancement organizations battled vigorously against the exclusion of blacks from other new public housing being built for war workers at Willow Run and in Detroit. In both campaigns they secured valuable assistance from the United Automobile Workers.

At first glance the site that the Detroit Housing Commission and the federal authorities in June 1941 selected for the Sojourner Truth project seemed logical enough. Although located just north of the predominantly Polish community of Hamtramck, some distance from the main black ghetto, the area—like Hamtramck itself—already had a number of Negro residents. Surrounding the site were white ethnic working-class homeowners, but only a few blocks away was a mixed neighborhood, including an enclave of homes owned by black business and professional families known as Conant Gardens.[2] Moreover, the pre-war history of black-Polish interaction in the Hamtramck area had been a relatively friendly one. J. Lawrence Duncan, who had lived there in the mid-1920's in the same neighborhood as Mayor Peter C. Jezewski, recalls that blacks and whites frequently occupied flats in the same buildings, and that relations between the high school students of both races were cordial. (One of his closest friends was the mayor's son, and the elder Jezewski personally drove the two youths to school each morning). With the Polish community still lacking a significant college-educated professional class, several Negroes were to be found among those who had established prosperous practices providing medical and legal services for the Hamtramck immigrant community.[3] When in 1936 Charles Diggs was elected to the state senate, his district included Hamtramck and had a constituency that was actually slightly more than half-Polish. Diggs's district did not include the Sojourner Truth site, but that of the area's U.S. Representative, Rudolph Tenerowicz, did, and he too represented a mixed constituency, in which blacks often exercised a political balance of power. Tenerowicz, regarded as a labor congressman, had been elected with strong backing from Local 600, and in fact he at first promised to support black occupancy of the Sojourner

Truth Project.[4] What neither the federal bureaucrats nor the black community leaders yet realized, however, was that at this juncture a generation of upwardly mobile American-born Poles was coming of age, resentful of competing with increasing numbers of blacks in the job market and bitterly opposed to them as neighbors.*

Paradoxically, opposition to the Sojourner Truth project at first came from both the well-to-do blacks of Conant Gardens, who were fearful of an influx of lower-class Negro migrants, and from Joseph Buffa, a white realtor who organized local Polish home-owners into an "improvement association." As the white protest mushroomed and the issue clearly became a racial one, the Conant Gardens group—along with Horace White, who as the one black man on the Detroit Housing Commission, served as their spokesman—reversed themselves. But with indignant letters from white home-owners raining on federal housing officials; with Ten-erowicz—who had switched his position—and the parish priest pressing Washington to reserve the project for whites; and with the Federal Housing Authority telling public housing administra-tors that black occupancy would dry up mortgage-lending in the neighborhood, the bureaucrats in the nation's capital wavered and seriously considered turning Sojourner Truth over to whites. At that point, however, black interests were well represented on the

---

* A government investigator for the Office of War Information reported in 1942: "The conflict over the Sojourner Truth Housing Project illustrates the changing atti-tude of the Poles toward the Negroes. Until the time when the project was to be occupied by Negroes, the Poles and Negroes lived amicably in Hamtramck on the same streets and in the same house. The Poles expressed no anxiety over depre-ciated property values in a mixed neighborhood until real estate agents and the sub-versive groups involved in the Sojourner Truth fight gave it to them when the proj-ect was to be opened. The second generation Poles were the first to take up the battle cry for segregation and discrimination. Like others of foreign descent in De-troit, they were beginning to fear the competition of young and status-conscious Negroes in jobs. The younger Poles are now inducing anti-Negro attitudes among the older generation and the Negroes are being forced out of Hamtramck." ("The Social Dynamics of Detroit," report prepared for Bureau of Intelligence, Office of War Information, Dec. 3, 1942, NA RG 44, Box 1814.) The same point was made by a Packard official in an interview with Lloyd Bailer in 1940. See Bailer, "The Negro Automobile Worker," *Journal of Political Economy* 51 (Oct. 1943): 421.

Detroit Housing Commission. Its secretary-director, former UAW organizer George Edwards, fully supported the blacks' demands, and Horace White emerged as an aggressive champion of their right to occupy the project. Indeed, when Washington officials encouraged the white protesters by offering to meet with them in Detroit, the black preacher's threat to call in a CIO picket line got the conference canceled. Finally in early January 1942, the government officially authorized the Detroit Housing Commission to assign the project to blacks.[5]

Yet the situation was highly unstable, and just two days later the same Washington officials suspended tenant selection.[6] It was probably no coincidence that Edwards departed that very same day to take his seat on the common council. His successor as secretary-director of the Housing Commission, Charles Edgecomb, though also a former UAW officer—having been president of Motor Products Local 203—was, unlike Edwards, hostile to blacks. In fact he had scarcely taken office when, at a January 15 conference with Tenerowicz and the federal housing administrators in Washington, he heatedly clashed with Horace White, and siding with the congressman, declared that riots would erupt unless the order that had awarded blacks Sojourner Truth was rescinded. That very same day the federal authorities promptly concurred and overturned their earlier decision, ruling that the project would be handed over to whites.[7]

This reversal finally propelled Detroit's black community to militant united action, in the form of a coalition known as the Sojourner Truth Citizens Committee. In many respects a prototype for the Citizens Committee for Jobs in War Industry which developed later in the year, this coalition was a broad-based umbrella group headed by Charles Hill. Louis Martin, Charles Diggs, LeBron Simmons, and James McClendon were highly visible participants in its activities; with Gloster Current serving as secretary and Mamie Thompson handling the monies, it was clear that the NAACP branch had a key role. Very shortly this black-initiated and black-controlled committee became interracial in mem-

bership, obtaining participation from Jewish groups, Protestant liberals in the Detroit Council of Churches,* and trade unionists.[8]
Not only did the Wayne County CIO—and even the County
AFL—condemn the government for reneging on its original com-
mitments but also their presidents figured prominently in the
Committee's activities.[9]† Although in the early stages the UAW
International office let the CIO Council (headed by the former
president of the Hudson Local, Tracy Doll) carry the ball, immediate and sustained support did come from Local 600. Horace Sheffield's well-organized efforts produced 5,000 postcards to President
Roosevelt from black foundry workers; both chairman Paul Ste.
Marie of the local's general council and Richard T. Leonard, director of the union's Ford Division, sent vigorously worded letters to
the mayor and common council; and the local made a substantial financial contribution to the Sojourner Truth Committee's work.[10]

The Citizens Committee, orchestrating an intensive campaign,
initiated nightly picketing of City Hall and the Detroit Housing
Commission offices. Mayor Jeffries had no choice but to confer
with Committee delegations: one group, with McClendon acting as
chief spokesman, read like a Who's Who of Detroit's Negro civic
leadership; while at another conference the CIO Council's Tracy
Doll and the AFL Council president Frank X. Martel spoke up
forcefully. Impressed with this demonstration of support for Sojourner Truth from both the united black community and a

---

* Prominent among them was the noted Methodist pacifist, Henry Hitt Crane. At
the start the list included only a rare Catholic. In the aftermath of the Sojourner
Truth riot, however, a scattering of concerned Catholics—the League of Catholic
Women, members of the faculty at the University of Detroit, leaders in the Catholic workers group and several priests—publicly voiced their support for the Negroes. (*News*, March 3, 17, 18, 1942, for role of Protestants and Crane, notably after
the rioting. On Catholic participation see *Tribune*, Jan. 24, 1942, and Bette Smith
Jenkins, "The Racial Policies of the Detroit Housing Commission and Their Administration" [M.A. thesis, Wayne State University, 1950], p. 95.)
† The AFL support was attributed to two factors: pressure from black members in
several AFL unions, and the Wayne County AFL president's disillusionment with
the mayor's refusal to grant pay raises to unionized municipal workers. (*Chronicle*,
Jan. 31, Feb. 7, 1942.)

number of influential white allies, the mayor and common council now lent their support to black occupancy and asked Washington officials to reverse themselves again. Then, following through on the advantage it had thus gained, the Citizens Committee, in an emergency interracial mass meeting, raised money to rush a large delegation of blacks and whites to Washington so that their case once more could be brought before the federal housing authorities. Faced with the militant and articulate blacks in this group like Charles Hill, LeBron Simmons, Geraldine Bledsoe, Horace White, and Charles Diggs, and impressed by the endorsement their position had received from the city's political leaders, the federal bureaucrats did another about-face, ruling that blacks could move into Sojourner Truth after all. [11]

But the blacks' opponents were not about to give up. The white homeowners in the area around the project, including some UAW members, immediately mounted their own picket lines and protests at City Hall. Fearing that these demonstrations might bring another turnabout from Washington, Horace White, joined by Diggs, Hill, and Bledsoe, led another interracial delegation to the nation's capital, where on February 12 they received firm reassurances from the federal housing coordinator and other officials. Indeed, despite sustained and frenzied pressures from the racist whites, the federal bureaucracy refused to back down, and announced that the first tenants would move in on February 28. [12]

At this juncture the Ku Klux Klan, operating with the tacit approval of the "improvement association," decided to intervene. The result was a violent confrontation at the Sojourner Truth site. The night before the scheduled move, 150 whites burned a cross and picketed outside the project, and early the next morning hundreds flocked to the scene, "as automobiles with horns blowing drove through the Polish section near the project, arousing people to come and defend their rights." When the small group of black tenants arrived, the angry mob attacked them and overturned their furniture vans. Yet the police began arresting the peaceful blacks. As the news of the disorders spread, hundreds of black youths came to the aid of the prospective tenants and defiantly fought back against both the mob and the police. Alarmed Negro leaders rushed in hoping to prevent a race war. Sheffield headed a team of black workers from Local 600 that tried to persuade the angry black youths to disperse, while Charles Hill and Horace White, speaking from UAW sound trucks, found themselves booed and nearly manhandled as they sought to calm things down. A score of people were injured in the melee, and by the early hours of the following morning over 200 blacks—along with a mere handful of whites—had been arrested.[13]

Detroit's public officials in effect also sided with the whites. Edgecomb, feeling that his dire predictions were vindicated, used the riot as an excuse to countermand—with common council backing—his previous directive that blacks could move in. In response Horace White and Gloster Current led a furious black delegation to see the mayor, denouncing the police and futilely demanding Edgecomb's removal. At first Jeffries reiterated his endorsement of black occupancy. But amidst white demonstrations at City Hall that at one point became so disorderly that police used tear gas to disperse the pickets, the mayor soon washed his hands of the controversy, blaming extremists on both sides and shifting to the federal government the responsibility for protecting the black tenants.[14]

While support from the Wayne County AFL became less forceful,[15] the stand of the CIO unions, particularly the UAW, was even more vigorous than before. Local 600's General Council called upon the FBI to investigate the Ku Klux Klan's role and condemned Tenerowicz as "a betrayer of labor's interests."* Walter Hardin joined Hill in still another Washington-bound delegation that urged officials there not to back down; in Detroit white trade unionists walked picket lines with blacks at City Hall; and a meeting of the Wayne County CIO Council gave Charles Edge-

---

* Later in the year Tenerowicz was defeated for reelection, and Louis Martin attributed his defeat to the congressman's double-cross on Sojourner Truth. (Louis Martin, "The Negro in the Political Picture," Opportunity 21 [July 1943]: 106.)

comb a withering time as he tried to justify his handling of the entire affair.[16] Most important of all, R. J. Thomas, with the unanimous backing of the International Executive Board, decided that a public stand on behalf of the blacks was necessary. In mid-March the UAW president informed the press that he was "more convinced than ever that justice requires that the project be occupied by Negro workers who are in need of public housing"; the only solution, in his view, was "immediate occupancy" by blacks under police protection. Thomas's stand elicited considerable opposition from many Polish union members in the Sojourner Truth neighborhood who circulated petitions denouncing him. But the UAW president refused to be intimidated, and at the union's War Emergency Conference in April, obtained from the 1400 delegates present a unanimous endorsement of his position.[17] UAW leadership was so united on the issue in fact that the Catholics among them now openly endorsed the blacks' side in the housing controversy. Prominent among the speakers at the Citizens Committee's final mass demonstration—a protest march and rally at Cadillac Square—was a representative of the Association of Catholic Trade Unionists.[18]

In the end federal officials stood firm, and the blacks began moving into the Sojourner Truth Housing Project at the end of April.[19] The impact of this struggle on black-union relationships was, however, paradoxical and ironic. On the one hand the February riot gave the auto companies an excuse for dragging their feet in transferring and upgrading black workers, and thus further inhibited UAW officials from redressing the Negroes' job grievances. On the other hand, the warm support of UAW leaders, ranging from those at Local 600 to R. J. Thomas, was deeply appreciated by black spokesmen and tightened the bonds that were developing between black Detroit and the UAW International.

Undoubtedly the Sojourner Truth victory would have been impossible if mixed housing had been the goal. It is inconceivable that the AFL or the mayor would have supported residential integration. Nor, as subsequent experience demonstrated, would

federal officials have yielded to such a demand. When blacks fron-
tally attacked this issue a year after the Sojourner Truth battle,
they again found their most influential allies among the UAW International's leaders. But this time black Detroit and their union
friends met decisive defeat.

Ever since the inception of the Federal Public Housing program
in 1937, official policy had virtually precluded integration, North
as well as South. Only in a few cases did blacks and whites live in
mixed projects, and in nearly all such instances each race was assigned to separate sections or buildings. The Federal Public Housing Authority (FPHA), although claiming that its policies merely
reflected local patterns, often demanded jim crow arrangements,
even in previously undeveloped areas, as it did in 1942 when residential units were erected at Ford's new Willow Run plant.[20]

Because blacks were completely excluded from housing near this
factory, Negro civic leaders decided to confront the segregation
issue head on. The Detroit NAACP provided the initiative for the
struggle, bringing in others like Louis Martin and Charles Hill,
sympathetic white clergymen, and black and white UAW leaders.
In February 1943 complaints were lodged simultaneously with the
Detroit Housing Commission about a new project in the Motor
City designed for blacks, and with the local director of FPHA
about the lily-white Willow Run development. However, the black
committee was frankly informed of Washington's segregation policy and told that Negro Willow Run workers would be accommo-
dated in separate Ypsilanti and Inkster developments. In response
to this negative reception the NAACP established a broad-based
steering committee in which UAW International representative Oscar Noble and several men from Willow Run Local 50 participated
prominently, and the branch quickly obtained from R. J. Thomas
and George Addes pledges to pressure federal authorities. Delighted, McClendon and Current told an enthusiastic "emergency
mass meeting" about the UAW's warm response, and then proceeded vigorously to solicit the union's participation in an inter-
racial delegation that departed for Washington in early March.

This group, in fact, included not only people like Current, Hill, and Martin, and a spokesman from the Michigan Council of Churches, but representatives from the Willow Run and Rouge locals, and Emil Mazey, recently reelected president of the Briggs Local as well.[21]

In the capital the delegation's conference with FPHA Commissioner Herbert Emmerich proved frustrating. Pointedly the Detroiters stressed that, since the Willow Run project involved previously undeveloped land, there was absolutely no precedent for segregation. Mazey went even further, insisting that "local custom" could no more justify jim crow housing than it could justify discrimination in employment. But Emmerich insisted that the color bar at Willow Run was unalterable.[22] In Detroit an angry NAACP branch responded with a mass indignation protest meeting and an interracial picket line at the local FPHA office. Unionists like Hardin and Sheffield were among those who joined McClendon and Current in this demonstration. Support came from UAW's top officials also; speaking on behalf of the International's leadership, George Addes denounced Charles Edgecomb for his "Fascist-like actions and speeches on housing issues," condemned the FPHA, and pointed to "UAW principles providing that public housing projects must be open on a first come first serve basis." Despite the blacks' and the union's pressure, however, Washington would not budge, and the Willow Run fight ended in failure.[23]*

Nor did the NAACP's campaign for public housing integration inside Detroit fare any better, although here again the struggle received UAW backing. After considerable temporizing, the Detroit Housing Commission granted the NAACP's request for a public hearing, and two in fact were held at the end of April. The impressive list of witnesses included McClendon, Hill, Martin,

---

*The Detroit Housing Commission also went ahead with its plans for the all-black George Washington Carver Homes in Inkster, which opened in November 1943. (*UAW, Ford Facts Edition*, Nov. 1, 1943.) Eventually, early in the summer of 1944, Willow Run began to accept Negro tenants.

Ray Hatcher of the Urban League, Dr. Henry Hitt Crane, secretary of the Detroit Council of Churches, Edward McFarland, head of the Metropolitan Detroit Council on Fair Employment Practices and a strong UAW contingent. At the first session, Tappes and Frank Winn, a sympathetic white official of Local 600, flatly declared that they intended to oppose vigorously lily-white occupancy at a project being built near the Rouge plant. Moreover, absolutely certain that racial mixing would not cause trouble between black and white tenants, they offered to be responsible for guaranteeing public order if both races were admitted to the development. The following week, to the accompaniment of boos and hisses from Joseph Buffa's followers, who had packed the meeting room, Emil Mazey and Victor Reuther similarly tried to allay the Commission's fears that mixed occupancy would lead to violence. To buttress their claim, the two union officials stressed how Detroit industry was integrating to an extent "many observers had believed impossible before."[24]

The hearings turned out to be a charade. After the first one, which was "unofficial" because it lacked a quorum, Edgecomb prevailed upon Mayor Jeffries and the common council to forestall the integrationists. Just hours before the second hearing, the council, urged on by the mayor, passed a resolution asking the Housing Commission to reaffirm its policy of conforming to neighborhood racial patterns. As Jeffries put it, "The Detroit Housing Commission will, in no way, change the racial characteristics of any neighborhood in Detroit through occupancy standards of housing projects under their jurisdiction." The *Chronicle* blamed Edgecomb, the "Negro-baiter," for pressing Jeffries to influence the other city officials. Yet the white housing commissioners, who had often declared that integration meant bloodshed, hardly required Edgecomb, Jeffries, or the council to tell them how to vote, and, ignoring Horace White's appeal, ringingly endorsed the maintenance of their jim crow policy. Only after the balloting did they open the hearing, and, even before any testimony was heard, the witnesses were flatly informed that the commissioners had no intention of reconsidering. A few days later, requests that the common council rescind its resolution produced another day of noisy and futile hearings, but the Detroit politicians remained obdurate. McClendon excoriated their unfairness, but his frustration only underlined the basic impotence of the city's Negroes and their white allies.[25]

With jim crow in public housing the policy of the federal agencies in Washington, the Detroit officials could ignore the integrationists' demands with impunity. Yet this battle, like the successful Sojourner Truth campaign, revealed that Detroit blacks had significant allies among some of the more sympathetic Protestant ministers, and most important, among key people in the UAW.* The union's efforts on the housing issue, well known in the Afro-American community, like its even more publicized actions on behalf of upgrading black workers, served to indicate that the UAW's top leadership was committed to fighting racial discrimination. Conceivably the UAW, unable to take much initiative in battling white hostility to black advancement on the job, may have sought instead to adopt public stands on other issues vital to the black community's welfare; although criticism from some white unionists would be inevitable, such steps may well have antagonized white workers less than actions interfering with their preferred status in the factories. Yet given the attitudes of most other influential whites in Detroit, the support and positive steps taken by the UAW indicated to blacks that the union's International leadership was their strongest ally in the Motor City.

## 2

Paralleling the Detroit NAACP's rising admiration for the UAW came the consolidation of the alliance between the union's leaders and the national officers of the Association. From the NAACP's perspective this development was laced with considerable ambigu-

* Charges aired by a *Chronicle* columnist that UAW leaders in both Local 600 and the International had deserted blacks on this issue were clearly without foundation. (*Chronicle*, May 22, 1943, and May 29, 1943.)

ity. Walter White greatly oversimplified matters in his 1948 autobiography, portraying the Ford strike as an historical turning point
in the relationship between blacks and organized labor, and flatly
asserting that thereafter the UAW had "assiduously" and "continuously" battled against racial discrimination.[26] Actually the alliance
was forged with the NAACP leader's full awareness of the UAW's
imperfections and with the knowledge that his organization had
the formidable task of persuading the union to live up to its principles.

While in Detroit during the 1941 Ford strike, White had frankly
discussed with UAW leaders the black workers' grievances. He
had learned from the union's officials how the racial attitudes of the
white rank and file had prevented the UAW from implementing
the 1939 convention's anti-discrimination resolution. Indeed, R. J.
Thomas and other leaders had admitted that, because of complex
promotion procedures (which as already seen were manipulated to
the blacks' disadvantage), no steps had been taken to improve
black economic opportunities at companies like Packard, GM, and
Chrysler.[27] Moreover, soon after returning to New York, White
became deeply disturbed by authenticated reports that UAW
locals in Cleveland had refused to fight lily-white hiring policies at
plants which they had organized.[28]

Nevertheless the NAACP leader was convinced of the sincerity
of the UAW's top officers, and was persuaded that the Association
had no other alternative than to cultivate its alliance with the leadership of the interracial industrial unions and prod them to advance the black workers' interests, despite the prejudice prevalent
among the white workers. As he wrote to the radical intellectual
A. J. Muste, who had congratulated him on his role in the Ford
strike: "It was a tough situation which Negroes faced there and
which they will face in the future. Thomas, Addes . . . and other
top officials of the UAW-CIO impressed me as being sincere in
their efforts to keep all of the promises to the Negro Ford workers.
But a large number of the [white] workers come from Mississippi,
Arkansas, Tennessee and other states of the the deep South. They

have brought with them to Detroit many of their prejudices, though some of these have been broken down. A great deal, however, remains to be done. If the union fails to keep its promises to the Negro, the NAACP and I are going to be on the spot. But that is just one of the chances that we have to take. The position we took seemed, to me, to be the only one to take." And in a blunt letter to the NAACP's old friend, Judge Ira Jayne, who had been reelected to the Circuit Court in Detroit with the CIO's support, White expressed the view that "Our greatest danger lies in the fact that there is really little difference fundamentally between the attitude of employers and of unions toward the Negro. Our task is to show labor unions that they have a most vital interest at stake."[29]

During the Ford strike White had characteristically grasped the opportunity presented by his presence in Detroit to press the union leaders for action. He got them to back his proposal to have CIO president, Philip Murray, come to the Motor City for a meeting with UAW and black civic leaders to explore ways of combatting white worker hostility. Hoping to have the conference held before the NLRB election at Ford, if at all possible, White pressed Murray vigorously, but the latter, reluctant to become involved, pleaded the rush of work and personal illness. By mid-summer the NAACP leader finally gave up.[30] White, who understood the dilemma faced by Thomas and his colleagues, was deeply perplexed about finding the right solution. To his close friend William H. Hastie, chairman of the NAACP's Legal Committee, he asked, "What is the answer?" The manipulation of "the seniority rule" perpetuated discrimination against blacks, yet to give up the principle for which the UAW had fought so hard "would mean destruction of or injury to the union and harm to union members, Negro as well as white." No practical steps seemed feasible to him except the friendly prod. Thus right after the UAW won the Ford NLRB election, White sent R. J. Thomas a congratulatory telegram that pointed out how the victory offered the UAW "an opportunity to demonstrate that it is one labor union which . . . can prove by demonstration that men can work together irrespective of race.

Knowing you and the other officers and members of UAW as I do, I am confident that in the Ford situation you will set a shining example of industrial democracy . . . which will inspire faith and hope of Negro workers all over the country in organized labor." Similarly when White learned of the hate strike at Curtiss-Wright in Columbus, he at once reminded Thomas of the "unequivocal stand you and other officials of the UAW-CIO took during the Ford strike . . . when the union needed the support of the colored workers. I am certain you will act promptly and uncompromisingly."[31]

Obviously White felt that neither he nor the national NAACP could fashion any other viable approach to the UAW. As already seen, such progress on employment bias as there was depended largely on pressure from the Detroit branch and other Negro spokesmen in the Motor City. Summoned to Detroit to address the branch-sponsored emergency mass meeting at the height of the hate strike wave that engulfed Detroit in the spring and summer of 1942, the NAACP executive could only join McClendon and Current in demanding a federal investigation of the "fifth columnists" responsible for these stoppages, and in applauding Thomas's supportive actions. Yet privately White was not satisfied that the union had done all within its power to fight racism in its ranks. As he advised the NAACP national board, the UAW could engage in far more "counter educational work to meet the propaganda of anti-Negro agents." Tentative arrangements for Thomas and White to address a series of shop stewards' meetings were never implemented, and about all the NAACP Secretary seems to have accomplished was to get posters placed on factory bulletin boards calling upon workers, in the name of Philip Murray, to "abandon race prejudice because it directly aided the Axis."[32]

Yet within the context of the times, the stance taken by the UAW's International leadership, constrained though it was by the white rank and file, was highly valued by the NAACP. Thus, when renewed discussions early in 1942 of a possible CIO-AFL merger aroused White's fears that labor unity would come at the price of sacrificing the egalitarian principles of the industrial unions,[33] the UAW's actions seemed by comparison more progressive than ever. Nothing made this clearer than the proceedings of the NAACP's Emergency Wartime Conference which met in Detroit early in June of the following year.

From the perspective of the leading participants, the situation must have been filled with ironies. Convening at Bradby's Second Baptist Church during the height of the Packard hate strike when 25,000 white unionists were actively resisting the upgrading of a handful of black workers, the conference exuded a spirit that contrasted markedly with the anti-union hostility pervading the conclave held in Detroit just six years before. In his keynote address, White held the Packard officials solely responsible, completely deflecting culpability from the firm's white employees. "Tokyo and Berlin tonight rejoice in the effective and unexpected aid given them" by the company's executives, White informed the assembled throng. As the pro-UAW authors Irving Howe and B. J. Widick later observed, "The sad truth would seem to be that [White] was wrong" in asserting that only a few Packard workers actually wished to walk out. Of course White knew better, but fearful of racial bloodshed—a concern that both he and NAACP chief counsel Thurgood Marshall expressed in their speeches— and fervently wishing to cement an alliance with the UAW, White calculatedly placed the entire blame on the company's management.[34]

Throughout the NAACP conference, in fact, the Packard walkout was the leading topic of conversation. When the whites returned to their jobs shortly before the conclave closed, Christopher C. Alston "stole the show" by informing the delegates how, in the face of the KKK's opposition, UAW leaders had broken the strike. Thomas himself received a tremendous ovation from the overflow crowd as he addressed the concluding mass meeting. Of course none who heard him could have known that he had accepted the NAACP's invitation only after the most careful deliberations. He had actually first gone to his International Executive

Board for guidance, and then after a "lengthy" discussion that body had referred the matter to the six Detroit area members who finally voted four to two that Thomas ought to appear. In his address, however, Thomas put on a militant face and gave no inkling of the constraints which the racial attitudes of the white rank and file imposed on his administration. The UAW, he declared, "will fight for equal rights for all workers regardless of color. If the KKK and the rest of the nightshirt boys want to fight the union on this issue, we are ready and willing to take them on." Horace White who was present undoubtedly summed up the spirit of the conference in praising Thomas's forceful words. They demonstrated, he said, "that unions can be made to protect the rights of all workers regardless of race, creed or color," and that clearly the greatest hope for black advancement "lies in our relationship with the labor movement."[35]

# 3

The NAACP leaders' deep-seated fear of massive racial violence was fully justified, and their strategy of cultivating close ties with the UAW was vindicated in the aftermath of the riot that swept Detroit within two weeks of the Association's national conference. For over a year confidential government intelligence reports had been predicting that Detroit, with its festering interracial hostility, housing shortages, and police brutality, was ripe for a major conflagration. In fact the Sojourner Truth episode had simply been the worst outbreak in a city characterized by endemic racial clashes. As the organ of the Motor City's Association of Catholic Trade Unionists put it, "The ugly truth is that there is a growing, subterranean race war going on in the City of Detroit which can have no other ultimate result than an explosion of violence, unless something is done to stop it."[36] No one in authority heeded either these secret reports or the *Life* magazine essay in which Louis Martin and Ted Poston warned, "Detroit Is Dynamite"—it "can either blow up Hitler or it can blow up the U.S." Mayor Edward J.

Jeffries seemed concerned only about the "scurrilous" publicity that this widely read article produced.[37] And after the 1943 riot erupted, black Detroiters discovered that the mayor whom they had helped elect once again betrayed them, and that their most influential support would come from the UAW.

Precipitated by an incident at an amusement park on Sunday evening, June 20, the rioting spread quickly. During its early stages some whites were physically assaulted, and subsequently many white-owned businesses were destroyed. Yet throughout Negroes bore the brunt of the violence—both from white mobs and from the city's white police—and about three-fourths of the twenty-five blacks killed were actually shot down by law officers.[38]

Monday noon, amidst growing alarm in the black community over this unchecked bloodshed, and over the failure of city officials to call for federal troops to restore order, Rev. Charles Hill convened an emergency meeting of black spokesmen and union leaders in a desperate attempt to talk to the mayor and get him to act. The complete spectrum of the city's Afro-American leadership was present—radicals like LeBron Simmons, conservatives such as Louis Blount, as well as centrists like McClendon. The racially mixed UAW contingent included Hardin, Alston, Hodges Mason (who had recently been named vice-president of the Wayne County CIO Council), Richard Leonard, and R. J. Thomas himself. Shocked by the police brutality and the mounting death toll, the gathering actually booed Jeffries when he expressed confidence in his lawmen and refused to request martial law or national guard reinforcements. Mason, for example, furiously confronted the mayor demanding that he "take a position for once in [your] life." Thomas, however, characteristically acting in the reconciliatory fashion that had brought him the union's top office, refrained at this point from attacking Jeffries, and even favored giving the city authorities a little more time to restore peace before resorting to federal troops. Yet he also angrily insisted on an immediate end to the violence against blacks, and pledged that he would ask all UAW officers to help dampen anti-black sentiment among riot-prone white workers in the auto plants. In fulfillment of these promises, Thomas later that day conferred with a hastily convened meeting of the union's shop stewards, and issued a public plea for a stop to this "lawlessness and racial hatred . . . which have disgraced our city."[39]*

Federal troops were finally called in that night, and by Tuesday morning the disorders had been reduced to sporadic outbreaks. Scarcely was the rioting over when Thomas, now quite clearly sensitized to the concerns of a thoroughly aroused Negro community, emerged as black Detroit's most vigorous white supporter. He at once released a press statement sharply attacking the police and proposing a "Community Action Program" to prevent future outbreaks. He recommended the creation of a biracial commission to alleviate friction, the construction of housing and recreation facilities, an enforceable program against job discrimination in Detroit's war plants, and, most important, a grand jury investigation to uncover the riot's causes and instigators and to assess the behavior of the law enforcement authorities during the disorders. With Detroit's industrialists silent and the blacks' other sympathizers slow to act, Thomas was, according to the *Free Press*, "the only Detroiter who has come forward with a set of formal recommendations looking toward a restoration of interracial accord for our riot-ravaged city."[40] The Detroit Interracial Fellowship, a coalition of religious, labor, and social welfare groups that the Detroit

---

* Union spokesmen generally took credit for the fact that no rioting occurred within the automobile factories. George Addes for example claimed, "The recent race riot furnished a shining example of the success the UAW-CIO had in welding the members of our Union into a united body of industrial workers. . . . White and Negro members of our Union kept on working side by side." (*Chronicle,* July 10, 1943; see also, *e.g.*, similar statements in *UAW,* July 1, 1943, and another by Otis Eaton cited in *Tribune,* Aug. 28, 1943.) Actually one reason that blacks were not attacked in the plants was high absenteeism among both races during riot—ranging between 50 percent and 90 percent for the blacks, and up to 30 percent for the whites. (*Chronicle,* June 26, 1943; *Free Press,* June 23, 1943; Anthony Luchek to Joseph D. Keenan, July 14, 1943, NA RG 179, box 1017.) The majority of the Negroes remained at home, while many of the absent whites were likely to be found on the streets among the rioters.

Council of Churches organized two days later, promptly endorsed Thomas's program. Blacks, including the UAW's new friend John Dancy, of course warmly applauded Thomas. Openly critical of the "timorous Jeffries," they were delighted with the UAW president's speech at the Michigan CIO convention a few days later when he condemned the mayor for his conduct during the riot and re-iterated the demand for a grand jury investigation. Equally wel-come was the strongly worded resolution that the state CIO con-ference passed in support of Thomas's program. [41]

Stung by all this criticism, Mayor Jeffries became increasingly hostile toward the black community. Not surprisingly he acted on only one of Thomas's proposals, appointing on June 25 a biracial commission that proved to be an impotent, though well-meaning, body. Its black members, although representative of the city's Negro community,* could do little to overcome either the moder-ate outlook of the six white members or the fact that the Commis-sion was the mayor's own political creation. Moreover, on the re-ally important issue of impaneling a special grand jury to investigate police misconduct, Jeffries was openly negative. [42] By the end of the month the mayor had become so irritated with the unrelenting black criticism that he issued a formal report warmly praising his racist law enforcement agency, and at the same time Jeffries pointedly warned that he was "rapidly . . . losing patience with those Negro leaders who insist that their people do not and will not trust policemen and the Police Department." [43]

The NAACP and other Detroit black spokesmen, however, were not to be intimidated. McClendon, speaking for a united black leadership, sharply condemned the mayor's "inflammatory state-ment." [44] For its part the national office of the NAACP also con-tinued to protest. Walter White himself had come to Detroit dur-ing the height of the holocaust and, appalled at the evidence of police bias during the disorders, had arranged for the Association

---

* The black members were Charles Hill, Beulah Whitby, Louis Martin, Walter Hardin, Rev. George W. Baber, and the conservative Republican state labor com-missioner, Charles Mahoney.

to conduct its own investigation. The report that NAACP chief counsel Thurgood Marshall forwarded to the governor amply documented the charges of police brutality. White's own widely circulated analysis of the riot—with its unmitigated condemnation of the police and its lavish praise for R. J. Thomas and the UAW— must have further inflamed the mayor and the city law officers.[45]

Resentful of this clamor for a grand jury investigation, Detroit police commissioner John Witherspoon and Wayne County prosecutor William E. Dowling took to the offensive. At the end of July they released a statement publicly blaming the black community for the riot, and charging that it was the agitation of the NAACP and the *Chronicle* that was really responsible for instigating the violence. The two white law enforcement officers were also influential members of the fact-finding commission that the governor had appointed, and when that body issued the "Dowling Report" a few weeks later, it naturally aired similar accusations. Detroit's Afro-American spokesmen were outraged. Dr. McClendon, reenforcing Walter White's denunciation of Dowling's "intemperate outburst," angrily questioned, ". . . . When did it become a crime to ask that all citizens be treated fairly in a democracy? When did it become a crime to ask that loyal colored Americans be given jobs commensurate with their skill and training? . . . No amount of NAACP militancy and propaganda could make the average Negro more mindful of discrimination and inequality than actual discrimination as practiced in the city. . . . ." Charles Hill excoriated "the spinelessness of Mayor Jeffries and the police department under Commissioner Witherspoon," and both he and Shelton Tappes charged Dowling with hiding the presence of subversive reactionaries on the city's police force. Why else, Tappes asked, did the police during the riot refuse to jail white rioters but showed "eagerness to send Negro rioters to the bullpen?"[46]

Again it was the CIO leadership, virtually alone among the city's influential whites, who came to the blacks' defense. With his position vigorously supported by the executive board of the Michigan CIO Council,[47] R. J. Thomas not only denounced the prosecutor and renewed his demand for a grand jury probe but uttered a heartening defense of the NAACP:

> "Prosecutor William Dowling's statements are the most serious incitation to race riots we have had since the riots themselves. . . . They sound like the hysterical alibi of a public official who either cannot or will not do his duty. . . . He is attacking that organization [NAACP] only to cover up his own ineffectiveness or unwillingness to act. The NAACP is an organization of which all Americans, regardless of race or color may be proud. It . . . is a trouble-making organization in the sense that unions are trouble-makers for unfair employers, and in the same sense that those who believe in liberty are trouble-makers for Hitler."

Unquestionably Robert Weaver was correct when he observed that it was Thomas's spirited defense in these post-riot days that did much to "impress the Negro community with the significance of a strong labor organization as an ally."[48]

### 4

That autumn in the riot's aftermath, a virtually united black community mobilized to seek Jeffries's defeat in his drive for reelection. During the campaign the blacks found themselves working for the first time in a close political coalition with the UAW. Paradoxically this partnership, suffering bitter defeat in the face of Jeffries's racist appeals to white workers, nevertheless marked the consolidation of the alliance between the UAW International and black Detroit.

In analyzing the role blacks played in Detroit politics and the rocky road toward the emergence of the UAW-black political coalition, the non-partisan character of Detroit's municipal elections must be noted. Under this system political alliances were personalized and unstable, and centered upon particular candidates rather than party machines. Black Democratic and Republican leaders generally formed blocs that were constantly dissolving and reforming, and yet with the right personality or issue they could on occasion unite in a virtually monolithic combination. Blacks were actively solicited by mayoralty candidates, but as a relatively small minority in a population composed largely of southern whites and European ethnics, they consistently experienced disappointment with politicians whom they had voted into City Hall. This fact, of course, heightened the tendency of blacks to shift allegiances between one municipal election and the next.[49]

If the party system that existed nationally and on the state level had functioned in Detroit's city elections during the 1930's, one might suppose that the city's black voters and the UAW, despite their divergent outlooks on collective bargaining, would have backed the same local candidates. Both were important elements in the New Deal coalition, and since blacks and strikers alike had been persistently manhandled by the city's lawmen, both were deeply concerned about police brutality. Yet even after the swing of Detroit's Afro-Americans into the Democratic column in 1936,[50] the local non-partisan system only accentuated the profound cleavage already existing between the UAW and most of the city's black leaders.* Accordingly, neither state senator Charles Diggs's close relationship with the CIO nor Louis Martin's regular editorial endorsement of CIO candidates represented any basic coalition between blacks and labor. Even in 1939, when most blacks and the CIO supported the same candidate for mayor, they acted without coordination.

The UAW had first entered Detroit municipal politics in 1937 when, following the sit-down victories, it ran several prominent union leaders for Common Council, and in the mayoralty race backed the liberal Democrat Patrick O'Brien against the business candidate Richard W. Reading. Not surprisingly the *Chronicle* warmly endorsed O'Brien, while both the *Tribune* and Willis Ward actively campaigned for Reading. Labor made some gestures toward the black vote with a platform urging an end to the blatant

---

* The same was true of the Wayne County AFL and CIO councils, which until 1943 were always to be found ranged on opposite sides in mayoralty contests.

employment discrimination in city government,* denouncing the police commissioner for the assaults suffered by blacks as well as by white strikers, advocating enforcement of the state civil rights laws, and even endorsing a black lawyer for a seat on the Common Council. Yet blacks, perceiving neither mayoral candidate to be the race's friend, and distrustful of the CIO at this time, displayed considerable apathy. In the end Reading, raising the specter of a radical CIO takeover of the city government, won handily, garnering as he did so the overwhelming majority of the black vote.[51]

Two years later, however, the black vote turned against the mayor and backed his successful challenger, Common Council president Edward J. Jeffries. The principal reason for this switch was Reading's failure to stop the mounting police brutality. In fact he had even retained in office the police commissioner whom the blacks and the CIO had so severely criticized. For Negroes the problem had become so aggravated that McClendon had managed to bring an extraordinarily diverse group of leaders ranging from LeBron Simmons to Rev. Robert Bradby into a coalition known as the Committee To End Police Brutality. Following unproductive conferences with Reading, McClendon openly charged that the mayor's retention of the police commissioner actually amounted to sanctioning the brutality, and the Committee, cooperating with the predominantly white Civil Rights Federation, secured petitions from tens of thousands of both races asking for his removal.[52] Running an astute campaign, Jeffries exploited this emotional issue and unhesitatingly opposed unnecessary violence by law enforcement authorities. Then, having emerged as the top vote-getter in the primary, with blacks in some wards deserting Reading, their longtime political ally, by margins of 8 to 1, Jeffries openly stepped up his appeals to them, promising to fire the police commissioner if elected.[53]

Pressures were so intense that the local black Democratic and

---

* For example, not a single fireman and only 40 of the 3,000 police were blacks. (Louis Martin, "The Big Stick in Detroit," *Crisis* 44 [December 1937]: 378.)

Republican organizations both departed from their policy of staying aloof from city elections. Senator Diggs easily swung the Michigan Federated Democratic Clubs behind the Common Council
president.[54] More complex were the actions of black Republicans,
working through the Wayne County Negro Voters District Association which Donald Marshall and state labor commissioner Charles
Mahoney had formed in the hopes of recapturing the black vote for
the GOP. Scarcely a purely political group, the Association actually functioned informally as part of the Ford personnel department's apparatus, providing jobs at the Rouge for its members,
and Ford officials actually tried to manipulate its role in the 1939
city election. Yet this attempt to exploit the company's influence
among blacks backfired in the face of the swelling Negro support
for Jeffries. Shortly before the general election a desperate Reading appealed directly to Henry Ford, and Willis Ward was instructed to have the Association endorse the incumbent mayor.
Then Jeffries bitterly complained to his good friend, Harry Bennett, who had the endorsement withdrawn. Undoubtedly Ward
was only too glad to be extricated from his awkward position, given
the decidedly pro-Jeffries sentiment of the rank and file.[55]*

   In contrast to the intense support for Jeffries exhibited by black
spokesmen, the UAW and other CIO unions eschewed an overtly
active role in this campaign. They had, of course, been badly
burned in the 1937 election; and what is more, with Reading repeating his strategy of denouncing his opponent as the instrument

---

*This was not the first case where Ford company officials had been charged with
using economic pressure to swing black voters behind a certain candidate. In 1932
an item in the *Crisis* stated: "It is charged that large numbers of Negroes working in
the Ford plants at Detroit have been discharged because they supported Mayor
Frank Murphy in the recent election. Several affidavits have come to THE CRISIS
asserting that Donald J. Marshall . . . has declared in several cases that 'You who
voted for the Honorable Frank Murphy ought not to be insulted when I advise you
who are out of work to go to Mayor Murphy for jobs.'" (*Crisis* 39 [Feb. 1932],
64–65). One can only speculate, but Du Bois's publication of this report may have
been related to the abrupt end in contributions made to the NAACP by Edsel
Ford, as mentioned in Chapter I.

of a Communist-dominated CIO conspiracy, Jeffries felt impelled actually to deny any CIO connection. With UAW support for the Council president thus covert, no black-labor political coalition was even remotely conceivable. In the end the strategy of both the unions and the black leaders paid off. The communist menace as a campaign issue was seen for the fantasy it was, and Jeffries trounced Reading with the support of the overwhelming majority of both black and white voters. The mayor-elect had carried the black wards by very heavy margins, especially in Diggs's stronghold on the East Side.[56]

McClendon, who had mobilized the city's Negroes so effectively on the police brutality issue, received major credit for the solid black political support that went to Jeffries.[57] The CIO's long-time supporter, Rev. Horace White received the most important political plum awarded by the new mayor to his black supporters—appointment to the Detroit Housing Commission. Appropriately enough White's first act was to vote for the appointment of the pro-black UAW staff member, George Edwards, as secretary-director of the Commission. Jeffries retained the backing of both the blacks and the UAW when he ran again in 1941 in a campaign that also brought the election of Edwards to the Common Council.[58] Yet afterwards the CIO unions and the blacks became disenchanted with some of the mayor's policies, and by the time of the 1943 election their original enthusiasm had so completely soured that they joined together in a united front to defeat him.

The blacks' anger at the mayor focused on two issues: his housing policy, culminating in his fervent endorsement of segregated public projects in April 1943, and the perennial problem of police brutality, which achieved greater salience than ever with the 1943 riot and the mayor's public defense of his law enforcement officers. Amidst the uproar following the charges made by the county prosecutor and Jeffries's police commissioner that the black press and the NAACP had instigated the 1943 riot, Louis Martin called editorially for a black-labor coalition in the autumn elections. Other black leaders found the idea appealing and quickly joined in supporting the UAW's mayoralty candidate, circuit court commissioner Frank Fitzgerald.[59]

Since Fitzgerald's record on racial matters was neutral, the blacks' backing was an act of faith and perhaps desperation. On the other hand, on Fitzgerald's slate was councilman George Edwards, a "shining example" (as Walter White would have termed it) of the potential in labor-black political cooperation. The youthful Edwards, whom *PM* described as one of the most "fearless" liberals holding office anywhere in America, and whom the *Chronicle* called "the lone incumbent who has won the respect and admiration of the Negro people," had left Harvard to become a UAW organizer during the sit-down strikes. Instrumental in bringing the Kelsey-Hayes Wheel Company workers into the UAW, he subsequently headed the UAW's WPA and welfare departments. Elected as labor's candidate to the Council in 1941, he took office during the Sojourner Truth controversy, and as his previous good record while secretary-director of the Detroit Housing Commission had shown, blacks found him helpful in resolving that particular crisis. Subsequently he alone among the councilmen opposed Jeffries's pro-segregation stand on public housing and pressed for a grand jury investigation of the police after the riot. In Louis Martin's words, Edwards had demonstrated that "no group in the city has interests which are more related to the interests of the Negro people than . . . the Congress of Industrial Organizations."[60]

With the Negro-labor political coalition well under way by the beginning of August, two distinct but cooperating black voter mobilization groups emerged: one consisting of trade unionists chaired by Horace Sheffield and the other of prominent civic leaders headed by Charles Diggs. At first Diggs sought to include under one roof nearly everyone from conservative Republican lawyers like Charles Mahoney to militant unionists like Hardin and Tappes. But in the end his Vote Mobilization Committee, although quietly backed by both Republican wheelhorses and the unionists, focused exclusively on enlisting important civic, religious, and business organizations.[61] Even though Fitzgerald's platform was vague on both law enforcement and racial issues, he pleased blacks by promising to appoint an unprejudiced police commissioner.[62] Consequently, with the lonely exception of Horace White, who publicly endorsed the mayor and defended his record,[63]* the black civic, social, and political elites in the Motor City were virtually unanimous in backing the CIO candidate. In addition to the activities of the Vote Mobilization Committee, Negro labor leaders were working out of the regular labor campaign headquarters. "Thousands of sample marked ballots were printed, women workers rang countless doorbells, and the preachers exhorted their flocks to go down the line for democracy and kick Jeff out of the city hall." On the Sunday before the primary, Councilman Edwards, running for reelection, was fulsomely presented to three black church congregations by their pastors. And the NAACP branch arranged a meeting of ministers, editors, and heads of civic organizations who demanded Jeffries's defeat. The primary vote itself was most encouraging: Fitzgerald ran well ahead of the mayor, particularly in Negro and union neighborhoods, blacks supporting labor's nominee by a margin of 20 to 1.[64]

Preparing for the general election the embattled Jeffries now resorted to an all-out labor-baiting and race-baiting campaign. Harping on the danger of two minorities—blacks and a clique of labor leaders—bent on capturing the city government, this strategy brought Negroes and the UAW spokesmen even closer together, but split the ranks of the white workers. Skillfully he differentiated between the average union worker and his leaders, asserting that "It is not the rank and file union man who wants to fas-

---

* White, Jeffries's appointee to the Housing Commission, was evidently motivated by political ambition. A member of the lower house of the state legislature in 1941–1942 (see obituaries in *Free Press*, Feb. 11, 1958, and *Chronicle*, Feb. 15, 1958) he had become embroiled in a political fight with Charles Diggs (*Tribune*, Aug. 22, 29, Sept. 5, 12, 1942. and *Chronicle*, Oct. 31, 1942), and at the time of the riot had actually openly defended Jeffries when the mayor refused to declare martial law. (Minutes of Citizens Meeting, June 21, 1943, in Michigan Civil Rights Congress Archives Box 70.)

ten a dictatorship on our city." Focusing on the NAACP as a "minority pressure group" demanding his defeat, Jeffries repeatedly accused the Negro of deliberately fomenting the June riot: "He threw the first stones . . . he ambushed, attacked and shot our policemen . . . he was responsible for most of the looting of stores." "Negro hoodlums started it [the riot]. . . . But the conduct of the Police Department, by and large, was magnificent." The mayor also charged that the Detroit NAACP—with the support of prominent "un-American" UAW leaders—was determined to invade white residential areas: "Arrayed against me are groups demanding mixed housing—the mingling of Negroes and whites in the same neighborhoods. I have said and will continue to say 'no.'" Singling out NAACP and UAW officials who had testified at the Housing Commission hearings, he denounced McClendon, Emil Mazey, and Frank Winn. "The Negroes of Detroit, in the primary, voted against me almost unanimously. I take it, therefore, that my opponent must have promised to make mixed housing the policy of his administration if elected."[65]

The NAACP became so worried that McClendon now openly abandoned even the thin pretense of non-partisanship that national NAACP policy required, and urged upon the branch "all-out support" for the Fitzgerald ticket. Even Horace White was dismayed; while not disavowing Jeffries, he nevertheless criticized him for stooping to racist appeals. As the campaign drew to a close, Jeffries's evident success with white workers prompted a frightened Fitzgerald to indulge in a few racist remarks of his own. Thus he charged the mayor with having encouraged black invasion of white neighborhoods by supporting Negro occupancy of the Sojourner Truth project and appointing Horace White, the "Negro radical" and advocate of mixed housing and interracial marriage to the Housing Commission. Although leading black and white supporters quickly prevailed upon Fitzgerald to drop this campaign style, for many Negro voters he had now become merely the lesser of two evils. And in order to minimize the damage, on election eve McClendon took to the airwaves, declaring his belief in

Fitzgerald's sincerity. In the end Jeffries won easily by splitting the labor vote, even though Fitzgerald carried the heavily UAW voting districts on the West Side as well as the black ghettos. All that labor and the blacks seemed to have salvaged from the balloting was Edwards's reelection to the Common Council, a contest he won quite handily.[66]*

As Louis Martin pointed out, Jeffries's margin of victory in the 1943 election, including as it did so many white workers, demonstrated the "political impotence" of labor's leadership when the race issue was raised.[67] This impotence was demonstrated again two years later when the popular UAW vice-president Richard T. Frankensteen futilely challenged Jeffries. Once more the mayor's racist appeal won the support of many white auto workers, thus guaranteeing his return to office, even though nearly 85 percent of the blacks supported the CIO candidate.[68] Nevertheless, in spite of these failures, the 1943 campaign had marked the emergence of a close political alliance between black Detroit and the UAW that would remain an important feature of Michigan's political landscape for years.[69]

These elections revealed the depth of black Detroit's faith in the

---

* Edwards had a large personal following among both blacks and white workers that gave him even more votes than Fitzgerald, and by 1945 this following would propel him into the Council presidency. On the other hand, as usual, white racism in Detroit blocked the effort to secure black representation on the Council. Edward Simmons, a young Negro attorney, won the endorsement not only of black organizations and the CIO but also of the conservative voice of the city's business interests, the Detroit Citizens League. He secured enough votes in the primary to appear on the final ballot but then went down to defeat, while polling the largest number of votes ever received by a black man in the city's history—100,000, some 40,000 of which came from white working-class districts (*Chronicle*, Sept. 25, Oct. 2, 9, 1943; *News*, Oct. 6, Nov. 3, 1943; Martin, "Detroit—Still Dynamite," *Crisis* 51 [Jan. 1944]: 10.) Actually, given the city-wide character of Common Council elections, it was virtually impossible in this period for a black person, lacking very substantial support among the white voters, to win a seat on that body. Thus back in 1939, *Chronicle* associate editor William Sherrill, with widespread endorsement from black organizations, received the largest primary vote ever given a black candidate up to that point, yet failed to make it into the general elections. (*Chronicle*, Sept. 30, Oct. 14, 28, 1939.)

UAW's top leadership and the viability of a union-black alliance. It is true that the UAW had certainly not delivered on the promises it had made at the time of the Ford strike to Walter White and the Negroes of Detroit. Yet at critical junctures the union's leadership had taken decisive stands on behalf of the black workers, and among the endemic racial crises that beset the Motor City it was in the UAW that the black community found its warmest and most dependable ally.

# V

## *The Image and the Reality: An Epilogue*

During the 1943 mayoralty election Louis Martin had optimistically anticipated that the coalition between blacks and the UAW would vindicate the strategy he had advocated for years: "We shall support the labor slate," he editorialized, "because we believe that the Negro people and organized labor are committed in theory and fact to the democratic ideals which must be upheld at all costs. . . . We are a race of workers and the best interests of the workers are identical with ours." In the sobering aftermath of the voting, however, he pessimistically wrote: "Here in Detroit was a partnership of the two groups wrecked on the shoals of racism. Until this bogey of color is dispelled, such an alliance will always be at the mercy of those who dare to exploit racial prejudice."[1]

Martin's vision and disappointment echoed the dilemmas and ambivalences that characterized the entire relationship between blacks and the United Automobile Workers. The UAW was one of the most racially egalitarian labor organizations in the country, yet prejudice among its white rank and file simply would not disappear. As a result blacks were compelled to continue their battle for access to better jobs; and while substantial advances were regis-

tered during the war and post-war period, virtual exclusion from
the higher-status and best-paying positions such as electricians and
tool-and-die makers lasted for a score of years. Some Negroes
could be officers of locals* and salaried International representatives, but not very many. Nor was the elevation of a black to the
International Executive Board possible so long as the rank-and-file
majority remained overwhelmingly racist. Yet because the UAW
in its racial policies was clearly far ahead of most other unions
(even in the CIO), it enjoyed a highly favorable image in the
Negro community, and the black-UAW alliance that had been
fashioned by 1943 would last for nearly two decades. As late as
1963 the UAW's president Walter Reuther was the one white labor
leader of national stature who was close to both the NAACP and
Martin Luther King, and could symbolize his commitment to
Negro rights by the prominent role he played in the historic
March on Washington.

## 1

Even at the height of the 1943 mayoralty election campaign, the
UAW's national convention revealed the ambivalent relations between blacks and the union. In a number of particulars the conclave, whose 160 black delegates (or 8 percent of those in attendance) were the largest Afro-American representation in the
UAW's history thus far,[2] went on record in support of black interests; yet the nearly unanimous pressure from Negro unionists for a
black member on the Executive Board was turned aside. At the

---

* Developments in black officeholding in the locals were quite mixed. Thus Hodges
Mason was elected president of Bohn Aluminum Local 208 in 1944, but in the
Midland Steel Local blacks lost their prominent role during the early years of the
war, with both Oscar Oden and Nelson Merrill failing to be reelected to their posts.
(Interview with Mason, Jan. 8, 1978; Minutes of Midland Steel Local 410,
1941–1943, *passim*, in Midland Steel Local 410 Archives, Box 1. See also George
W. Crockett's column in *Chronicle*, May 26, 1945, reprinted in *Detroit Would Be
Twenty Years Ahead with George Crockett as Councilman* [Detroit, 1965], for
losses by blacks in local elections of 1945.)

outset, in a move warmly applauded by Detroit's black spokesmen, the union switched the convention site from St. Louis to Buffalo because the Missouri city's hotels and restaurants refused to guarantee equal treatment to all delegates.[3] Moreover the blacks were encouraged by the passage of a resolution that went beyond the standard rhetoric of "firm opposition to any form of racial discrimination" and "sharp condemnation of mob hatred," to direct explicitly "that all instigators of, or participants in 'hate strikes' be immediately disciplined by the local union with the unqualified support of the international union."[4] The hate strikes of course were evidence that anti-Negro sentiment among the whites was so pervasive that a black candidate could not be elected to the International Executive Board through normal procedures. Accordingly Negro union leaders now decided to press forcefully for representation on that body by bringing to the convention floor their demand for a specially designated seat for blacks.

This proposal, first presented and rejected in 1939 had achieved considerable prominence in 1942 when Oscar Noble and Walter Hardin had both entertained hopes of being the person elected to fill such a seat; but in the end the black delegates that year simply took the symbolic step of nominating Noble and James Anderson to new vice-presidencies intended for Walter Reuther and Richard Frankensteen, and futilely ran Sheffield for the Board as a Detroit regional representative.[5] In 1943, however, the Negro unionists were more insistent, hoping to exploit the factional split between the "left-wing" Addes-Frankensteen bloc and the "right-wing" bloc centered upon Walter Reuther. At this highly divided convention both sides courted the black delegates in an effort to win the closely contested election for secretary-treasurer between the incumbent George Addes and his Reutherite opponent, Richard T. Leonard. Accordingly the Negroes, seeing themselves as a "balance of power," sought to exact maximum advantage from the situation—much as they had tried to do five years before during the factional cleavage between Homer Martin and his opponents.

The initiative appeared to come from the blacks in the UAW's left wing. Shelton Tappes was the one who submitted the resolution proposing the creation of a minorities department headed by an elected board member who would be black. Although cool to Tappes's announced candidacy for the new job, Noble, Hardin, and Sheffield endorsed the resolution, pointing out that black "representation on our policy-making body" would do much to "stem the tide of the anti-Negro movement which has resulted in hate strikes." Because it was NNC-oriented unionists Shelton Tappes and Hodges Mason who spearheaded the campaign for a Negro board member, and because communist-oriented people in the Addes faction—like the well-known party functionary Nat Ganley—were championing the cause, there was a widespread belief that the Communists were exploiting the issue to garner needed votes for Addes. In any event they were supporting a very genuine aspiration among black unionists. The latter, fully aware of the leverage they had acquired because the two blocs were nearly equal in strength, lined up overwhelmingly behind Tappes and Mason in a marked show of unity. As Otis Eaton, Tappes's rival in Local 600, put it, "because of the all out fight . . . to gain undisputed control of the UAW, the Negro delegates were looked upon . . . as . . . the balance of power."[6]

With Tappes publicly attacking Leonard, the Addes-Frankensteen group endorsed the demand for a black seat well before the convention began. In reply Reuther and Leonard averred their own support for a Negro on the Executive Board, but flatly opposed electing anyone "on a jim-crow basis." Then, despite the well-organized pressure coming from the caucus of black delegates after the conclave had opened, the Reutherites continued to reject the idea of a special black seat but did offer to back the creation of a minorities department with its own director appointed by the UAW president. Naturally this compromise proved unacceptable, and with the blacks voting overwhelmingly for Addes, they did indeed function as a "balance of power" and easily accounted for his small margin of victory.[7]

Unfortunately this election was held before the Tappes proposal was brought to the floor, and the very narrowness of Addes's victory suggested that he might not be able to hold enough of his supporters together to give the blacks a special seat on the board. Accordingly, to hold wavering white votes in line, the "left-wing" bloc watered down Tappes's resolution by allocating the head of the proposed minorities department only a single vote on the Executive Board instead of the thirty that Tappes had specified.* Finally, at a tense night session the issue reached the floor in two reports from the constitution committee—a majority recommendation supporting the Reuther compromise, and a minority one endorsing the modified Tappes proposal. In the impassioned debate that followed, the convention heard emotional appeals not only from Tappes and Mason but also from nearly all the International's top leaders—Frankensteen, Addes, Victor and Walter Reuther, and President Thomas himself. Thomas, remaining consistent with his previous position, personally backed Reuther's view by denouncing the special black seat as a "hypocritical" demand for racism in reverse. Most of the black delegates of course supported the minority report; as one remarked, "We are getting desperate for real representation on that board and if we have to take it 'Jim Crow,' we'll take it." But Sheffield and Hardin, in an unpopular step among their fellow blacks, abandoned the minority report. Explaining that the Addes bloc's compromises had reduced the proposed black position to one of impotence, the two men announced their support for the stand taken by Reuther and Thomas. Not surprisingly the convention rejected both proposals.[8]†

* Members of the Executive Board cast multiple and highly varied numbers of votes, ranging from ten to eighty-two, depending on the size of the constituencies they were regarded as representing. One of the fears of the Reuther faction, in fact, had been that, if Tappes's proposal passed, the black elected to the Board would be a member of the Addes group, and his thirty votes would be enough to place the secretary-treasurer in a dominant position on the closely divided Executive Board. (See *Workers' Age*, Oct. 23, 1943.)

† Some scholars who have read this book in manuscript form, or with whom we have discussed it prior to publication, wonder if we should not have given greater attention to the role of Communists in shaping the union's policies toward blacks. Actually we ourselves began our research with the assumption that Communist in-

But the issue did not die. Sheffield and Hardin were bitterly attacked by other black unionists,[9] and at the 1944 convention the black delegates, now larger in number than ever (250 out of 2300) again tried their balance-of-power strategy in another fruitless effort to win their point.[10] Thereafter the subject would continue to be raised with painful regularity at the UAW annual conclaves.

Similarly there was persistent dissatisfaction over the representation of blacks on the UAW International's salaried staff. Not only was the number of Negro clerical workers minuscule, but at the close of World War II there were only a dozen blacks among the 400 International representatives, although the 100,000 blacks in the UAW formed about ten percent of the union's membership. As George Addes pointed out, "We have more international representatives who are colored than any other union. But we should and eventually will have more."[11] On the other hand the International proved to be a pioneer among labor organizations in establishing new administrative machinery to deal with the continuing problem of discrimination in the factories.

The old Inter-Racial Committee, long relegated to a marginal position, had been dissolved directly after the Packard strike in

fluence would be an important subject to analyze. Certainly, as we point out, a number of Communists and Communist sympathizers were active; most of the early black UAW staff organizers were either Communists or ex-Communists; and the Communists in the union were strongly identified in the early 1940's with the blacks' desire for representation on the International Executive Board. However, our findings indicated that opposition to the union among Detroit blacks rarely, if ever, involved charges of Communist influence; and, more important, the Communists within the union were usually very similar to other factional groupings in the way they *acted* on racial matters. All the leaders in the UAW's major factions believed in the soundness of interracial trade unionism and would have liked to have seen the elimination of racial discrimination from the automobile industry; but all were also faced with the deep-seated prejudices and discriminatory acts of rank-and-file white workers. Neither Walter Reuther, who headed the GM division, nor George Addes, who was allied with the Communists and had close ties to the Packard local, felt able to take effective steps against racial discrimination in the very locals in which they had the greatest influence. Thus the Communists and their allies, like the leaders in the other factions, operated with a heavy dose of pragmatism.

June 1943, ostensibly because Hardin often operated at cross-purposes with the union's regional directors.[12] Thereafter Hardin's relations with Thomas became increasingly strained until he was dismissed from the staff late in 1944.[13]* By then, at its October 1944 convention, the UAW had established a Fair Practices Committee, headed by the former labor department lawyer and FEPC staff member, George W. Crockett, to deal with problems of discrimination posed by both manufacturers and union locals.[14] Two years later the anti-discrimination work of the union was further institutionalized by giving it the status of a department financed by one percent of all annual dues payments. Headed by a black unionist, William Oliver, who had come up from the ranks in the Ford Highland Park plant (where he had served as recording secretary of Local 400 since 1942), the new Fair Practices and Anti-Discrimination Department functioned along the lines of its predecessor, helping to solve many grievances in local plants "from upgrading on the job to the use of facilities in halls rented for union meetings."[15]

The creation of this machinery within the UAW, like the national FEPC itself, suggests the importance of the Second World War as a watershed that did much to establish new job opportunities for blacks. Nowhere, probably, was this more true than in Detroit. The policies of the UAW's International leaders, combined with labor shortages and federal intervention, had produced significant changes both in the number and kinds of jobs that blacks held. Thus during the year after May 1942, blacks in the Detroit auto industry rose from 5.5 percent to 8.8 percent of the total employed, and by the spring of 1945 they comprised 15 percent. At Chrysler, for example, the proportion of blacks rose from 2.5 percent to 15 percent; at Packard from 4 percent to 15 percent; and at Briggs from 10 percent to about 19 percent. More difficult to assess is the degree to which blacks actually moved out of foundry and unskilled work into more desirable job categories. In

* Subsequently, during the period 1944–1947, Hardin "was frequently on and off the payroll." (Emil Mazey to authors, Jan. 18, 1978.)

the middle of the war, USES figures for Detroit indicated that 60 percent of the blacks were doing unskilled labor compared with 18.5 percent of the whites. As G. James Fleming observed at the time, "All these auto companies have areas of employment where Negroes may move a few steps above the lowest unskilled brackets [but] . . . there are skills and sections to which Negroes are not upgraded or placed. . . ." On the other hand, especially during the latter part of the war, there was a significant amount of upgrading—even at firms like GM and Packard—into many types of inspection jobs, machine production, and assembly-line work.[16]

Yet tensions over black transfers and promotions did not disappear. Several minor white hate strikes and black walkouts occurred,[17] and Packard was again the scene of major confrontations. In October and November 1944 there were brief wildcat strikes by white workers in protest against the introduction of blacks into departments from which they had hitherto been excluded, and then, when 4 more Negroes were upgraded to metal polishing, 39,000 walked out, completely closing the plant again. Union leaders quickly got the whites back, but with the transfers suspended, the angry blacks staged their own walkout, returning only when UAW officials pledged themselves to rectify the situation.[18]

Exacerbating the tensions that led to these disturbances were fears that with peacetime reconversion there would be serious competition for a sharply reduced number of jobs.[19] And indeed in the tightened post-war labor market, many blacks with seniority rights were compelled to return to former foundry and unskilled jobs, while certain employers reverted to outright discrimination.[20] UAW officials seeking to strengthen the anti-discrimination clauses in their contracts found that all the companies refused to pledge themselves to eliminate racial bias in the hiring of Negro workers, and GM was still absolutely adamant against signing any kind of non-discrimination clause at all. Crockett and Oliver, directing the union's new fair practice machinery, experienced considerable success in resolving a number of complaints of bias inside the union, ranging from getting blacks admitted to a southern local by threatening charter revocation to forcing northern locals to stop sponsoring social affairs that barred blacks.[21] On the other hand, outside Detroit charges of racism in the enforcement of seniority and equal pay provisions, especially where management and local white union officials acted in collusion, proved far harder to rectify, with results spotty at best.[22]

Yet by and large the United Automobile Workers' seniority rules operated to the Negroes' benefit, and, once the painful transition to peacetime was over, blacks found that they retained the foothold in semi-skilled machine production and assembly-line work which they had won during the war. Not only was the UAW's commitment evident in the creation of the Fair Practices Committee and Department, but there were cases where International leaders, faced with recalcitrant managements and hostile white workers, protected the blacks' seniority rights by firmly invoking the union contract and threatening hate strikers with loss of jobs. In the Southern locals, of course, discrimination died a much slower death,[23] but in Detroit by mid-century the blacks' position in semi-skilled jobs was secure, and the new battle lines focused on the highly skilled trades such as tool-and-die making, from which blacks were still virtually barred.[24]

## 2

Even though discrimination in the industry was by no means eliminated, and even though there were periodic expressions of dissatisfaction with the UAW, the union nevertheless enjoyed enormous support among Detroit blacks and acquired among the major race advancement organizations an image of forceful racial egalitarianism. The contrast with Detroit blacks' previous experience with labor organizations, the indubitable job protection afforded by the UAW, the well-publicized cases where the International took vigorous action on behalf of black workers, as well as the fact that the UAW's racial policies were indeed in the forefront among the industrial unions, made the UAW a highly valued organization. As early as December 1942, an Office of War Information investigator privately reported, "It is remarkable how thoroughly the whole Negro community supports and believes in the UAW. . . . The leadership of the UAW . . . has converted them into a solid union asset. It is as common in interviewing to hear Negro workers recite their change of heart towards unions as to hear the same from white Southerners." Few blacks would have disagreed with the evaluation of the black director of the CIO's National Committee To Abolish Race Discrimination, George L. P. Weaver, when he wrote in the National Urban League's magazine, *Opportunity*, that the UAW's "race relations is second to the record of no other American union."[25]

UAW officials, though conceding that much remained to be done, spoke proudly of their accomplishments and aggressively publicized them among blacks and liberal whites, insisting that the union was courageously working on behalf of the black workers' interests. Shortly after the war Walter Reuther, reaching an influential biracial audience through *Opportunity*, pointed to the UAW's precedent-setting Fair Practices Committee and maintained that the auto workers had "gone seriously about the business of making practice square with principle." Similarly, Reuther's archrival, George F. Addes, boasting that blacks in the UAW were "the largest single group of organized Negro workers in this country," asserted, "We do not claim a perfect record; but we do claim for ourselves the best record in this field of human relations of any comparable organization in American life—including the churches. . . . discrimination within our own ranks is becoming a thing of the past."[26]

*PM*, the liberal New York daily, took such statements literally, crediting the "uncompromising" UAW not only with having "fought out and settled . . . the issue of economic equality for Negroes with whites" but also with having produced white members whose conduct during the riot furnished a model of tolerance and good will. Leaders of black advancement organizations like the NAACP and the National Urban League also were enthusiastic about the UAW. The NUL fostered the impression that in the wartime hate strikes the UAW and R. J. Thomas consistently took "prompt disciplinary action" and unhesitantly risked "the wrath of the unenlightened thousands of transplanted Southerners." The League's executive secretary, Lester Granger, asserted that Thomas had ended the Hudson walkout quickly by telling strikers "to return to work or be expelled from the Union," and subsequently praised the UAW's "courageous leadership" which ended a Packard wildcat by "immediately order[ing] the white strikers to return to work or suffer loss of union membership and employment."[27]

Over the following years the union developed even closer ties with the NAACP than with the Urban League. Thus in 1945 Thomas circularized all UAW locals, urging full cooperation with the Association's membership drive. "Long in the vanguard of organizations working for the same interracial principles for which the UAW-CIO stands," the NAACP "has recognized that the solidarity of labor . . . is the soundest foundation for constructive interracial relations." Ignoring the clear-cut historical record, he added, "we have invariably found the NAACP a strong support in all our organizing efforts." Walter White similarly glossed over the hard realities in his autobiography and engaged instead in facile exaggeration as he remembered the half dozen years since the 1941 Ford strike: The UAW "has vigorously and continuously fought racial discrimination within the union and in American life generally. . . . During the terrible race riots in Detroit in 1943 white union members fought against white mobbists to protect Negroes, and Negro unionists fought Negroes in protection of white fellow workers."[28]

The two organizations grew still more intimate after Walter Reuther became UAW president in 1946. Although his base was among the General Motors workers on the West Side of Detroit, he had found it impracticable to mount a vigorous assault on that intransigent corporation's notoriously discriminatory policies. On the other hand, during the wartime crises over black transfers and upgrading, he supported a firm stance and disciplinary action on the union's part, and consistently expressed support for black concerns. Thus it was Reuther rather than Thomas who was the International's spokesman at the Cadillac Square demonstration in 1943. Speaking to the CIO convention several months earlier, he had characteristically exhorted the delegates to "take up the fight against racial discrimination, not as a secondary consideration, not as something you think about after you get your closed shop and your wage increases and your seniority agreements, but this fight against racial discrimination must be put on top of the list with union security and other major union demands."[29]* As president he proved no more able than his predecessor to bring about full equality in the industry, and like Thomas he consistently blamed management, although he was deeply aware of the problems arising from within the ranks of his own organization. On the other hand Reuther enhanced the status of the UAW's anti-discrimination work by personally assuming the co-directorship (with William Oliver) of the Fair Practices and Anti-Discrimination Department, and over the following years he was highly visible in championing federal FEPC legislation.[30] Reuther's positive image among blacks

---

* Reuther had also been among those strongly in favor of Thomas accepting the invitation to address the NAACP Emergency Wartime Conference in June 1943. (UAW Executive Board Minutes, April 10–21, 1943, in UAW Board Minutes, Box 2.) On the other hand, J. Lawrence Duncan recollects Reuther as articulating pro-black sentiments but in practice acting no better than his colleagues: "I had to build a fire under him and often still couldn't get anywhere. . . . He would talk about integration . . . but was just like everybody else." (Interview with J. Lawrence Duncan, April 9, 1977.)

On occasion Reuther did take effective action on a local level. In 1945 he personally went to Atlanta and forced the GM local there to admit blacks employed in the plant. ("Digest of Cases Considered by the International UAW-CIO Fair Practices Committee, First Quarter 1945" [April 1945], Norman Matthews Collection, Box 1.) Early the following year, in the case of a California GM factory which refused to hire any blacks at all, Vice-President Reuther, with the support of the UAW local there, successfully pressed management to hire qualified Negroes. (Walter Reuther and William Oliver, co-directors, Fair Practices and Anti-Discrimination Department, to UAW-CIO International Executive Board Fair Practices Committee, Dec. 10, 1946, Matthews Collection, Box 1.)

was so great that in January 1949 he was elected to the NAACP national board. As Walter White enthusiastically explained, the NAACP took this step as "a tribute to his unyielding fight against racial discrimination throughout the labor movement."[31]

Back in the 1930's the national NAACP and the National Urban League had been far in advance of most black Detroiters in admiration for industrial unions like the UAW. But during World War II and the post-war era black enthusiasm in the Motor City coincided with the attitudes of those national spokesmen. To a black unionist like Sheffield, wartime improvements in job opportunities showed that "the only real and potent ally that the Negro has in the struggle for survival in industry is the organized labor movement," and Louis Martin recalled that, after leaving Detroit in the mid-forties, his return visits to the Motor City revealed a continuous growth in sentiment favorable to the UAW. So admired was the UAW that when John Dancy published his autobiography he suppressed his early anti-union position and pictured himself as an early and warm supporter of the UAW.[32] In effect the Union now occupied the esteemed place once held by Henry Ford.

## 3

During the late 1950's the close cooperative relationship between the black community and the industrial unions gradually broke down. The merger of the CIO with the AFL in the middle of the decade indicated to many blacks a declining commitment to the battle for job equality. And this came at the very time that the multiplying NAACP legal victories and the dramatic rise of Martin Luther King to public prominence signified a revolution of expectations that was spawning a new militance among black Americans. In this context the old, still unsolved issues of job discrimination in the factories and the lack of representation in the highest councils of the auto union assumed new urgency. In Negro labor circles the black UAW leaders were in the vanguard of the rising protest. In 1957 Horace Sheffield and his colleagues formed the Trade Union

Leadership Conference (TULC) to upgrade the status of blacks
both in the plants and the unions of the Motor City. This organization of Detroit unionists provided the prototype for the federation
of similar groups, the Negro American Labor Council, established
by A. Philip Randolph two years later.

To the TULC the UAW Fair Practices Department was ineffec-
tual. While blacks were a much larger proportion of the work force
than ever before, severe discrimination nevertheless still existed in
access to the highly skilled jobs. As Sheffield informed the U.S.
Civil Rights Commission in 1960, blacks constituted a fraction of
one percent in such trades as carpentry and tool-and-die making.
Even at the Rouge where there were 12,500 black workers, less
than 250 of them were among the 7,000 in the skilled trades. With
blacks now 25 percent of the work force at major Detroit companies like Chrysler and GM, the situation was becoming increasingly volatile, and their grievances about exclusion from the skilled
trades represented one of the principal issues raised by TULC.[33]

TULC also protested the extremely low number of paid international staff representatives who were Negroes[34] and gave new salience to the problem of securing black representation on the Executive Board. The latter issue had been raised several times at
conventions in the decade following the war, usually in the form of a
proposal for a Negro vice-president. Even after Reuther had consolidated his control and attained the presidency, it remained intertwined with the union's factionalism and typically was championed by Communists and the union's left wing.[35] Then at the
1959 convention the matter was taken up by Sheffield and other
long-time Reuther loyalists. While still opposed to the left wing's
old proposal for a constitutional amendment guaranteeing a Negro
seat, they had become discouraged at the prospects of a black
being elected through normal channels, and Sheffield, though a
paid staff member, nevertheless challenged the union's International leadership by nominating the head of the Chicago Amalgamated Local 734, Willoughby Abner, for a vice-presidency. This
particular effort failed, but the TULC agitation, reenforced by the

growing proportion of blacks in the factories, finally paved the way for the election of a black to a newly created vice-presidency in 1962.[36]

The work of TULC proved to be a prelude to the militant agitation of the 1960's—a complex subject that is of course beyond the scope of this volume. In the context provided by the civil rights protest movement early in that decade, the black revolutionary nationalism several years later, and the rapidly growing proportion of Detroit area blacks in the industry's labor force (with Negroes comprising about 25 percent of the UAW members before the end of the 1960's), black workers would make more progress on all of these issues than ever before. Expectations continued to exceed actual change, but the number of local officers and International representatives grew rapidly, a second Negro was elected to the International Executive Board in 1968, and barriers in apprenticeships and skilled trades started to fall.[37]

### 4

The entire history of the relations between black Detroit and the UAW had been characterized by a striking ambiguity. On the one hand the union had protected seniority rights, fostered greater economic security, and aided the blacks' movement into production and assembly-line jobs outside the foundry. On the other hand, the constraints placed upon the International leadership by the white rank and file often inhibited implementation of the union's constitutional provisions prohibiting racial discrimination, and blacks from the beginning waged protests against the union's failure to eliminate job bias and the lack of representation in the highest councils of the organization. Although by the 1960's the warm relationship between rank-and-file black auto workers and the UAW International leaders, on the one hand, and between those leaders and the national black protest organizations, on the other hand, would deteriorate, the alliance had endured so long precisely because the UAW had been in the vanguard of the labor movement and indeed of the larger American society in its support for black aspirations. The tensions between the UAW's principles and what the union actually delivered were crucially important. Nevertheless, with the possible exception of the Packinghouse workers, the UAW had done more in the factory and in the larger civil rights struggle than any other trade union. It was just because the UAW had been in the forefront of the struggle for economic and social change that Detroit blacks had found it to be such an indispensable ally.

## Abbreviations Used in Notes

**I  SERIAL PUBLICATIONS**

| | |
|---|---|
| *Afro-American* | Baltimore *Afro-American* |
| *Chronicle* | Michigan *Chronicle* |
| *Courier* | Pittsburgh *Courier* |
| *Defender* | Chicago *Defender* |
| *Free Press* | Detroit *Free Press* |
| *NAACP, Annual Report for* [*year*] | Short form for NAACP Annual Reports, title and imprint vary. |
| *News* | Detroit *News* |
| *Times* | New York *Times* |
| *Tribune* | Detroit *Tribune* |
| *UAW* | *United Automobile Worker* |
| *UAW* [*year*] *Convention Proceedings* | Short form for United Automobile Workers Convention Proceedings, title and imprint vary. |

## II    COLLECTIONS IN THE NATIONAL ARCHIVES

| | |
|---|---|
| FEPC, followed by reel number | Fair Employment Practices Committee. Citations are to the microfilm made of documents from this archival collection. (This is Record Group 228 in the National Archives.) |
| NA RG 44 | National Archives, Record Group 44, Office of Government Reports. |
| NA RG 80 | National Archives, Record Group 80, General Records of the Department of the Navy. (Citations are to General Correspondence files, 1940–1942.) |
| NA RG 179 | National Archives, Record Group 179, War Production Board. |
| NA RG 202 | National Archives, Record Group 202, War Labor Board. |
| NA RG 208 | National Archives, Record Group 208, Office of War Information. |
| NA RG 211 | National Archives, Record Group 211, War Manpower Commission. |
| NA RG 211-Chicago | National Archives, Record Group 211, War Manpower Commission, Records for Region 5, in Federal Records Center, Chicago. |
| NA RG 212 | National Archives, Record Group 212, Committee for Congested Production Areas. |
| NA RG 280 | National Archives, Record Group 280, Federal Mediation and Conciliation Service, Department of Labor. (Citations are to Dispute Case Files, 1914–1948.) |

## III    OTHER MANUSCRIPT AND ARCHIVAL COLLECTIONS

| | |
|---|---|
| AFL Archives | American Federation of Labor Archives. |
| ANP | Associated Negro Press Archives. |
| CIO Archives | Congress of Industrial Organization Archives. |
| DUL | Detroit Urban League Archives. |
| NAACP, followed by box number (e.g. NAACP C 322), or by name of file where box numbers had not yet been | National Association for the Advancement of Colored People Archives, Library of Congress. |

assigned (e.g.
NAACP, Ford
Strike File)

| | |
|---|---|
| NAACP-NYC | Executive Board Minutes and Monthly Reports of the Secretary to the Board, at the national NAACP office in New York City. |
| NNC followed by reel number | National Negro Congress Archives. Citations are to the microfilm copy. |
| NUL | National Urban League Archives. |
| UAW Archives | United Automobile Workers Archives. |

## CHAPTER I

1. George S. Schuyler, "Reflections on Negro Leadership," *Crisis* 44 (Nov. 1937): 328. Among the most useful background works on the history of the relationships between blacks and organized labor since the opening of the century are Sterling D. Spero and Abram L. Harris, *The Black Worker* (New York, 1931); Horace R. Cayton and George S. Mitchell, *Black Workers and the New Unions* (Chapel Hill, 1939); Philip S. Foner, *Organized Labor and the Black Worker, 1619–1973* (New York, 1974); Ray Marshall, *The Negro and Organized Labor* (New York, 1965); Harvard Sitkoff, *A New Deal for Blacks* (New York, 1978), chap. 7. Pertinent articles include Bernard Mandel, "Samuel Gompers and the Negro Workers, 1886–1914," *Journal of Negro History* 40 (Jan. 1955): 34–60; Paul B. Worthman, "Black Workers and Labor Unions in Birmingham, Alabama, 1897–1904," *Labor History* 10 (Summer 1969): 375–407; Herbert G. Gutman, "The Negro and the United Mine Workers of America: The Career and Letters of Richard L. Davis and Something of Their Meaning, 1890–1900," in Julius Jacobson, ed., *The Negro and the American Labor Movement* (Garden City, 1968). For discussions of the role of organized labor in two important race riots see Elliott Rudwick, *Race Riot at East St. Louis, July 2, 1917* (Carbondale, 1964), and William M. Tuttle, *Race Riot: Chicago in the Red Summer of 1919* (New York, 1972).

2. Paul Oliver, *Blues Fell This Morning: The Meaning of the Blues* (New York, 1960), 32. We are indebted to Leon Litwack for calling this item to our attention.

3. Walter White to Senator James Couzens, April 11, 1934. NAACP C257.

4. Lloyd H. Bailer, "The Automobile Unions and Negro Labor," *Political Science Quarterly* 59 (Dec. 1944): 548.

5. George Edmund Haynes, *Negro New-Comers in Detroit, Michigan: A Challenge to Christian Statesmanship* (New York, 1918), 12–14; Arthur Turner and Earl R. Moses, *Colored Detroit: A Brief History of Detroit's Colored Population* (Detroit, 1924), 54–57; quotation from John Ragland, "The Negro in Detroit," *Southern Workman* 52 (Nov. 1923): 535.

6. See p. 18.

7. Haynes, *Negro New-Comers in Detroit*, 14; David L. Lewis, "History of Negro Employment in Detroit Area Plants of Ford Motor Company 1914–1941" (paper submitted in partial fulfillment of the requirements of History 334, University of Michigan, 1954), copy at Reuther Library, 7; [J. C. Dancy], "Unemployment" [1921], DUL Box 1; Ragland, "The Negro in Detroit," 534; Mayor's Inter-racial Committee, "The Negro in Detroit" (Detroit, mimeographed, 1926), section III, 4–5, 9–10; Dancy to J. S. Jackson, May 4, 1931, DUL Box 2; "Ford Motor Company River Rouge Plant, Proportion of Colored Employes in Each Building," Oct. 5, 1937, copy in UAW Archives: Public Relations Department—Ford Motor Company Box 2.

8. Mayor's Inter-racial Committee, "The Negro in Detroit," 4–5; on GM in 1941, see also Dancy to Eugene Kinckle Jones, March 10, 1941, DUL Box 4; Dancy to Lester Granger, May 8, 1941, DUL Box 4; "The Integration of Negroes into Defense Training," Feb. 17, 1942, NUL Series VI, Box 14; and interview with Oscar Noble, April 8, 1978.

9. Lloyd H. Bailer, "The Negro Automobile Worker," *Journal of Political Economy* 51 (Oct. 1943): 415–16.

10. See *e.g.* correspondence in DUL relating to Milwaukee, St. Louis, St. Paul, and Kansas City: Dancy to William F. Kelley, March 6, 1930, Box 3; John T. Clark to Dancy, Nov. 21, 1934, Box 3; Charles W. Washington to Dancy, April 7, 1936, Box 3; E. K. Jones to Dancy, March 1, 1937, Box 4.

11. Lloyd H. Bailer, "Negro Labor in the Automobile Industry" (Ph.D. dissertation, University of Michigan, 1943), 45; interview with Oscar Noble, April 8, 1978.

12. Bailer, "The Negro Automobile Worker," 419–20.

13. Robert W. Dunn, *Labor and Automobiles* (New York, 1929), 69;

Michael D. Whitty, "Emil Mazey: Radical as Liberal: The Evolution of Labor Radicalism in the UAW" (Ph.D. dissertation, Syracuse University, 1968), 126 for Briggs.

14. Herbert R. Northrup, *et al., Negro Employment in Basic Industry: A Study of Racial Policies in Six Industries* (Philadelphia, 1970), 57; Lewis, "History of Negro Employment in Detroit Area Plants of Ford Motor Company," 29; and detailed breakdowns given in "Ford Motor Company, Rouge Plant: Proportion of Colored Employees in Each Building," Oct. 5, 1937, and "Ford Motor Company, Rouge Plant: Proportion of Colored Employees in Each Department," Oct. 5, 1937, both compiled by S. W. Harrison of the Ford Motor Company, copies to be found in UAW Archives, Public Relations Department-Ford Motor Company, Box 2.

15. Interviews with Oscar Oden, former worker at Midland, Jan. 2, 1978, and with Peter Friedlander, the leading scholarly authority on the Midland UAW local, April 7, 1977.

16. Dancy to T. Arnold Hill, April 15, 1938, DUL Box 4; Lloyd H. Bailer, "The Negro Automobile Worker," chapter X in Paul H. Norgren, "Negro Labor and Its Problems" (a research memorandum prepared for the Carnegie-Myrdal Study of the Negro in America, 1940), 554, copy in Schomburg Collection of New York Public Libary.

17. Lewis, "History of Negro Employment in Detroit Area Plants of Ford Motor Company," 8, 13–14, 31; Dancy to T. Arnold Hill, Dec. 7, 1938, DUL Box 1; Northrup *et al., Negro Employment in Basic Industry,* 53; *Courier,* March 15, 1941; *Tribune,* May 10, 1941; Bailer, "Negro Labor in the Automobile Industry," 59–60, 71; interviews with J. Lawrence Duncan, son of a black Ford foreman, Nov. 18, 1977, and June 24, 1978.

18. Northrup, *et al., Negro Employment in Basic Industry,* 57.

19. Lewis, "History of Negro Employment in Detroit Area Plants of Ford Motor Company," 12; and for Detroit Urban League, see especially minutes, DUL Board of Trustees 1926–1928, *passim,* DUL Box 11.

20. Lewis, "History of Negro Employment in Detroit Area Plants of Ford Motor Company," 17–18. Lewis, on the basis of interviews, records the date of the luncheon as 1918. Actually it could not have been before 1919, since Sorensen had not been connected with Ford's auto manufacturing for the four years beginning in 1915. See Allan Nevins and Frank E. Hill, *Ford: Expansion and Challenge, 1915–1933* (New York, 1957), 15.

21. Lewis, "History of Negro Employment in Detroit Area Plants of Ford Motor Company," 18, 20, 21–26; Bailer, "Negro Labor in the Automobile Industry," 140, 147–48; Willis F. Ward, "The Reminiscences of

Mr. Willis F. Ward" (typescript, May 1955), 65–67, Ford Company Archives; interview with James J. McClendon, Aug. 17, 1976, and Gloster Current, Aug. 5, 1977.

22. See Horace White, "Up the Wrong Tree," *Tribune*, Aug. 28, 1937, for general and highly critical discussion of hiring system at Ford involving ministers and politicians; also transcript of oral history interview with Malcolm Dade, n.d., Reuther Library.

23. Allan Nevins and Frank Ernest Hill, *Ford: Decline and Rebirth, 1933–1962* (New York, 1962), 497; Lewis, "History of Negro Employment in Detroit Area Plants of Ford Motor Company." 9.

24. Editorial, Dearborn *Independent*, Feb. 23, 1924; Henry Ford's Page, *ibid.*, Oct. 21, 1922; editorials, *ibid.*, Aug. 5, 1922, July 4, 1925, Feb. 20, 1926, Nov. 14, 1925.

25. Editorials, *ibid.*, Dec. 10, 1921, Nov. 14, 1925.

26. Ford's Page, *ibid.*, June 17 and Oct. 21, 1922.

27. For discussion of the history of the radical but weak industrial union, the United Carriage and Wagon Workers' International Union, later known as the Auto Workers Union, see esp. Joyce Peterson, "A Social History of Automobile Workers Before Unionization, 1900–1933" (Ph.D. dissertation, University of Wisconsin, 1976), 241, 247, 267–69, 275–84; and Roger R. Keeran, "Communists and Auto Workers: The Struggle for a Union, 1919–1941" (Ph.D. dissertation, University of Wisconsin, 1974), 4–6, 31, 39–41, 125, 184. For discussion of the similarly weak efforts of the IWW in the early part of the century, particularly the brief effort to organize at Ford's in 1913 and the Studebaker strike of the same year, see Peterson, "A Social History of Automobile Workers . . . ," 248–51, and Henry Faigin, "The Industrial Workers of the World in Detroit and Michigan from the Period of Beginnings Through the World War" (M.A. thesis, Wayne University, 1937), 73–86.

28. Keith Sward, *The Legend of Henry Ford* (New York, 1948), 51–52, 56.

29. Editorials, Dearborn *Independent*, Aug. 5, 1922, May 15 and June 12, 1920; Ford's Page, *ibid.*, Nov. 22, 29, Dec. 6, 1919.

30. Ford's Page, *ibid.*, Oct. 21, 1922; anonymously authored article, *ibid.*, March 26, 1921; Llewellyn Smith, "The Jewish Attempt To Bolshevize the Negro," *ibid.*, Dec. 22, 1923; Ford's Page, *ibid.*, Oct. 21, 1922; editorial, *ibid.*, Jan. 9, 1926.

31. See *e.g.*, retrospective article on the Ford-Carver friendship in *Chronicle*, Sept. 5, 1953; Rackham Holt, *George Washington Carver* (Garden City, 1943), 312–14.

32. *Tribune,* Nov. 23, 1935; retrospective discussion in *Chronicle,* Aug. 15, 1953.

33. *Chronicle,* Aug. 22, 1953; Sward, *The Legend of Henry Ford,* 229–30; [J. C. Dancy], "The Negro Population of Detroit" [1926], DUL Box 1; *Times,* Dec. 17, 1931.

34. Bailer, "Negro Labor in the Automobile Industry," 179.

35. Press release, "Negro Worker Got Break Under Henry Ford," April 16, 1937, Associated Negro Press Archives; Bailer, "Negro Labor in the Automobile Industry," 176.

36. Ralph J. Bunche, *The Political Status of the Negro in the Age of FDR,* ed. Dewey W. Grantham (Chicago, 1973), 587; Lewis, "History of Negro Employment in Detroit Area Plants of Ford Motor Company," 26.

37. Bailer, "Negro Labor in the Automobile Industry," 165, for quotation; Horace Cayton's column in *Courier,* Jan. 25, 1941.

38. Bailer, "Negro Labor in the Automobile Industry," 174; Lewis, "History of Negro Employment in Detroit Area Plants of Ford Motor Company," including quotation from Henry Ford notebook no longer accessible to scholars.

39. On history of Negro churches in Detroit, see David Katzman, *Before the Ghetto: Black Detroit in the Nineteenth Century* (Urbana, 1973), *passim;* Haynes, *Negro New-Comers in Detroit,* 33; Turner and Moses, *Colored Detroit,* 17–20, 66–67. On their relationship to the class structure of black Detroit, interviews with Gloster Current, Aug. 5, 1977; James J. McClendon, Aug. 17, 1976; and Shelton Tappes and Marcellus Ivory, Aug. 15, 1976. 'On Daniel's career, obituaries in *Chronile,* Sept. 9, 16, 1939, and Claudia Timmons, office of the registrar of New York University to authors, Feb. 22, 1978.

40. For biographical sketches of Peck, see *Chronicle,* Dec. 26, 1942, and Nov. 11, 1944. For Booker T. Washington Trade Association and Peck's role in it, see Richard Thomas, "From Peasant to Proletarian: The Formation and Organization of the Black Industrial Working Class in Detroit, 1915–1945" (Ph.D. dissertation, University of Michigan, 1976), 140–43. On Peck recommending workers to Ford, see Bailer, "Negro Automobile Worker," in Norgren, "Negro Labor and Its Problems," 611. For biographical sketch of Woodson, see *Chronicle,* Dec. 19, 1942.

41. *Guide to the Microfilm Edition of the Detroit Urban League Papers* (Ann Arbor, 1974), 1; DUL Board of Trustees minutes, Jan. 14, 1926, DUL Box 11; Spero and Harris, *The Black Worker,* 140. For role of Employers Association, see David Allan Levine, *Internal Combustion: The Races in Detroit, 1915–1926* (Westport, Conn., 1976), 28–29, 80–81. For

Dancy's career, see *News*, June 11, 1943; *Tribune*, June 19, 1943; and his autobiography, *Sand Against the Wind* (Detroit, 1966).

42. See esp. Detroit Urban League Board of Trustees minutes, 1926–1928, *passim*, DUL Box 11.

43. Dancy, *Sand Against the Wind*, 128–34; Ragland, "The Negro in Detroit," 536; unsigned, untitled memorandum, Oct. 28, 1918, DUL Box 1. For Winegar being member of Detroit Urban League Trustee Board 1937–1945, various materials in DUL and NUL archives too numerous to list. On the two men's very warm relationship, see especially Board of Trustees minutes, April 24, 1936, DUL Box 11. For references to Dodge recruiting through the Detroit League during 1920's, see Board of Trustees minutes, 1920's *passim*, DUL Box 11. For sketches of Winegar's career, see obituaries in *Times*, Jan. 15, 1945, and *Free Press*, Jan. 15, 1945.

44. [Dancy], "Unemployment" [1921], DUL Box 1; Ragland, "The Negro in Detroit," 536–37.

45. Thomas, "From Peasant to Proletarian," 72, 147–48; minutes of National Urban League Steering Committee, Dec. 26, 1919, June 9, 1920, NUL Series XI, Box 2.

46. See various requests for Dancy's intercession with Ford: *e.g.*, Lester Granger to Dancy, Nov. 5, 1934, and Elmer A. Carter to Dancy, Feb. 19, 1935, both in DUL Box 3.

47. Spero and Harris, *The Black Worker*, 140. National Urban League, *Annual Report for 1916–1917* (New York, 1917), 18, confirms that the Employers Association paid the salary of the Employment secretary.

48. Dancy to Charles S. Johnson, July 9, 1934, and Dancy to John T. Clark, May 1, 1934, both in DUL Box 3. See also interview with Dancy in 1926 quoted in Glenn E. Carlson, "The Negro in the Industries of Detroit" (Ph.D. dissertation, University of Michigan, 1929), 189.

49. For discussion of the evolution of the National Urban League's policies toward organized labor, see Nancy J. Weiss, *The National Urban League, 1910–1940* (New York, 1974), chaps. 13 and 18.

50. Detroit Urban League Board of Trustees minutes, April 26, 1934, DUL Box 11; Bailer, "Negro Labor in the Automobile Industry," 192–93.

51. *Crisis* 4 (July 1912): 125.

52. *Tribune*, Nov. 30, 1935.

53. Interview with Gloster Current, Aug. 5, 1977; statement by Bradby in *Tribune*, Aug. 28, 1937.

54. List of Detroit branch presidents in *Afro-American*, May 21, 1940, and materials in national NAACP branch files in NAACP G 94–G 97.

55. L.C. Blount to Roy Wilkins, April 13, 1934, NAACP G 97. See also

Blount's statement in *Afro-American*, April 28, 1934. For Blount's career, see *Chronicle*, Oct. 7, 1939, Dec. 12, 1942.

56. "Urban League Staff Attends Tea at the [Edsel] Ford Home," Feb. 8, 1926, DUL Box 1, and Granger to Dancy, Nov. 5, 1934, DUL Box 3. Materials in NAACP G 95 *passim* (for Mrs. Dodge, see "Detroit Contributors December 1923.") For Couzens, see Robert Bagnall to James Weldon Johnson, Oct. 29, 1919, NAACP C 62. Ira W. Jayne to Mary White Ovington, Dec. 18, 1922, and Ovington to Jayne, Dec. 22, 1922, both in NAACP G 95; on Ovington see also reference in Walter White, *A Man Called White* (New York, 1948), 212–13.

57. Jayne to Edsel Ford, Nov. 23, 1923, Ford to Jayne, Dec. 5, 1923, and Walter White to Edsel Ford, Jan. 22, 1924, all in Ford Company Archives, Accession 572, Box 33; Detroit Branch, "Annual Report, July 1, 1921, to June 17, 1922," NAACP G 95; list of contributors to Detroit Branch, Dec. 1923, NAACP G 95; White to Jayne, March 2, 1925, NAACP G 95; White to Edsel Ford, July 7, 1933, NAACP C 156; White to Jayne, July 7, Sept. 12, 1933, NAACP C 156; correspondence concerning the William Rosenwald matching offer, 1929–1932, NAACP C 158 and C 159, *passim*.

58. Bailer, "Negro Labor in the Automobile Industry," 192.

59. For this conscious division of the field of black advancement, see esp. James Weldon Johnson to Moorfield Storey, April 5, 1927, NAACP C 66; Minutes of NAACP Annual Meeting, Jan. 3, 1916, NAACP A 1.

60. NAACP Board minutes, Feb. 11, March 11, April 8, July 8, 1918, NAACP A 1; 1918 and 1919 documents and correspondence in NAACP C 319, esp. "Synopsis of Conference Held at Office of American Federation of Labor Between Committee Representing the A. F. of L. and Committee Representing the Colored Workers," April 22, 1918; "The Negro and the Labor Union: An N.A.A.C.P. Report," *Crisis* 18 (Sept. 1919): 239–41.

61. Walter White, "Solving America's Race Problem," *Nation* 128 (Jan. 9, 1929): 42; John P. Frey, "Attempts To Organize Negro Workers," *American Federationist* 36 (March 1929): 296–305; relevant correspondence in NAACP C 232 and in Frey Papers, Box 12.

62. For discussions of this, see B. Joyce Ross, *J. E. Spingarn and the Rise of the NAACP, 1911–1939* (New York, 1972), chaps. 6 and 8 *passim;* Raymond Wolters, *Negroes and the Great Depression* (Westport, Conn., 1970), chaps. 9 and 12 *passim;* and materials on 1935 NAACP annual conference in NAACP B 11. See also materials on 1933 Amenia Conference, in NAACP C 229; and on Harris Committee in NAACP A 29, including quotations from "Future Plan and Program of the NAACP, A Report of the Committee on Future Plan and Program," 1935.

63. See correspondence in NAACP C 413; *Report of the Proceedings of the 54th Convention of AFL* (Washington, 1934), 54–55, 330–34; *Report of Proceedings of the 55th Annual Convention of AFL* (Washington, 1935), 808–20; "Investigation of Charges of Discrimination Against Negroes, Authorized by Action of the San Francisco Convention 1934 on Resolution No. 41," Transcript of Proceedings of Hearings, July 9 and 10, 1935, copy in William Green's files, AFL Archives; John Brophy to William Green, Nov. 6, 1935, in *ibid.*; John E. Rooney *et al.* to Executive Council of AFL, Sept. 14, 1935 (report of the committee), in *ibid.*; correspondence in American Federation of Labor folder, NAACP C 413. For standard account of the history of the split between the AFL and CIO, see Walter Galenson, *The CIO Challenge to the AFL: A History of the American Labor Movement, 1935–1941* (Cambridge, Mass., 1960). For Brophy's role in the fight against race discrimination, see also John Brophy, *A Miner's Life* (Madison, Wisconsin, 1964), 245–46, and Sister M. Camilla Mullay, "John Brophy, Militant Labor and Reformer: The CIO Years," (Ph.D. dissertation, Catholic University, 1966), 41–49.

64. Minutes of the Committee for Industrial Organization, 1935–1937, Katherine Pollak Ellickson Collection; minutes and proceedings of the meetings of the Executive Board of the Congress of Industrial Organizations (title varies), 1938–1940; *Proceedings of the First Constitutional Convention CIO, November 14–18, 1938* (no imprint, 1938), 126, 178–80, 185; *Daily Proceedings of the Second Constitutional Convention of the Congress of Industrial Organizations, October 10–13, 1939* (no imprint, 1939), 172; *Daily Proceedings of the Fourth Constitutional Convention of the CIO, November 17–22, 1941* (no imprint, 1941), 260–61.

65. Correspondence with Clinton S. Golden of Steel Workers Organizing Committee, 1937, *passim*, NNC Archives, Reel 1189; "Statement by Philip Murray, November 8, 1936," CIO Archives, Box A7-33; White to John L. Lewis, Nov. 29, 1935, and John Brophy to White, Dec. 2, 1935, both in CIO Archives, Box A7A-13; *Courier*, Aug. 19, 1937.

66. *CIO News*, April 28, May 6, June 21, 1940. Discussions at the 1941 CIO Convention made clear the relationship between black agitation for war jobs and the increased salience of the anti-discrimination issue in the CIO. See *Daily Proceedings of the Fourth Constitutional Convention of the CIO . . . ,* 227–29.

67. "Address of John L. Lewis at the 31st Annual Conference of the National Association for the Advancement of Colored People," NAACP subject file 1940: Labor, folder labelled John L. Lewis; *Daily Proceedings of the Fourth Constitutional Convention of the CIO . . . ,* 260–61.

68. "Report of Resolutions Committee, 27th Annual Conference N.A.A.C.P., Baltimore, Md., July 3, 1936," NAACP B 12.

69. This analysis of the National Negro Congress is based on a study of primary and secondary sources too numerous to be cited here. In addition to the organization's archives at the Schomburg Collection, the most useful items included Ralph J. Bunche, "Extended Memorandum on the Programs, Ideologies, Tactics and Achievements of Negro Betterment and Interracial Organizations" (A research memorandum prepared for the Carnegie-Myrdal Study of the Negro in America, 1940), copy in Schomburg Collection, 319–71; Cayton and Mitchell, *Black Workers and the New Unions*, 415–24; Lawrence S. Wittner, "The National Negro Congress: A Reassessment," *American Quarterly* 22 (Winter 1970): 883–901; "Toward Negro Unity," *Nation* 142 (March 11, 1936): 302; *Official Proceedings, Second National Negro Congress, October 15–17, 1937* (Washington [1937]); John L. Lewis, "Equal Opportunity" ([Washington], 1940) speech delivered at NNC Convention. On Walter White's attitude, see correspondence in NAACP Archives too voluminous to be cited here.

70. White to James Couzens, April 11, 1934, NAACP C 257.

71. On Auto Workers Union, see Note 27 above. For specific references to its stand on blacks, see Peterson, "A Social History of Automobile Workers Before Unionization," 241, 275, and Keeran, "Communists and Auto Workers," 39–41. See also anti-discrimination planks in list of AWU's demands, *Auto Workers News*, June 1929, cited in William Ellison Chalmers, "Labor in the Automobile Industry: A Study of Personnel Policies, Workers' Attitudes and Attempts at Unionism" (Ph.D. dissertation, University of Wisconsin, 1932), 220; interview with Phil E. Raymond, leader in Auto Workers Union, April 9, 1977.

72. Sidney Fine, "The Origins of the United Automobile Workers, 1933–1935," *Journal of Economic History* 18 (Sept. 1958): 250.

73. *Afro-American*, July 1, 1933; Nahum Daniel Brascher to William J. Cameron, June 25, 1933, Associated Negro Press Archives.

74. Louis Blount to Roy Wilkins, April 13, 1934, NAACP G 97; *Afro-American*, Jan. 13, 1934; William Collins to William Green, Nov. 18, Dec. 15, 1933, cited in Fine, "Origins of the United Automobile Workers," 258.

75. Report of the Secretary for the April 1934 NAACP Board of Directors Meeting, NAACP-NYC; Fine, "Origins of the United Automobile Workers," 262–64, 280–81; *Constitution of the International Union, United Automobile Workers of America and Laws Governing Local Unions, Adopted . . . 1935* [Detroit, 1935], 9.

76. Ernest Calloway, "The C.I.O. and Negro Labor," *Opportunity* 14 (Nov. 1936): 330.

77. On origins of National Negro Congress in Michigan, see hazy discussion in untitled interview with LeBron Simmons, n.d., in William McKie Papers in the Nat Ganley Collection, Series VI, Box 33; *Negro Congress News*, I, 1 (Jan. 1936), mimeographed, in Schomburg Collection vertical file; correspondence of John P. Davis with Snow Grigsby and Robert Evans, 1935–1936, in National Negro Congress Archives, Reel 1185. Although Wittner, "The National Negro Congress: A Reassessment," finds considerable activity on the part of the local NNC chapters, our data on Detroit support the opposite conclusions reached by Cayton and Mitchell, *Black Workers and the New Unions*, 422, and Bunche, "Extended Memorandum on the Programs, Ideologies, Tactics and Achievements of Negro Betterment and Interracial Organizations," 347–48.

78. Turner and Moses, *Colored Detroit*, 29; Diggs's obituary, *Free Press*, April 26, 1967; Thomas R. Solomon, "Participation of Negroes in Detroit Elections" (Ph.D. dissertation, University of Michigan, 1939), 55, 22–23. For Diggs's activities in legislature, see *e.g.*, *Tribune*, Feb. 4, 1939; *Defender*, Dec. 30, 1939, Jan. 13, June 15, 1940; Diggs's column in *UAW*, Oct. 29, 1938.

79. Interview with Louis Martin, Oct. 21, 1976; on White, see *Chronicle*, March 18, 25, April 1, Nov. 8, 1939; *Tribune*, Feb. 24, March 16, Nov. 9, 1940; obituaries in *Free Press*, Feb. 11, 14, 1958.

## CHAPTER II

1. Irving Howe and B. J. Widick, *The UAW and Walter Reuther* (New York, 1949), 211; Lloyd H. Bailer, "Negro Labor in the Automobile Industry" (Ph.D. dissertation, University of Michigan, 1943), 200; J. C. Dancy to T. Arnold Hill, Jan. 27, 1937, DUL Box 3; Sidney Fine, *Sit-Down: The General Motors Strike of 1936–1937* (Ann Arbor, 1969); Peter Friedlander, "The Social Basis of Politics in a UAW Local: Midland Steel, 1933–1941" (unpublished paper delivered at meeting of Organization of American Historians, April 1977); interview with Raymond Boryczka and Friedlander, April 7, 1977; interview with Oscar Oden, Jan. 2, 1978.

2. *UAW*, December, n.d., 1936; interview with James Landfair, a black worker at Plant No. 3, Jan. 8, 1978. Hodges Mason, who worked at Plant No. 2, recalls a sit-down strike with high black participation in his plant, but contemporary evidence does not support his recollection. (Interview with Mason, Jan. 9, 1978.)

3. *Courier*, Feb. 13, 1937, George S. Schuyler article in *Courier*, Sept.

4, 1937, and Bailer, "Negro Labor in the Automobile Industry," 200, for a degree of black participation in sit-down strike at GM; *Courier*, Jan. 23, 1937, for statements by UAW leaders; NAACP press release, Feb. 19, 1937, NAACP C 322.

4. Interview with Raymond Boryczka, April 7, 1977; circular addressed to "Negro Workers of Dodge and Chrysler" [March 1937], Reuther Library vertical file; *Afro-American*, March 20, 1937. On Fanroy, see Herbert Hill, Oral History interview with Nick De Gaetano, June 17, 1968, Reuther Library; Howe and Widick, *The UAW and Walter Reuther*, 211, and esp. Bailer, "Negro Labor in the Automobile Industry," 199–200.

5. Sources do not indicate any significant black participation in the Briggs sit-down. The problem Mazey faced with many southern white workers is discussed in Michael D. Whitty, "Emil Mazey: Radical as Liberal" (Ph.D. dissertation, Syracuse University, 1968), 48, 52.

6. George S. Schuyler, "Reflections on Negro Leadership," *Crisis* 44 (Nov. 1937): 328.

7. *Afro-American*, Jan. 30, 1937, and White's recollection of the debate in *Chronicle*, Oct. 30, 1943; *Courier*, Jan. 23, 30, 1937.

8. Walter White to Roy Wilkins, March 2, 1937; NAACP press releases, Feb. 19, March 19, 1937; John L. Lewis to Wilkins, March 19, 1937; Wilkins to Homer Martin, April 1, 1937; Martin to Wilkins, April 22, 1937; NAACP press release, April 23, 1937, all in NAACP C 322. Also see *Crisis* 44 (May 1937): 150.

9. *Courier*, March 27, 1937.

10. Bailer, "Negro Labor in the Automobile Industry," 201; *Afro-American*, Jan. 5, 1937; *UAW*, Jan. 1, 1938.

11. *Defender*, April 24, 1937; *Courier*, April 24, 1937, and esp. Sept. 4, 1937; *UAW*, May 22, 1937; interview with Kirk, July 24, 1977.

12. *UAW*, July 31, 1937; Walter Hardin, "UAW Champion of Negro Workers," *ibid.*, Aug. 21, 1937; Francis Henson to White, July 26, 1937, NAACP C 323; *Courier*, Aug. 14, 1937.

13. *CIO News*, June 26, 1939; *UAW*, July 31, 1937; *Courier*, Sept. 4, 1937; Pontiac *Daily Press*, Nov. 13, 16, 17, 1931; interviews with Jay Lovestone, Oct. 14, 1977; with Leonard Schiller, Oct. 17, 1977; with Phil E. Raymond, Oct. 24, 1977; with William Bowman, Nov. 3, 1977; with Oscar Noble, Nov. 3, 10, 1977.

14. Both Walter White and John P. Davis urged, evidently at the behest of black unionists, the hiring of more black organizers. See Henson to Davis, July 8, 1937, NNC Archives, reel 1187; Henson to White, July 8, 1937, and White to Henson, July 14, 1937, both in NAACP C 323.

15. *UAW 1937 Convention Proceedings*, 187; *UAW*, Sept. 4, 1937.

16. *Tribune*, Oct. 9, 1937; *UAW*, Oct. 9, 1937, Jan. 8, ·1938; Richard Frankensteen, "Tactics, Strategy, Conditions of Ford Organizing Drive," Jan. 12, 1938, Walter Reuther Pre-presidential Papers, Box 1.

17. On Nowell, see Statement of William Odell Nowell, Nov. 30, 1939, in U.S., Congress, House, 75th Congress, 3rd Session, Special Committee To Investigate Un-American Activities and Propaganda in the U.S., *Hearings*, vol. XI (Washington, 1939), 6984–98, *passim*, and 7007; Richmond *Planet*, Sept. 13, 1930. On Billups, *ibid.*; *Tribune*, Feb. 22, 1941; Alex Baskin, "The Ford Hunger March—1932," *Labor History* 13 (Summer 1972): 357; interview with Mrs. Billups, July 2, 1977.

18. Interview with Frank Evans, July 27, 1977.

19. Interviews with William Bowman, Nov. 3, 1977, March 15, 1978; and with Oscar Noble, Nov. 3, 1977, March 16, 1978.

20. On use of Communist organizers in the UAW, and on Auto Workers Union as important source of early UAW activists, see especially Roger R. Keeran, "Communists and Auto Workers: The Struggle for a Union, 1919–1941" (Ph.D. dissertation, University of Wisconsin, 1974), 183–84, 236, 287. For discussion of importance of black Communists as organizers and source of activism among Negroes in the early years of the UAW, see also transcript of Herbert Hill's oral history interviews with Shelton Tappes, Oct. 27, 1967, and Feb. 1968, *passim*, Reuther Library.

21. For role of Lovestoneites in Homer Martin's faction, see Keeran, "Communists and Auto Workers," 290–91.

22. Testimony of Ralph Knox, former president of Local 212, in U.S., Congress, House, 75th Congress, 3rd session, *Hearings Before House Special Committee on Un-American Activities* (Washington, 1938), 1528; Statement of William Odell Nowell, Nov. 30, 1939, *op. cit.*, 7018. For list of officers of the Sub-Organizing Committee, see letterheads on Kirk to Davis, Aug. 16, 1937, NNC Archives, reel 1187; and on Kirk to Dear Sirs and Brothers, June 30, 1937, in Briggs Local 212 Archives, Box 4. On Nowell being Lovestoneite, interviews, especially with Frank Evans, July 27, 1977.

23. Interview with Christopher Columbus Alston, March 19, 1978; Kirk to Davis, July 16, 1937, NNC Archives, reel 1187; *Ford Worker News*, June 16, 1934.

24. Statement of William Odell Nowell, Nov. 30, 1939, *op. cit.*, 7029; correspondence, 1937, *passim*, in NNC Archives, reel 1187.

25. Interviews with Jay Lovestone, Oct. 14, 1977, and Frank Evans, July 27, 1977. Oscar Noble in interview, Nov. 3, 1977, recalled that Hardin joined the Lovestoneites in late 1933.

26. Cleveland *Call and Post*, Oct. 14, 1937; *UAW*, Oct. 9, 1937.

27. Interview with Oscar Noble, Nov. 3, 1977.

28. Hardin, "UAW Champion of Negro Workers"; Frankensteen, "Tactics, Strategy, Conditions of Ford Organizing Drive"; minutes, UAW International Executive Board, Jan. 23, 1938, George Addes Papers, Box 2.

29. *Tribune*, Oct. 23, 30, 1937.

30. Frankensteen, "Tactics, Strategy, Conditions of Ford Organizing Drive"; for the two specific incidents, see *UAW*, Nov. 6, 1937, Jan. 15, 1938.

31. See *e.g.*, *Tribune*, June 12, 26, July 17, 1937. Files of the *Chronicle* are not extant for this period, but Louis Martin recalls publishing these columns. (Interview with Martin, Oct. 21, 1976.)

32. *UAW*, July 24, 1937; Kirk to Davis, July 6, 1937, NNC Archives, reel 1187; *Courier*, Aug. 14, 1937.

33. Frankensteen, "Inside the Ford Campaign," *UAW*, Aug. 21, 1937; *UAW*, Jan. 29, March 12, 1938.

34. *UAW*, Nov. 13, Aug. 21, 1937; Hardin, "Remnants of Ford Myth Still Exist," *UAW, Packard Edition*, Jan. 1, 1938; William Nowell, "The Ford Worker and the Negro," *UAW, Ford Edition*, Feb. 5, 1938.

35. *UAW*, June 12, 19, 30, 1937.

36. *Ibid.*, June 5, Aug. 21, Sept. 13, Nov. 13, Oct. 18, 1937.

37. George S. Schuyler, article on Detroit auto industry, *Courier*, Sept. 4, 1937. Accurate overall statistics are not available, and the rosy estimates supplied by Kirk and Hardin during the summer of 1937 are clearly inflated. (*Ibid.*, and Hardin, "UAW Champion of Negro Workers.")

38. Frank Winn, "Labor Tackles the Race Question," *Antioch Review* 3 (Fall 1943): 347.

39. Associated Negro Press dispatch by Robert Crump, in *Courier*, March 27, 1937.

40. Kirk, "Negro Labor Forum," *Tribune*, July 17, 1937; Hardin quoted in Cleveland *Call and Post*, Oct. 14, 1937; Hardin, "UAW Champion of Negro Workers."

41. Frankensteen, "Inside the Ford Campaign"; *UAW, Packard Local 190 Edition*, November 20, 1937; paraphrase of Frankensteen's remarks in Cleveland *Call and Post*, Oct. 14, 1937; *UAW*, Nov. 13, 1937.

42. Lloyd H. Bailer, "The Negro Automobile Worker," chapter X in Paul H. Norgren, "Negro Labor and Its Problems" (a research memorandum prepared for the Carnegie-Myrdal Study of the Negro in America, 1940), copy in Schomburg Collection, New York Public Library, 637–38; Schuyler article in *Courier*, Sept. 4, 1937.

43. *UAW*, Oct. 30, 1937; *Tribune*, Oct. 30, 1937; Frankensteen, "Tactics, Strategy, Conditions of Ford Organizing Drive."

44. Hardin, "UAW Champion of Negro Workers."

45. Schuyler article in *Courier*, Sept. 4, 1937. On Midland Steel, see minutes of Local 410, Nov. 7, 1937, Midland Steel Local 410 Archives, Box 1; interview with Oscar Oden, Jan 2, 1978; Friedlander, "The Social Basis of Politics in a UAW Local: Midland Steel, 1933–1941." For Newman see article in *Chronicle*, Feb. 23, 1957, observing 20th anniversary of the local's founding. On Noble and Pontiac, interview with Noble, March 16, 1978. On Sneed, see *UAW*, Oct. 18, 1937, and for his reelection *ibid.*, March 13, 1940.

46. Bailer, "Negro Labor in the Automobile Industry," 260; Kirk to Dear Sirs and Brothers, June 30, 1937, Briggs Local 212 Archives, Box 4; Schuyler article in *Courier*, Sept. 4, 1937.

47. *West Side Conveyor*, July 20, 27, Aug. 10, 1937; *Voice of Local 212*, Aug. 21, 1937¡

48. Louis Martin in *Defender*, July 3, 1937; David L. Lewis, "History of Negro Employment in Detroit Area Plants of Ford Motor Company, 1914–1941" (paper submitted for History 344, University of Michigan, 1954), copy in Reuther Library, citing interview with Daniel's son, and Bradby to Charles Sorensen, May 28, 1937, a letter subsequently removed from the Ford Company Archives.

49. *E.g.*, *Courier*, Aug. 14, 1937.

50. Untitled interview with LeBron Simmons, n.d., in William McKie papers in Nat Ganley Collection, Series VI, Box 33; *Official Proceedings, Second National Negro Congress* (Washington [1937]), unpaged.

51. Kirk to Davis, July 16, 1937, NNC Archives, reel 1187; H. Easton, Jr., letter to editor, *Tribune*, June 12, 1937.

52. Wilkins to Davis, June 16, 1937, NAACP B 13; *Crisis* 44 (July 1937) 212, and (Aug. 1937), 249; Wilkins to Dancy, May 25, 1937, DUL Box 3.

53. Article by Louis Martin in *Defender*, July 3, 1937; *Tribune*, July 10, 1937; NAACP press release, June 18, 1937, NAACP B 13, printed in various papers, *e.g.*, *Courier*, June 26, 1937; Walter White, *A Man Called White* (New York, 1948), 212; Wilkins to Catherine Freeland, June 29, 1937, NAACP B 14.

54. *Tribune*, July 10, 1937; *Courier*, July 10, 1937; Homer Martin, "Address to the Convention of the National Association for the Advancement of Colored People," June 30, 1937, Homer Martin Papers.

55. *Tribune*, July 3, 10, 1937; Norfolk *Journal and Guide*, July 10, 1937.

56. *Crisis* 44 (Aug. 1937): 246; "Tentative Draft of Suggested Resolution for Consideration by the Detroit Conference, June 29–July 4, 1937," June 26, 1937, NAACP B 14; Norfolk *Journal and Guide*, July 17, 1937; "Reso-

lutions Adopted By the Twenty-Eighth Annual Conference of the N.A.A.C.P. in Detroit, Michigan, June 29–July 4, 1937," NAACP B 14.

57. White's address, July 4, 1937, in NAACP B 14; *Tribune*, July 10, 1937; editorial, " 'Mind Your Own Business,' " *Crisis* 44 (Aug. 1937): 241.

58. *Tribune*, Aug. 21, 28, 1937; Daniel and Marshall quotes in *Courier*, Aug. 28, 1937; Horace White, "Up the Wrong Tree," *Tribune*, Aug. 28, 1937; interview with Louis Martin, Oct. 21, 1976. Unfortunately files of the *Chronicle* for this period are no longer extant.

59. Kirk, "Negro Labor Forum," *Tribune*, July 17, 1937, and Hardin's column in *UAW*, Aug. 21, 1937.

60. *Tribune*, Jan. 8, 1938; A. J. Allen, "Selling Out the Workers," *Crisis* 45 (March 1938): 80; Horace White, "Who Owns the Negro Churches?", *Christian Century* 55 (Feb. 9, 1938): 175–76; *Tribune*, Jan. 29, Feb. 5, 1938.

61. *Tribune*, Jan. 8, 1938; Horace White, "Who Owns the Negro Churches?", 176–77; Schuyler in *UAW*, March 5, 1938.

62. Louis E. Martin, "The Big Stick in Detroit," *Crisis* 44 (Dec. 1937): 378; for example of skepticism toward UAW among Detroit's black bourgeoisie, see "We Soliloquize on Labor," *Club News Review* I (Oct. [1937]): 13–14, copy, courtesy Chicago Historical Society.

63. Walter Galenson, *The CIO Challenge to the AFL: A History of the American Labor Movement, 1935–1941* (Cambridge, Mass., 1960), 169.

64. Interviews with Frank Evans, July 27, 1977, and with Oscar Noble, Nov. 3, 1977.

65. For accounts of the larger factional struggle, see esp. Galenson, *The CIO Challenge to the AFL*, 150–71, and Jack Skeels, "The Development of Political Stability Within the United Auto Workers Union" (Ph.D. dissertation, University of Wisconsin, 1957), *passim*. For dissolution of the Negro Department, see UAW press release, Dec. 30, 1938, in Reuther Library vertical file; interviews with Frank Evans, July 27, 1977, and with Oscar Noble, Nov. 3, 1977; see also statement by Frank Evans in *Tribune*, Dec. 2, 1939.

66. UAW press release, Dec. 30, 1938, Reuther Library vertical file; *UAW*, Jan. 7, 1939; clipping from unidentified organ of Homer Martin faction, May 2, 1939, in Reuther Library vertical file: *UAW*, March 11, 1939.

67. Minutes of Special Executive Board Meeting, Dodge Local 3, Feb. 28, 1939, John Zaremba papers, Box 2; *UAW*, Nov. 19, 1938, and Cleveland *Call and Post*, April 6, 1939.

68. Minutes, UAW International Executive Board, May 9–25, 1938, George Addes Papers, Box 2; Frank Evans, letter to editor, *UAW*, Nov. 26, 1938.

69. *Chronicle*, Jan. 14, 1939. For his participation in the Federal Screw strike, see *UAW*, April 23, 1938. For his re-election in 1939, see *UAW, West Side Conveyor Edition*, Aug. 16, 1939.

70. *Chronicle*, Feb. 11, 1939.

71. Galenson, *The CIO Challenge to the AFL*, 167–68.

72. *UAW*, March 13, 1939; *Chronicle*, March 4, 1939; *Courier*, March 8, 1939; interview with Oscar Noble, March 16, 1978.

73. *Defender*, Aug. 1, 1942.

74. *Proceedings of the Special Convention of the International Union United Automobile Workers of America, Detroit, Michigan, March 4 to 8, 1939* (Detroit, 1939), 117, 147–51, 168. Copy courtesy of Dominick D'Ambrosio, president, Allied Industrial Workers of America, AFL-CIO; clipping from unnamed Martin faction paper, May 2, 1939, Reuther Library vertical file.

75. *Defender*, April 8, 1939; Cleveland *Call and Post*, April 6, 1939; *Proceedings of the Special Convention of the United Automobile Workers of America, 1939* (Detroit, 1939), 569–71; *Report of R. J. Thomas, Submitted for the International Executive Board to the Special Convention,* March 27, 1939 (Detroit, 1939), 33, 34. Tracy Doll statement in *Chronicle*, Feb. 11, 1939.

76. Clipping from unnamed Martin faction paper, May 2, 1939, Reuther Library vertical file; Henry Clark, letter to editor, *Tribune*, April 29, 1939.

77. *CIO News*, June 26, 1939; *Chronicle*, July 1, 1939 and *Tribune*, July 1, 1939.

78. Galenson, *The CIO Challenge to the AFL*, 173–74.

79. Frank Winn, "Labor Tackles the Race Question," 348, has good summary of sequence of events; for employee statistics, see *Chronicle*, Dec. 2, 1939.

80. Schuyler article in *Courier*, Sept. 4, 1937; Bailer, "Negro Labor in the Automobile Industry," 207–8. Bailer's discussion is based on interviews with men who participated in the back-to-work movement.

81. Interview with Louis Martin, Oct. 21, 1976, for Urban League. *Chronicle*, Dec. 9, 1939, Feb. 10, 1940; *Tribune*, Dec. 9, 1939, March 9, 1940; *CIO News, Michigan Edition*, Dec. 11, 1939, clipping Reuther Library vertical file; statements of Curtis Davis and Vincent Bogadich, attached to minutes, Dodge Local 3 Executive Board meeting, Nov. 24, 1939, Zaremba Papers, Box 2.

82. Minutes, Dodge Local 3 Executive Board, Nov. 24, 1939, and attached statements by Davis, Bogadich, and L. Donaby, *ibid.*; *News*, Nov. 24, 1939; *Free Press*, Nov. 25, 1939.

83. Teletype dispatch from Detroit, Nov. 27, 1939, Case 199/4520, NA RG 280; Statement of Alvin Wroblewski, Nov. 27, 1939, in Zaremba Papers, Box 8; quotation in *Tribune*, Dec. 2, 1939.

84. Minutes, Dodge Local 3 Executive Board meetings, Nov. 24, 25, 1939, and statements by Davis and Donaby, *op. cit.*, all Zaremba Papers, Box 2; *News*, Nov. 24, 28, 1939; *Free Press*, Nov. 25, 1939.

85. Interview with Louis Martin, Oct. 21, 1976; transcript of Oral History interview with Malcolm Dade, n.d., Reuther Library; for Hill's career, see obituaries in *News*, Feb. 10, 1970, and Free Press, Feb. 10, 1970.

86. *Chronicle*, Dec. 2, 1939; *UAW*, Nov. 29, 1939; *News*, Nov. 27, 1939.

87. *News*, Nov. 27, 28, 1939; *Free Press*, Nov. 28, 29, 1939; *UAW*, Nov. 29, 1939; *Times*, Nov. 29, 1939; *Michigan Labor Leader*, Dec. 1, 1939; *Chronicle*, Dec. 2, 1939; *Courier*, Dec. 2, 1939; teletype news dispatch from Detroit, Nov. 28, 1939, Case 199/4520, NA RG 280. Information on Fanroy in transcript of Herbert Hill oral history interview with Nick DiGaetano, June 17, 1968, Reuther Library. Union leaflets will be found in Zaremba Papers, Box 8 (quotation from *Dodge Bulletin*, Nov. 27, 1939).

88. *News*, Nov. 29, 1939.

89. *Tribune*, Dec. 2, 1939; letters from Paul Kirk, Luke Fennell, and Frank McDonald, *Chronicle*, Dec. 9, 1939; *UAW*, Dec. 6, 1939.

90. Complaints on this matter were being made as late as early 1939. See *Courier*, March 18, 1939.

91. "Agreement Entered on the 29th Day of November 1939, Between Chrysler Corporation and the United Automobile Workers of America . . . ," Case 199/4520, NA RG 280; anti-discrimination seniority clauses in various contracts quoted in *Ford Facts*, April 5, 1941; for black criticism of General Motors contract, see "Minutes of Conference of Local Officers and Stewards of Region 1 in Connection with Ford Drive," Jan. 26, 1941, Walter Reuther Pre-presidential Papers, Box 1.

92. Excellent discussion of the complicated seniority and promotion provisions in UAW contracts and how they were applied to the blacks' disadvantage, in Bailer, "Negro Labor in the Automobile Industry," chap. XI; interview with Negro Dodge foundry worker in Bailer, "The Negro Automobile Worker," 586–87.

93. "Suggested Policy on Negro Problem in the Ford Drive, Adopted by Joint Organizing Committee of Locals 51, 155, and 208, UAW-CIO and Negro Ford Organizing Committee," and "Minutes of Conference of Local Officers and Stewards of Region 1 in Connection with Ford Drive," Jan.

26, 1941, both in Reuther Pre-presidential Papers, Box 1; Addes quoted in *UAW, West Side Conveyor Edition,* Feb. 15, 1941, and in *Daily Worker,* Feb. 10, 1941.

94. *UAW 1940 Convention Proceedings,* 677; interview with a white teacher of Chrysler local educational classes, Feb. 24, 1940, quoted in Bailer, "The Negro Automobile Worker," 585.

95. Bailer, "Negro Labor in the Automobile Industry," 280–81; *UAW 1940 Convention Proceedings,* 184–85.

96. Bailer, "The Negro Automobile Worker," 629; *UAW,* May 22, 1940 (for Fennell and Mason): minutes of Midland Steel Local 410, Feb. 3, 1940, Midland Steel Local 410 Archives, Box 1.

97. *Defender,* April 8, 1939; Walter White, Notes Made in Detroit, April 8, 1941, NAACP Ford Strike File.

98. Bailer, "The Negro Automobile Worker," 629, for Local 235, Midland Steel, and Bohn Aluminum; *Chronicle,* Jan. 14, 1939, for Key; *UAW, West Side Conveyor Edition,* March 29, 1938, May 6, 1939, June 5, 1940, for Hatcher; *Ford Facts,* May 10, 1941, for Noble's reelection; minutes of Local 410, Nov. 7, 1937, April 4, 1938, Feb. 3, 1940, Feb. 11, 1941, in Midland Steel Local 410 Archives, Box 1; interview with Oscar Oden, Jan. 2, 1978; Friedlander, "The Social Basis of Politics in a UAW Local: Midland Steel, 1933–1941"; interview with James Landfair, former worker at Bohn Aluminum, Jan. 8, 1978; *UAW, Local 212 Edition,* March 11, 1939, Feb. 28, 1940, March 15, April 1, 1941, for Briggs.

99. Bailer, "The Negro Automobile Worker," 636; R. J. Thomas's statement at meeting of Conference of Negro Trade Unionists, Feb. 22, 1940, cited in *ibid.,* 628; *Tribune,* March 2, 1940; *UAW,* Feb. 21, 1940.

100. *UAW 1940 Convention Proceedings,* 604–5.

101. Bailer, "The Negro Automobile Worker," 625–28; *Tribune,* March 2, 1940.

102. Bailer, "Negro Labor in the Automobile Industry," 273.

103. Interview with Hardin, quoted in *ibid.,* 270, 273; *Chronicle,* Jan. 14, 1939, for Key; *UAW,* May 22, 1940, for Fennell and Mason.

104. Interview with James Landfair, Jan. 7, 1978.

105. *NAACP, Annual Report, 1937,* 24; *1938,* 22; *1939,* 26, for contributions to national office; *Tribune,* June 12, 1937, Nov. 1, 1939, and *Crisis* 45 (Dec. 1938): 400, for membership statistics.

106. *Tribune,* Dec. 18, 1937; for biographical details see Program honoring McClendon, May 24, 1945, copy in Michigan Civil Rights Congress Papers, Box 70.

107. *Chronicle,* June 24, 1939; interview with Dr. James J. McClendon, Aug. 17, 1976.

108. *Tribune*, Jan. 15, June 18, 1938, Nov. 18, 1939, Jan. 13, 20, 1940; *Crisis* 45 (Dec. 1938): 400; *Courier*, May 14, 1938.

109. *Tribune*, May 12, 1938, on Dairy Workers Union; *ibid.*, March 2, 9, 1940, and *Chronicle*, Feb. 10, 24, 1940, on NAAW.

110. Transcript of Oral History interview with James J. McClendon, 1967, Reuther Library; *Tribune*, Dec. 18, 1937, Nov. 18, 1939; 1939 letterhead of Detroit branch NAACP on Horace White to Frank X. Martel, in Wayne County AFL-CIO Archives, Box 12; correspondence between Robert Evans and John P. Davis, spring and summer 1936, *passim*, NNC Archives, reel 1185; *UAW, West Side Conveyor Edition*, July 23, 1938; letterheads of Michigan Division of NNC, June 1939, NNC Archives, reel 1191.

111. *Chronicle*, June 10, 1939.

112. *Tribune*, Oct. 16, 1937; *Crisis* 45 (May 1938): 153; Gloster Current, "Detroit's Multiple Youth Councils," *ibid.* 46 (May 1939): 146; interviews with Horace Sheffield, Aug. 17, 1976, and March 15, 1978; interview with Marcellus Ivory and Shelton Tappes, Aug. 15, 1976.

113. *Crisis* 45 (May 1938), 153; *Tribune*, Aug. 13, 27, Oct. 15, 1938; *Chronicle*, Jan. 28, Feb. 25, March 4, 11, 25, 1939; Current, "Detroit's Multiple Youth Councils," 157. For further successes of this jobs campaign, see *Tribune*, Aug. 9, 1939; *Chronicle*, July 8, Sept. 2, 1939.

114. Interviews with Horace Sheffield, Aug. 17, 1976, Jan. 6, 1977; interview with Shelton Tappes and Marcellus Ivory, Aug. 15, 1976.

115. Current, "Detroit's Multiple Youth Councils," 155; *Tribune*, Feb. 22, 1941; interview with former youth council leader Theodore B. Smith, Aug. 15, 1976.

116. *Voice of the Ford Worker*, Feb. 26, 1940, and April [n.d.] 1940.

117. *UAW, Local 212 Edition*, Feb. 15, 1941; *Daily Worker*, Jan. 5, 27, 1941; Keeran, "Communists and Auto Workers: The Struggle for a Union, 1919–1941," 343; "Minutes of Conference of Local Officers and Stewards of Region 1 in Connection with Ford Drive," Jan. 26, 1941, Reuther Pre-presidential Papers, Box 1. On Kirk as member of Local 155, see *UAW*, Aug. 30, 1939, and *Chronicle*, Dec. 9, 1939. On charges of Communist domination of the three locals, see also *Michigan Labor Leader*, Sept. 27, 1940, Feb. 27, March 27, 1942, and *Wage Earner*, May 28, Sept. 3, 1943, Feb. 18, 1944.

118. Walter Hardin, "Negro Organization at Ford's" [1941], Reuther Library vertical file; *Ford Facts*, April 5, 19, 23, May 10, 1941; interview with William Bowman, Nov. 3, 1977; interview with John Conyers, Sr., March 17, 1978.

119. *Chronicle*, Feb. 23, 1957 (article on 20th anniversary of the local);

Whitty, "Emil Mazey: Radical as Liberal," 68, 126–27; *UAW, Local 212 Edition*, May 15, 1940; Mazey, "The Negro Question," *ibid.*, Nov. 26, 1938.

120. Minutes of UAW International Executive Board, March 17–21, 1941, George Addes Papers, Box 2; Hardin, "Negro Organization at Ford's."

121. *Ford Facts*, April 5, 1941; Hardin, "Negro Organization at Ford's."

122. *Chronicle*, Feb. 11, 1939; Christopher Columbus Alston, *Henry Ford and the Negro People* [Detroit, 1941], *passim*; Alston to John P. Davis, Feb. 20, 1940, NNC Archives, reel 1191; interviews with Alston, July 23, 1977, March 19, 1978.

123. Horace Cayton's column in *Courier*, Feb. 1, 1941; Bailer, "Negro Labor in the Automobile Industry," 210–13, 215–16; Hodges Mason quotation from "Minutes of Conference of Local Officers and Stewards of Region 1 in Connection with Ford Drive," Jan. 26, 1941, Reuther Pre-presidential Papers, Box 1; *Afro-American*, April 8, 1941.

124. *Ford Facts*, April 5, 19, May 10, 1941; *PM*, April 4, 1941; on Tappes's being on negotiating committee, see Louis E. Martin, "The Ford Contract: An Opportunity," *Crisis* 48 (Sept. 1941): 285.

125. Bailer, "Negro Labor in the Automobile Industry," 213; Wilkins column in New York *Amsterdam News*, April 19, 1941, and *Crisis* 48 (May 1941): 161.

126. *Ford Facts*, Dec. 30, 1940; *Courier*, Feb. 1, 1941, and *Tribune*, Feb. 1, 1941, April 12, 1941.

127. *Tribune*, March 15, 1941.

128. Thomas's reply in *Tribune*, Jan. 11, 1941; Widman's in *Chronicle*, March 22, 1941, reprinted in *UAW*, April 5, 1941.

129. Bailer, "Negro Labor in the Automobile Industry," 213–14; *Courier*, Feb. 1, 1941; Walter White, handwritten notes made in Detroit [April 7, 1941], marked "Filed 6-3-41" NAACP Ford Strike File; Walter White to Edward Levinson, April 24, 1941, *ibid.*

130. Interview with Geraldine Bledsoe, March 9, 1977; also for biographical sketch of Beulah Whitby, see *Tribune*, Nov. 1, 1941. Early in the 1940's especially, the black press in Detroit contained many references to their activities, too numerous to be cited here.

131. Bailer, "Negro Labor in the Automobile Industry," 217–18, 220, 222; *Tribune*, April 5, 1941; *News*, April 6, 1941; Dancy to Jones, April 9, 1941, DUL Box 4; incident regarding member of Horace White's church from Walter White, handwritten notes April 7, 1941, NAACP Ford Strike File.

132. Allan Nevins and Frank Ernest Hill, *Ford: Decline and Rebirth, 1933–1962* (New York, 1964), 163; *News*, April 7, 1941.

133. *NAACP Bulletin* I (April 1941): 1; Ford Organizing Committee press release, 1:30 P.M., April 3, 1941, NAACP Ford Strike File.

134. *News*, April 2, 1941. See also accounts in *Times*, April 3, 1941; PM, April 3, 1941; and UAW press release, April 3, 1941, in NAACP Ford Strike File.

135. *Ford Facts*, April 2, 1941, and interview with John Conyers, Sr., March 17, 1978; *Courier*, April 12, 1941; *Times*, April 3, 1941, *Chronicle*, April 5, 1941, clipping in Michigan Civil Rights Congress Papers.

136. *News*, April 3, 4, 1941; *Free Press*, April 3, 1941; *Times*, April 4, 1941; *Tribune*, April 5, 1941; *Afro-American*, April 12, 1941; *PM*, April 3, 1941.

137. Walter White, *A Man Called White* (New York, 1948), 214.

138. *News*, April 3, 1941.

139. *Tribune*, April 5, 1941; Ford Organizing Committee press release, 8:00 P.M., April 2, 1941, NAACP Ford Strike File; leaflet, "To All Negro Ford Workers," April 2, 1941, NAACP Ford Strike File; leaflet, "To All Negro Ford Workers," April 3, 1941. Nat Ganley Papers, Box 33.

140. Interview with Horace Sheffield, Aug. 17, 1976; *Crisis* 48 (May 1941): 169.

141. *Free Press*, April 3, 4, 1941; *News*, April 3, 4, 1941.

142. *Free Press*, April 4, 1941; NAACP press release, April 5, 1941, NAACP Ford Strike File; transcript of Oral History interview with Malcolm Dade, n.d., Reuther Library; Ford Organizing Committee press release, 1:30 P.M., April 3, 1941, NAACP Ford Strike File.

143. Martin, "The Ford Contract: An Opportunity," 284.

144. Ford Organizing Committee press release, 8:54 P.M., April 3, 1941, NAACP Ford Strike File; *Ford Facts*, April 5, 1941; *Tribune*, April 12, 1941.

145. *Courier*, April 12, 1941.

146. *Ford Facts*, April 5, 1941; Walter White to A. Philip Randolph, April 7, 1941, NAACP Ford Strike File; *News*, April 8, 1941; *Courier*, April 12, 1941.

147. Charles A. Hill, Owen A. Knox, and Louis Martin, "An Open Letter to the Ford Motor Company," leaflet [April 5, 1941], Reuther Library vertical file; *Tribune*, April 5, 1941; Cayton column in *Courier*, April 19, 1941.

148. Hardin, "Negro Organization at Ford's"; interview with Horace Sheffield Aug. 17, 1976; *Courier*, April 12, 1941; Walter White, telegram to McClendon, April 5, 1941, NAACP Ford Strike File.

149. Interview with Geraldine Bledsoe, March 9, 1977; DUL Board of Trustees minutes, April 10, 1941, DUL Box 41; Dancy to Eugene Kinckle Jones, April 9, 1941, DUL Box 4.

150. *News*, April 5, 7, 1941; *Free Press*, April 5, 7, 1941. On increased number of black pickets, see *PM*, April 4, 1941, and Dancy to Jones, April 9, 1941, DUL Box 4.

151. Ford Organizing Committee news release, April 6, 1941, NAACP Ford Strike File; *Ford Facts*, April 5, 1941.

152. *News*, April 5, 1941; *Free Press*, April 5, 10, 1941; quotation in Cayton column, *Courier*, April 19, 1941.

153. Walter White to Harry Davis, April 17, 1941, NAACP Ford Strike File; Ford Organizing Committee press release, 7 P.M., April 6, 1941, *ibid.*; copy of advertisement in *Free Press*, April 7, 1941.

154. *News*, April 7, 1941.

155. *News*, April 6, 1941; *Free Press*, April 6, 10, 1941.

156. *News*, April 7, 1941; Walter White, undated memorandum [April 7, 1941], marked "Filed 6–3–41," and undated handbill [April 6, 1941], "To All Ford Workers," both in NAACP Ford Strike File.

157. Charles A. Hill, Owen Knox, and Louis Martin, "An Open Letter to the Ford Motor Company"; *Free Press*, April 7, 1941.

158. *News*, April 7, 1941; *Free Press*, April 8, 1941; *PM*, April 8, 1941; *Tribune*, April 12, 1941.

159. *Free Press*, April 7, 1941, and *PM*, April 8, 1941, for Dewey; Walter White, telegrams to Eddie Levinson and John F. Dewey, April 7, 1941, NAACP Ford Strike File.

160. NAACP Board minutes, April 14, 1941, NAACP-NYC; NAACP press release, April 5, 1941, and White, telegram to McClendon, April 5, 1941 in NAACP Ford Strike File; interview with Horace Sheffield, August 17, 1976.

161. See correspondence in the NAACP Labor File 1941, esp. Roy Wilkins to William H. Knudsen, Feb. 29, 1940; McClendon to Walter White, Jan. 4, 1941; White to Knudsen, Jan. 8, 1941; H. C. Wide to White, Jan. 25, 1941. See also exchanges between White and Knudsen reported in the press: *Crisis* 48 (Feb. 1941): 54; *Courier*, Jan. 18, March 15, 1941; *Defender*, Jan. 25, Feb. 15, 1941.

162. Walter White, telegram to McClendon, April 5, 1941; White, telegram to Associated Press, April 5, 1941; NAACP press release, April 5, 1941; White to A. Philip Randolph, April 7, 1941, all in NAACP Ford Strike File; interview with Shelton Tappes, Aug. 15, 1976; NAACP Board minutes, April 14, 1941, NAACP-NYC.

163. Edward Levinson to Walter White, May 12, 1933, NAACP Ford

Strike File; White, *A Man Called White*, 213–15; White, notes handwritten in Detroit, April 7, 1941, NAACP Ford Strike File.

164. White, *A Man Called White*, 215; *News*, April 9, 1941; *Free Press*, April 10, 1941; *The Ford Picket*, April 8, 1941, copy in Nat Ganley Papers.

165. White to Philip Murray, April 12, 1941, and White, handwritten notes made in Detroit, April 7, 8, 1941, both in NAACP Ford Strike File.

166. Interview with Shelton Tappes, Aug. 15, 1976; information based on Tappes's personal recollections of interaction between White and the top UAW leaders.

167. NAACP press release, April 9, 1941, NAACP Ford Strike File.

168. Walter White to Earl Brown, April 14, 1941, NAACP Ford Strike File; White, *A Man Called White*, 215.

169. Harry Davis to Walter White, April 14, 1941, and White to Davis, April 17, 1941, NAACP Ford Strike File.

170. Howe and Widick, *The UAW and Walter Reuther*, 219; R. J. Thomas, *Automobile Unionism, 1940–1941: A Report Submitted to the 1941 Convention of the UAW-CIO* (Detroit, 1941), 22–23.

171. White to McClendon, April 12, 1941, NAACP Ford Strike File.

172. *Washington Afro-American*, April 19, 1941; *Tribune*, April 19, 26, 1941; *Defender*, April 19, May 31, 1941; Hardin, "Negro Organization at Ford's"; *Ford Facts*, April 15, 17, 19, 23, May 1, 10, 1941; interview with Miriam Lee, April 29, 1978.

173. *Courier*, April 19, 1941; National NAACP press release, April 18, 1941, NAACP Ford Strike File.

174. Edward Levinson to Walter White, April 24, 1941, NAACP Ford Strike File; *UAW*, May 1, 1941; *Afro-American*, April 22, 1941; *Defender*, April 26, 1941; *Courier*, April 26, 1941; White, telegram to Gov. M. D. Van Wagoner, April 22, 1941, NAACP Ford Strike File; McClendon to White, April 24, 1941, NAACP Ford Strike File; *Ford Facts*, April 19, 23, 1941; *News*, April 18, 19, 20, 21, 27, 1941; *Tribune*, May 3, 1941.

175. *Courier*, April 26, 1941; Wilkins column in New York *Amsterdam News*, April 19, 1941; *Tribune*, April 26, May 10, 1941.

176 . *Ford Facts*, April 19; text of statement in *Tribune*, May 17, 1941 and *Daily Worker*, May 16, 1941.

177. *Defender*, May 24, 1941; *Tribune*, May 17, 31, 1941; *Ford Facts*, April 23, May 17, 1941; Hardin, "Negro Organization at Ford's."

178. *Ford Facts*, May 20, 1941; *Daily Worker*, May 21, 1941.

179. *News*, May 23, 1941; *UAW*, June 1, 1941; *Tribune*, May 31, 1941; *Courier*, April 26, 1941; *Defender*, May 31, 1941.

180. Bailer, "Negro Labor in the Automobile Industry," 237; Martin, "The Ford Contract: An Opportunity," 285; and *Chronicle*, June 28, 1941,

for role of Tappes; *Tribune*, June 14, 1941, for text of the anti-discrimination clause.

181. Eugene Hall, "Memorandum on Ford Labor Situation, Based upon Observations of a Ford Worker," June 27, 1941, NAACP Ford Strike File; *Tribune* June 21, July 26, 1941; Martin, "The Ford Contract: An Opportunity," 285.

182. *Tribune*, Nov. 15, 29, 1941; *Chronicle*, June 27, 1942.

## CHAPTER III

1. Lloyd H. Bailer, "Negro Labor in the Automobile Industry" (Ph.D. dissertation, University of Michigan, 1943), 250; also interview with Louis Martin, Oct. 3, 1977.

2. Herbert R. Northrup *et al.*, *Negro Employment in Basic Industry: A Study of Racial Policies in Six Industries* (Philadelphia, 1970), 61.

3. See esp. Lester Granger, "The President, The Negro and Defense," *Opportunity* 19 (July 1941): 204–7; Herbert Garfinkel, *When Negroes March* (Glencoe, Ill., 1959), 78–79; Louis Ruchames, *Race, Jobs, and Politics: The Story of FEPC* (New York, 1953), 27, 46; John Beecher, "8802 Blues," *New Republic* 108 (Feb. 22, 1943): 248–50; Committee on Fair Employment Practice, *FEPC: How It Operates* (Washington, [1944]), 4; Fair Employment Practices Committee, *Final Report, June 28, 1946* (Washington, 1947), 24; Robert Weaver, *Negro Labor: A National Problem* (New York, 1946), chap. IX.

Unfortunately, given the fact that most of the OPM, WPB, and WMC records have been destroyed, it is difficult to trace Weaver's activities except as he reported them in his own publications and the numerous references to his work to be found in the FEPC Archives. A few documents do survive in other federal record groups. For a good example of how Weaver worked at WPB through tactful urging, see Weaver to Donald M. Nelson, April 22, 1942, NA RG 179, Box 1017. For his work with WMC, see his weekly reports, June to September 1942, NA RG 211, Box 12-620. Interviews with Robert Weaver, March 15, May 20, June 7, Oct. 19, 1977, and with J. Lawrence Duncan, April 9, 10, 1977, were also very helpful for our understanding of how Weaver's office operated.

4. For specifics of arrangements between FEPC and Weaver's office, see Lawrence W. Cramer to Sidney Hillman, Aug. 13, 1941, FEPC Reel 41; Ruchames, *Race, Jobs, and Politics*, 137–38. For Weaver's public criticism of FEPC, see Weaver, *Negro Labor*, 138–39. For evidence of the rivalries masked behind polite negotiations, see Cramer to Will W. Alexander and Weaver, July 15, 1942; [Weaver], "Relationship Between Presi-

dent's Committee on Fair Employment Practice and War Manpower Commission in the Field" [July 15, 1942], and Cramer to Weaver and Alexander, July 16, 1942, all in FEPC Reel 41. For dissolution of Weaver's department, see Charley Cherokee, "Twelve Rounds for the Championship," *Opportunity* 21 (Jan. 1943): 7; *Chronicle*, Oct. 31, 1942.

5. The story of the struggle to preserve FEPC has been told in several places. See esp. Ruchames, *Race, Jobs, and Politics*, 48–56, *passim*. For arrangements regarding disposition of Weaver's former field investigators, see G. James Fleming to John Beecher, Oct. 15, 1942, FEPC Reel 41; Cramer to Harper, Feb 22, 1943, FEPC Reel 1.

6. *Tribune*, May 31, 1941; interview with Duncan, April 9, 1977.

7. Report of Membership Committee in minutes of Detroit Branch NAACP Annual Meeting, Dec. 13, 1942, Gloster Current Papers; NAACP, *Annual Report for 1943*, 21.

8. For NAACP efforts, see *Tribune*, Dec. 21, 28, 1940, Jan. 18, 25, 1941, and discussion below; for NNC, see *Tribune*, March 15, 1941.

9. *Tribune*, Jan. 31, 1942; *Chronicle*, Jan. 31, Feb. 7, 1942; *News*, March. 26, April 9, 16, 1942; Walter Hardin to Victor Reuther, Jan. 19, 1942, UAW War Policy Division, Box 6; "Minutes, Meeting of a Provisional Group to Discuss a Detroit Council on Fair Employment Practice— January 16, 1942," in *ibid.*; Raymond G. Hatcher to Warren Banner, June 29, 1942, NUL Archives Series VI, Box 15; Clarence W. Anderson, *Unfinished Business: A Fair Employment Practice Handbook* (Detroit, 1944), unpaged, copy in Donald March Collection, Box 5; "Constitution of Metropolitan Detroit Council on Fair Employment Practice" [1942], DUL Box 4; and "Minutes of Metropolitan Detroit Council on Fair Employment Practice," April 18, 1942, *ibid.*

10. For references to essentially stillborn establishment of committee in May, see *Tribune*, May 16, 1942; *Chronicle*, Nov. 7, 1942; and J. Lawrence Duncan to Weaver, May 28, 1942, FEPC Reel 54 FR, which also makes the point about the role of people in Local 600. Quotation from "The Social Dynamics of Detroit" (author unidentified), report prepared for Bureau of Intelligence, Office of War Information, Dec. 3, 1942, NA RG 44, Box 1814.

11. James J. McClendon, "To Officers and Members of Detroit Branch NAACP," Dec. 13, 1942, Current Papers; Minutes of Detroit NAACP Executive Board, Nov. 9, 1942, Feb. 1, 2, 1943, *ibid.*; *Chronicle*, Nov. 21, Dec. 5, 1942.

12. *Chronicle*, Nov. 21, Dec. 5, 12, 19, 26, 1942; NAACP Detroit Branch minutes, Dec. 13, 1942, Current Papers; interview with Gloster Current, Aug. 5, 1977.

13. *Chronicle*, Dec. 26, 1942, April 10, 24, 1943; *Crisis* 50 (May 1943): 140–41.

14. Minutes of Detroit NAACP Executive Board, Feb. 1–2, 1943, Current Papers; *Chronicle*, March 6, 1943; G. James Fleming to George M. Johnson, May 21, 1943, FEPC Reel 40.

15. "The Social Dynamics of Detroit," NA RG 44, Box 1814, *op. cit.*; Weaver, "With the Negro's Help," *Atlantic Monthly* 169 (May 1942): 702–4; *Opportunity* 20 (March 1942): 88; interviews with Robert Weaver, March 15, 1977, and with J. Lawrence Duncan, April 9, 10, 1977; see also *Detroit Labor News*, April 24, 1942, attributing improvements in black job opportunities to close cooperation between organized labor, management, and Weaver's office.

16. Detroit Branch NAACP press release [July 1941], and Louis Martin to Walter White, Oct. 2, 1941, both in NAACP Labor 1941 File.

17. For abuses in seniority practices and situations that developed with the conversion to war industry, see Bailer, "The Negro Automobile Worker," 423; Weaver, "Detroit and Negro Skill," *Phylon* 4 (Second Quarter, 1943): 134–35; Lester Granger, "Negroes and War Production," *Survey Graphic* 31 (Nov. 1942): 469. See also complaints of blacks in UAW Executive Board minutes, Sept. 15–23, 1941; in R. J. Thomas Papers; in *UAW, Local 190 Edition*, July 15, 1941; and in *Dodge Main News*, Sept. 15, 1941. For terms of "Six Point Transfer Program" agreement, see documents in UAW War Policy Division, Box 8.

18. For Dodge Truck, see the following all in NAACP Labor 1941 Files: affidavit of Eddie Kemp, Sept. 13, 1941; "Report of Interview with Chrysler Corporation, Mr. C. T. Winegar—Personnel Manager," Aug. 15, 1941; extract from "Dodge Truck Plant Meeting Minutes," July 14, 1941; and "Dodge Truck Plant Meeting Minutes," July 17, 1941. For Dodge Main, see Weaver, "Detroit and Negro Skill," 139, and Current to White, Sept. 25, 1941, NAACP Labor 1941 File.

19. Detroit Branch NAACP press release [July 1941], NAACP Labor 1941 file; Martin to White, Oct. 2, 1941, *ibid.*; *UAW 1941 Convention Proceedings*, 212, and *Tribune*, Aug. 23, 1941; UAW Executive Board minutes, Sept. 15–23, 1941, R. J. Thomas Papers; *UAW*, Oct. 1, 1941. For number of black delegates at the convention, see Bailer, "Negro Labor in the Automobile Industry," 258.

20. Current to White, Sept. 25, 1941, NAACP Labor 1941 File; *Crisis* 48 (Nov. 1941): 356; minutes, Special Meeting UAW International Executive Board, Jan. 22–23, 1942, George Addes Papers, Box 2; *Tribune*, Oct. 11, Nov. 8, 1941.

21. Current to Lawrence Cramer, Sept. 16, 1941, Weaver to Current, Sept. 20, 1941, Duncan to Weaver, Oct. 15, 1941, and Weaver to Cramer, Oct. 27, 1941, all in FEPC Reel 50 FR; *Tribune*, Nov. 8, 1941; *UAW, Dodge Main News Edition*, Jan. 15, 1942; *Opportunity* 20 (March 1942): 88.

22. Duncan, Field Report, Jan. 18, 1942, FEPC Reel 55 FR.

23. *Tribune*, June 21, 1941; Duncan, Field Report, Jan. 10, 1942, FEPC Reel 60 FR; *Opportunity* 20 (March 1942): 88.

24. The following all in FEPC Reel 58 FR: Current to Cramer, Aug. 19, 28, 1941; Duncan to Weaver, Sept. 23, 1941; Weaver to Briggs president W. D. Brown, Sept. 25, 1941; Weaver to Cramer, Sept. 26, Oct. 27, Dec. 29, 1941, Jan. 7, 1942; Weaver to Martin Carpenter of USES, Oct. 27, 1941; Duncan, field report, Feb. 9, 1942; Duncan to Weaver, July 14, 1942. See also Brown to Ernest Kanzler, May 5, 1942, NA RG 179, Box 1016.

25. For situation at GM in 1941, see statistics in Oscar Noble's reports on employment patterns at various GM divisions, titles vary, October 1941, in Walter Reuther Pre-presidential Papers, Box 3.

26. The following in FEPC Reel 58 FR: Duncan, field reports, Jan. 10, Feb. 8, 1942. Duncan to Weaver, Jan. 8, 1942; Harrison Johnson to Cramer, Nov. 5, 1941, and June 22, 1942. Also Terrell Thompson to Victor Reuther, Dec. 23, 1941, and Reuther to Noble, Dec. 31, 1941, both in UAW War Policy Division, Box 6.

27. The following all in FEPC Reel 58 FR: Duncan, field reports, Jan. 10, Feb. 8, 1942, and n.d. (page 1 missing) [October 1942]; Duncan to Weaver, June 12, 1942; Duncan to Joseph Wickware, July 15, 21, Oct. 2, 1942.

28. The following in FEPC Reel 58 FR: Duncan to John L. Thurston, July 10, 1942; Duncan to Colonel George Strong, July 15, 1942. Also Weaver, "Report to General Frank McSherry," July 20, 1942, NA RG 211, Box 12-620.

29. Weaver, "With the Negro's Help," 705; Lester Granger, "The Problems of Minorities in War Time," May 14, 1942, NUL Archives, Series VI, Box 14; Granger, "Negroes and War Production," *Survey Graphic* 31 (Nov. 1942): 544; Weaver, *Negro Labor*, 209.

30. Negro Committee, consisting of Arthur Perry, Christopher C. Alston, and Tom January, to Inter-racial Committee, Nov. 13, 1941, UAW War Policy Division, Box 6; "The Negro's War," *Fortune* 25 (June 1942): 158; Duncan and Ted Poston to Weaver, Dec. 8, 1941, FEPC Reel 55 FR.

31. Duncan and Poston to Weaver, Dec. 8, 1941, FEPC Reel 55 FR;

R. J. Thomas to president and Executive Board, Packard Local 190, Nov. 21, 1941, in UAW War Policy Division, Box 6; Curt Murdock to Thomas, Nov. 27, 1941, *ibid.*

32. The following in FEPC Reel 55 FR: Duncan and Poston to Weaver, Dec. 8, 1941; Thomas to Murdock, Dec. 4, 1941; Duncan field report to Weaver, Dec. 18, 1941; Hardin and Noble to Duncan, Dec. 11, 1941.

33. The following in FEPC Reel 55 FR: Duncan field reports to Weaver, Dec. 18, 31, 1941; Thomas to C. E. Weiss, Dec. 16, 1941; Sidney Hillman to M. M. Gilman, Dec. 31, 1941; Gilman to Hillman, Jan. 17, 1942.

34. Duncan, field report, Jan. 18, 1942, FEPC Reel 55 FR; minutes, Special Meeting of the UAW International Executive Board, Jan. 22–23, 1942, Addes Papers, Box 2; *Chronicle*, Jan. 31, 1942. For discussions of the racial issue during the Local 190 election and the subsequent suspension proceedings, see *PM*, Feb. 13, 1942; *News*, Feb. 17, April 4, 13, 1942; *Tribune*, Feb. 21, 1942; *Free Press*, Feb. 21, April 4, 14, 1942; *Chronicle*, April 4, 11, 18, 1942; *UAW Local 190 Edition*, Feb. 15, April 15, 1942; *Michigan Labor Leader*, Feb. 27, 1942; *Wage Earner*, April 10, 1942.

35. Duncan to Weaver, March 16, 1942, FEPC Reel 55 FR; *UAW*, April 1, 1942; Murdock to Weiss, March 17, 1942, FEPC Reel 55 FR; *Chronicle*, April 18, 1942.

36. Weaver, "Detroit and Negro Skill," 139; Bailer, "Negro Labor in the Automobile Industry," 342; Duncan to Omar Taylor, April 30, 1942, NA RG 179, Box 1017; *Chronicle*, April 25, 1942.

37. Weaver, "Detroit and Negro Skill," 140; Duncan to Weaver, June 12, 1942, FEPC Reel 59 FR; *Times*, June 3, 1942; *PM*, June 4, 1942; interviews with Duncan, June 2 and 3, Oct. 10, 1977; interview with Weaver, Oct. 10, 1977; Weaver to Frank J. McSherry, Sept. 9, 1942, NA RG 211, Box 12-620; *Chronicle*, June 6, 1942; *Tribune*, June 6, 1942.

38. Comments of both men in *Chronicle*, June 13, 1942.

39. Weaver, "Detroit and Negro Skill," 138–39; interview with Duncan, June 3, 1977; *Chronicle*, Jan. 31, Feb. 7, April 11, 25, 1942; R. G. Waldron to Capt. A. S. Wotherspoon, June 26, 1942, Navy Department General Correspondence 1940–1942, NA RG 80, P8-1(3) (42062); Waldron to McSherry, May 15, 1942, and Rear Admiral C. W. Fisher to McSherry, June 11, 1942, both in *ibid.*, P8-1(3) (420602-8); *UAW, Local 154 Edition*, June 1, 1942.

40. Weaver, "Detroit and Negro Skill," 140–41; *PM*, June 19, 21, 1942; Waldron to Wotherspoon, June 26, 1942, *op. cit.*; *News*, June 20, 1942; *Chronicle*, June 27, July 4, 1942; *UAW*, July 1, 1942; R. J. Thomas to

Local 154 president W. A. Germain, June 18, 1942, in Navy Department General Correspondence 1940–1942, NA RG 80, P8-1(3) (42062); Frank A. Knox, telegram to Wotherspoon, June 18, 1942, and Ralph A. Bard to Thomas, June 20, 1942, both in *ibid.*, P8-1(3) (420603-8); transcript of Oral History interviews with Richard Frankensteen, Oct. 10, 23, Nov. 6, 1959, and Dec. 7, 1961, Reuther Library.

41. *Chronicle*, June 27, July 4, 1942; *UAW*, July 1, 1942.

42. *Tribune*, July 11, 18, Aug. 1, 1942; Weaver, Report to Mc-Sherry, July 20, 1942, NA RG 211, Box 12-620; Noble, memorandum, n.d. [Fall 1942], UAW War Policy Division, Box 6.

43. *Chronicle*, July 25, 1942; *Defender*, Aug. 1, 8, 1942.

44. *Tribune*, July 18, 1942.

45. *UAW 1942 Convention Proceedings*, 185, 282–84; *Tribune*, Aug. 15, 1942; *Chronicle*, Aug. 15, 1942, clipping Reuther Library vertical file.

46. Untitled document, May 19, 1942, UAW War Policy Division, Box 6, tracing developments through mid-May; *Tribune*, Feb. 21, 1942; *Chronicle*, Feb. 28, 1942; Duncan to Weaver, March 11, April 24, May 6, 1942, FEPC Reel 54 FR.

47. *Tribune*, April 18, May 2, 23, 30, 1942; *Chronicle*, May 9, June 6, 1942; Zaio A. Woodford, memorandum re Meeting with Harry Bennett on May 29, 1942, dated June 1, 1942, NA RG 211-Chicago, Series 278, Box 3530; Woodford, "Ford Motor Company Panel Report," June 17, 1942, FEPC Reel 54 FR.

48. Interviews with Duncan, April 9, Oct. 13, 1977; Duncan to Weaver, May 28, 1942, FEPC Reel 54 FR.

49. Duncan to Harry Bennett, May 27, 1942, and Duncan to Weaver, May 28, 1942, both in FEPC Reel 54 FR.

50. *Chronicle*, June 6, 13, 27, 1942; *Tribune*, June 13, 1942.

51. Duncan to Ernest Kanzler, July 24, 1942, FEPC Reel 54 FR; Duncan to Edsel Ford, July 29, 1942, and Ford to Duncan, Aug. 5, 1942, both in FEPC Reel 54 FR; Duncan to Weaver, Aug. 7, 1942, NA RG 211-Chicago, Series 278, Box 3530.

52. Sheffield, Conyers, and Noble to Bennett, July 27, 1942, and Tappes and Sheffield to Edsel Ford, Aug. 14, 1942, both in NA RG 211-Chicago, Series 278, Box 3530; *UAW 1942 Convention Proceedings*, 282; Resolution Adopted by Local 600 General Council, Aug. 17, 1942, NA RG 211-Chicago, Series 278, Box 3530; *Tribune*, Aug. 22, 1942.

53. Sheffield to Walter Reuther, Aug. 20, 1942, and Leo R. Werts to Victor Reuther, Aug. 26, 1942, UAW War Policy Division, Box 6; Current to Cramer, Aug. 6, 1942, Current to Paul McNutt, Aug. 7, 1942, and McClendon to McNutt, Aug. 7, 1942, all in FEPC Reel 54 FR.

54. Duncan to Weaver, Aug. 24, 1942, FEPC Reel 54 FR; Duncan, Memorandum, Oct. 26, 1942, NA RG 211-Chicago, Series 278, Box 3530; Duncan to Willis Ward, Aug. 24, 1942, FEPC Reel 54 FR; Werts to Victor Reuther, Aug. 26, 1942, UAW War Policy Division, Box 6; Theodore A. Jones to Cramer, Nov. 20, 1942 (reviewing earlier events), FEPC Reel 54 FR.

55. Weaver to Current, Aug. 22, 1942, and Current to McNutt ("Attention: Mr. Robert C. Weaver"), Aug. 26, 1942, both in FEPC Reel 54 FR; *Tribune*, Sept. 5, 1942; Sheffield to Victor Reuther, Oct. 20, 1942, NA RG 211-Chicago, Series 278, Box 3530.

56. Sheffield to Victor Reuther, Oct. 20, 1942; Duncan, Memorandum, Oct. 26, 1942; and Resolution Adopted by Production Foundry of Local 600, Oct. 11, 1942, all in NA RG 211-Chicago, Series 278, Box 3530. Also Duncan to Cramer, Nov. 12, 1942, FEPC Reel 54 FR; Tappes to Sheffield, Oct. 23, 1942, FEPC Reel 54 FR; and *Ford Facts*, Oct. 15, 1942.

57. *Tribune*, June 13, Oct. 10, 1942.

58. *Tribune*, Oct. 24, 31, Nov. 7, 1942; *Chronicle*, Oct. 31, 1942.

59. Interview with Weaver, Oct. 19, 1977; McSherry to Robert C. Goodwin, Dec. 7, 1942, NA RG 211-Chicago, Series 278, Box 3530.

60. Memorandum on Long Distance Phone Call from Robert Lieberman, Oct. 27, 1942, FEPC Reel 54 FR; Cramer to Arthur S. Flemming, Jan. 13, 1943, FEPC Reel 54 FR (regarding earlier events).

61. *Chronicle*, Nov. 7, 1942; *Tribune*, Nov. 7, 1942.

62. *Chronicle*, Nov. 7, 1942; Theodore A. Jones to Cramer, Nov. 20, 1942, FEPC Reel 54 FR; interview with Geraldine Bledsoe, March 9, 1977; Morris Weitz to Edward Swan, Sept. 5, 1944, FEPC Reel 54 FR (regarding earlier events).

63. *Tribune*, Nov. 14, 1942; *Chronicle*, Nov. 14, 1942.

64. Duncan to Weaver, July 23, 1942, FEPC Reel 54 FR; *Chronicle*, Nov. 14, 21, Dec. 5, 1942; recollection of demonstrations in transcript of Oral History interview with William Oliver, March 5, 1963, Reuther Library; *Ford Facts*, Dec. 1, 15, 1942.

65. Theodore A. Jones to Cramer, Nov. 20, 1942, FEPC Reel 54 FR; retrospective account in Cramer to Arthur S. Flemming, Jan. 13, 1943, FEPC Reel 54 FR; Victor Reuther to McSherry, Nov. 13, 1942, UAW War Policy Division, Box 6.

66. *Chronicle*, Nov. 28, 1942; *Ford Facts*, Dec. 1, 1942.

67. *Chronicle*, Nov. 28, Dec. 5, 1942. On McNutt having given approval, see G. James Fleming to George M. Johnson, Jan. 7, 1943, FEPC Reel 48.

68. *Chronicle*, Dec. 12, 1942; *Tribune*, Dec. 12, 1942; Duncan to Cramer, Dec. 7, 18, 1942, FEPC Reel 54 FR; *Ford Facts*, Dec. 15, 1942.

69. *Automobile Unionism: Report of R. J. Thomas, Submitted in Behalf of the International Executive Board, UAW-CIO to 5th Convention, UAW-CIO, Oct. 4, 1943* (Detroit 1943), 87–88; for issue in Local 600 election, see *Chronicle*, March 13, 20, April 10, 1943; *Tribune*, March 13, 1943.

70. UAW Research Department, "Negro Women Employees," Jan. 5, 1943, UAW War Policy Division, Box 6; G. James Fleming to George M. Johnson, March 13, 1943, FEPC Reel 40; Fleming to Maceo Hubbard, May 12, 1943, FEPC Reel 37; *Tribune*, Sept. 11, 1943; *Chronicle*, Sept. 25, 1943; untitled report by Metropolitan Detroit Council on Fair Employment Practice, accompanying Col. George Strong to Clarence W. Anderson, Oct. 1, 1943, FEPC Reel 50; J. Dudley to Mr. Nottingham, June 16, 1943, E. E. Fitzpatrick to Cy Newcomb, July 8, 1943, both FEPC Reel 40.

71. References in black press and FEPC Archives too numerous to be cited here.

72. Anthony Luchek to Joseph D. Keenan, July 14, 1943, NA RG 179, Box 1017; UAW Research Department, "Negro Women Employees," Jan. 5, 1943, UAW War Policy Division, Box 6.

73. Both reported in *Chronicle*, Nov. 14, 1942.

74. Duncan to Weaver, July 14, 24, Sept. 4, 1942, FEPC Reel 58 FR; Duncan to Cramer, Nov. 18, 30, 1942, FEPC Reel 58 FR; Duncan to Cramer, Dec. 17, 1942, FEPC Reel 40.

75. Luchek to Keenan, July 14, 1943, *op. cit.*; *Chronicle*, Sept. 25, 1943; *Tribune*, Nov. 6, 1943.

76. *Tribune*, May 23, 1943.

77. WMC, Reports and Analysis Section, "Utilization of Negroes in War Production in Wayne County Area," Jan. 22, 1943, copy in UAW War Policy Division, Box 6; Geraldine Bledsoe, "A Statement About the Ford Motor Company Based on Employment Service Records, Experiences, and Observations," March 17, 1943, FEPC Reel 54 FR.

78. The following documents in FEPC Reel 54 FR: Duncan to Current, Aug. 24, 1942; Current to Walter White, Aug. 26, 1942; Cramer to White, Sept. 21, 1942; John L. Craig to E. L. Keenan, Aug. 31, 1942.

79. G. James Fleming, "Detroit Field Office Activity," July 17, 1943, FEPC Reel 6; Report dated Feb. 19, 1943, accompanying Geraldine Bledsoe to Fleming, Feb. 22, 1943, FEPC Reel 54 FR.

80. *Chronicle*, Oct. 31, 1942. Text of clause to be found in *ibid.*, June 28, 1942.

81. *Chronicle*, May 18, 1943; *Free Press*, May 1, 2, 1943; *News*, May 1, 2, 1943; *Ford Facts*, May 15, 1943.

82. Luchek to Keenan, July 14, 1943, *op. cit.*; Herbert R. Northrup,

*Organized Labor and the Negro* (New York, 1944), 204; *Chronicle*, May 29, 1943.

83. *Chronicle*, May 7, 15, 22, June 19, Aug. 21, 1943; *Tribune*, May 22, Aug. 21, Sept. 11, 25, 1943; *Ford Facts*, Sept. 1, 1943; Maceo Hubbard to Cramer, June 7, 1943, FEPC Reel 40; Tappes to Earl Dickerson, May 15, 1943, FEPC Reel 40; McClendon and Current, telegram to Earl Dickerson, May 17, 1943, FEPC Reel 37.

84. Fleming to Cramer, May 4, 1943, FEPC Reel 37; Fleming to Hubbard, May 12, 1943, FEPC Reel 37; Hubbard to Cramer, June 7, 1943, FEPC Reel 40; Fleming to Will Maslow, July 23, 1943, FEPC Reel 40.

85. Jack Burke, E. G. Trimble, and G. James Fleming to George M. Johnson, Sept. 25, 1943, FEPC Reel 50; undated memo, no author, "Ford Motor Company—Willow Run and Rouge Plants," FEPC Reel 63. On Bennett's refusal to confirm arrangements made, see William T. McKnight to Will Maslow, Oct. 23, 1943, FEPC Reel 40, and Nov. 23, 1943, FEPC Reel 50; and Emanuel Bloch to Maslow, Feb. 1, 1944, FEPC Reel 6.

86. Eugene Davidson to Edward Swan, June 1, 1945, FEPC Reel 40.

87. George M. Johnson to Fleming, Dec. 30, 1942, FEPC Reel 3; Fleming to Johnson, Jan. 5, 1943, FEPC Reel 40. On Fleming's earlier career, see *Opportunity* 19 (Oct. 1941);310.

88. Fleming to Johnson, Jan. 19, 1943, FEPC Reel 1; Fleming to Cramer, March 26, 1943, FEPC Reel 48; Fleming to Johnson and Hubbard, May 21, 1943, FEPC Reel 40.

89. Fleming to Hubbard, May 12, 1943, FEPC Reel 37.

90. D. R. Donovan to Cramer, Dec. 10, 1942, FEPC Reel 49, and especially "Area War Manpower Commission Letter to Keenan, Deputy Regional Director, WMC," abstract by D.R.D. [Donovan], n.d., FEPC Reel 49 FR. A handwritten notation indicates that this is an abstract from a letter to Keenan by the Detroit WMC area director in June 1943, but it is obviously the document Fleming identifies as Montague A. Clark to Edward Keenan, Dec. 30, 1942, and as having been drawn up by Clark's deputy, Edward Cushman. See Fleming to Johnson, Jan. 7, 1943, FEPC Reel 48.

91. Fleming to Cramer, May 3, 1943, FEPC Reel 48; *Times*, April 11, 1943; Jack Burke to Cramer, April 13, 1943, FEPC Reel 40.

92. Fleming's remarks to a staff meeting summarized in Clarence Mitchell to Fleming, April 5, 1943, and Fleming to Francis J. Haas, July 2, 1943, both FEPC Reel 40, as well as a number of specific cases, a few of which are referred to in the discussion that follows.

93. *PM*, Jan. 11, 14, 1943; *Times*, Jan. 12, 1943; *Tribune*, Jan. 16, 1943; Ralph A. Bard to McNutt, Jan. 1, 1943, FEPC Reel 40.

94. Fleming to Johnson, Jan. 19, 1943, FEPC Reel 1.

95. *Tribune*, Jan. 16, 23, 30, 1943; *Defender*, Jan. 23, 1943.

96. Fleming to Johnson, Jan. 19, 1943, FEPC Reel 1; Fleming to Haas, July 2, 1943, FEPC Reel 40; Fleming to Cramer, May 4, 1943, FEPC Reel 37.

97. Fleming to Johnson, March 5, 1943, FEPC Reel 48; Fleming to Dickerson, May 15, 1943, FEPC Reel 37; *Chronicle*, May 1, 1943; interview with Christopher Alston, Oct. 29, 1977; *UAW 1943 Convention Proceedings*, 389.

98. Fleming to Cramer, May 4, 1943, FEPC Reel 37.

99. *Courier*, April 10, 1943; *Defender*, April 24, 1943; [Maceo W. Hubbard], "Detroit Hearings" [July 1943], FEPC Reel 2.

100. Fleming to Earl B. Dickerson, May 15, 1943 (containing the quotation); Noble to Dickerson May 15, 1943; Tappes, telegram to Dickerson, May 15, 1943; McClendon and Current, telegram to Dickerson, May 17, 1943, all in FEPC Reel 37. *Chronicle*, May 22, 1943.

101. [Maceo W. Hubbard], "Detroit Hearings" [July 1943], FEPC Reel 2. Dickerson, telegrams to a number of individuals, including C. C. Alston, May 20, 1943, FEPC Reel 37; *Defender*, May 22, 1943; *Courier*, May 22, 1943.

102. On further delays and Haas's visit, see Cramer to Hubbard, June 12, 1943, FEPC Reel 37; [Hubbard], "Detroit Hearings" [July 1943], FEPC Reel 2; Fleming, "Father Francis J. Haas in Detroit" [early July 1943], FEPC Reel 40; George M. Johnson to Haas, Sept. 20, 1943, FEPC Reel 55 FR.

103. *Courier*, April 10, 1943; *News*, June 6, 1943; *Chronicle*, May 22, June 12, 1943; " 'Hate' Strikes in Which Services of President's Committee on Fair Employment Practice Have Been Requested" [July 1943], attached to Fleming to Jack Raskin, July 20, 1943, in Michigan Civil Rights Congress Archives, Box 54.

104. Michael D. Whitty, "Emil Mazey: Radical as Liberal" (Ph.D. dissertation, Syracuse University, 1968), 128–29; transcript of Oral History interview with Jess Ferrazza, May 26, 1961, Reuther Library.

105. *Chronicle*, March 6, 27, 1943.

106. *Chronicle*, March 27, 1943; Fleming, "Work Stoppages at Chrysler Corporation, Highland Park Plant by Department 25, March 16, 1943," dated March 25, 1943, FEPC Reel 48; Fleming to Cramer, March 25, 1943, FEPC Reel 48; Fleming, telegram to Jack Carter, black steward who led the Highland Park walkout, March 20, 1943, FEPC Reel 48.

107. *Chronicle*, March 27, April 3, 1943; Fleming to Hubbard, May 12, 1943, FEPC Reel 37; Fleming to Hubbard, July 14, 1943, FEPC Reel 55 FR.

108. *Chronicle*, March 27, 1943.

109. See discussion of dissolution of Inter-Racial Committee in Chapter V.

110. *Chronicle*, March 6, 13, 20, 1943; minutes, Detroit Branch NAACP Executive Board, April 5, 1943, Current Papers; *Tribune*, April 17, 1943; *Crisis* 50 (May 1943): 54; leaflet, "The Cadillac Charter," in UAW War Policy Division, Box 5.

111. *Chronicle*, April 21, 1943; minutes of Detroit Branch NAACP Executive Board, April 12, 1943, Current Papers.

112. *Chronicle*, May 29, 1943; *Courier*, April 10, 1943.

113. "Work Stoppages—Packard Motor Company," March 3, 1943, FEPC Reel 48; Jack Burke to Johnson, Aug. 31, 1943, FEPC Reel 40; Burke to Fleming, Feb. 27, 1943, FEPC Reel 55 FR.

114. Fleming to Will Maslow, July 23, 1943, FEPC Reel 55 FR.

115. *UAW, Local 190 Edition*, June 15, 1943.

116. See complaints of seniority rights violations, *Chronicle*, May 1, 1943.

117. *UAW, Local 190 Edition*, Feb. 1, 1943; Burke, "Report on Work Stoppage," March 3, 1943, FEPC Reel 48; "Report on Complaints of Work Stoppage at Packard Motor Company on Feb. 12, 1943" [Feb. 22, 1943], FEPC Reel 55 FR; *Chronicle*, March 6, 1943.

118. " 'Hate' Strikes in Which Services of President's Committee on Fair Employment Practice Have Been Requested," *op. cit.*; "Report on Complaints of Work Stoppage at Packard Motor Company on Feb. 12, 1943" [Feb. 22, 1943], FEPC Reel 55 FR; Burke to Fleming, Feb. 27, 1943, FEPC Reel 55 FR; Fleming to Montague Clark, March 4, 1943, FEPC Reel 48; Fleming to Johnson, March 4, 1943, FEPC Reel 48; John Q. Jennings to J. R. Steelman, telegrams, March 2 and 3, 1943, Case 300/62, NA RG 280; *Tribune*, March 6, 1943; *Chronicle*, March 6, 13, 1943.

119. Fleming to Johnson, March 5, 1943, Fleming to Cramer, March 13, 1943, and Burke to Fleming, March 24, 1943, all in FEPC Reel 48; Jennings, Special Report, May 5, 1943, Case 199/9438, NA RG 280; *Tribune*, March 27, 1943; *Chronicle*, March 27, 1943.

120. Fleming to Dickerson, May 15, 1943, FEPC Reel 48; Fleming to Cramer and Johnson, June 3, 1943, FEPC Reel 55 FR; Fleming to Alston, June 1, 1943, FEPC Reel 55 FR; Fleming to Maslow, retrospective account, July 23, 1943, FEPC Reel 55 FR; Fleming to Johnson, May 29, 1943, FEPC Reel 55 FR.

121. Interview with Alston, Oct. 29, 1977.

122. Edward Miller, untitled reports, May 26 and 28, 1943; Jennings to

E. E. Witte, May 27, 1943; and Miller, telegrams to Steelman, May 26 and 27, 1943, all in Case 199/9931, NA RG 280. Fleming to Johnson, May 29, 1943, FEPC Reel 55 FR; *News*, May 25, 26, 1943; *Free Press*, May 27, 1943; *Chronicle*, May 29, 1943; On Alston being a chief steward, see *Chronicle*, March 13, 1943.

123. *Chronicle*, June 5, 1943; Fleming to Cramer and Johnson, June 3, 1943, FEPC Reel 55 FR.

124. Miller, untitled report, June 8, 1943; teletype news report from Detroit, June 1, 1943; W.C.P., Memorandum for the Record, re: Telephone Call from Commissioner Thompson in Detroit to Mr. Cunningham, June 2, 1943 (containing the quotation) all in Case 199/9931, NA RG 280. Fleming to Cramer and Johnson, June 3, 1943, FEPC Reel 55 FR; *Free Press*, June 3, 1943; *News*, June 4, 1943; *Tribune*, June 5, 1943.

125. Francis Haas to Staff, June 4, 1943, FEPC Reel 3; UAW International Executive Board minutes, June 7–11, 1943, UAW Board minutes Box 2.

126. E.J.C. [Cunningham], Memorandum for the Record, June 1, 1943, based on phone call from Edward Miller in Detroit, Case 199/9931, in NA RG 280; "Telephone Conversation, June 2, 1943, between Father Haas and Mr. Ed Cunningham," FEPC Reel 55 FR; *Free Press*, June 3, 1943; *Tribune*, June 5, 1943; Fleming to Cramer and Johnson, June 3, 1943, FEPC Reel 55 FR; J.R.S. [Steelman], telegram to Edward Miller, June 2, 1943, and Cunningham to Steelman, June 3, 1943, both in Case 199/9931, NA RG 280.

127. Interview with George Strong, June 24, 1978; teletype news report from Detroit, June 3, 1943, Case 199/9931, NA RG 280; Cunningham to Steelman, June 3, 1943, *ibid.*; *Free Press*, June 4, 1943.

128. *Free Press*, June 4, 5, 1943; *News*, June 5, 1943; *Times*, June 5, 1943; *Washington Post*, June 5, 1943.

129. *Free Press*, June 4, 1943; *Tribune*, June 5, 1943.

130. AP dispatch, June 3, 1943, in *Times*, June 4, 1943; Haas, Memo to Staff, June 4, 1943, FEPC Reel 3; E. Trimble, Report of Phone Conversation with Truman K. Gibson, Jr., of War Department, June 5, 1943, FEPC Reel 55 FR; interview with Gibson, July 18, 1977.

131. *Washington Post*, June 5, 1943; *Free Press*, June 5, 1943; *Times*, June 5, 1943; interview with George Strong, June 24, 1978. See also inconclusive discussion in War Labor Board minutes; transcript of Executive Sessions, June 5, 1943, NA RG 202 (War Labor Board), Series 25, copies courtesy of Nelson Lichtenstein of the Ohio Historical Society and Joseph B. Howerton of the National Archives.

132. *Free Press*, June 6, 1943, has most detailed account; see also

*Chronicle*, June 12, 1943, and supportive resolution in Draft of Resolutions of National UAW-Ford Conference, June 1943, in UAW Ford Department Archives, Box 1.

133. News teletype from Detroit, June 5, 1943, Case 199/9931, NA RG 280; *Times*, June 6, 1943; *News*, June 5, 6, 7, 1943; *Free Press*, June 7, 1943; *PM*, June 6, 1943; Miller, Special Report, June 8, 1943, Case 199/9931, NA RG 280.

134. *News*, June 9, 1943; UAW International Executive Board minutes, June 7–11, 1943, UAW Board minutes, Box 2; *Chronicle*, Aug. 28, 1943; *UAW, Local 190 Edition*, Nov. 1, 1943.

135. Julius A. Thomas, "Race Conflict and Social Action," *Opportunity* 21 (Oct. 1943): 166.

136. Burke to Hubbard, June 9, 1943, FEPC Reel 55 FR; Hubbard to Cramer, June 24, 1943, FEPC Reel 1; Fleming to Maslow, July 17, 1943, FEPC Reel 6; Hubbard and Fleming to Local 190, Aug. 9, 1943, FEPC Reel 55 FR; Burke, recording statement of local leader, in report to Johnson, Aug. 31, 1943, FEPC Reel 40.

137. E. G. Trimble to C. E. Weiss, Aug. 23, 1943; Burke to Johnson, Aug. 31, Sept. 9, 1943; Donovan and Burke to Johnson, Sept. 6, 1943; Trimble to Haas, Oct. 4, 1943, all in FEPC Reel 55 FR.

138. *UAW 1943 Convention Proceedings*, 389; Edward Swan to William T. McKnight, weekly report, Nov. 13, 1943, and McKnight to Maslow, Nov. 22, 1943, both in FEPC Reel 51.

## CHAPTER IV

1. Robert C. Weaver, *The Negro Ghetto* (New York, 1948), 9; Lester Velie, "Housing: Detroit's Time Bomb," *Colliers*, Nov. 23, 1946, 15.

2. Nelson Foote, "Special Report on Negro Housing Situation in Detroit," March 5, 1942, 3–5, in Office of Facts and Figures, Bureau of Intelligence, Division of Surveys, Box 33, NA RG 208; *News*, March 8, 1942; unsigned, untitled document, n.d. [March 1942], Chronology section, 1–2, Office of Government Reports, United States Information Agency, Box 1814, in NA RG 44. This last and very useful document is divided into two sections separately paged—an analytical and narrative essay, and a day-by-day chronology. It will hereafter be cited as "Untitled USIA Document"; unless the chronology section is indicated, the citations will be to the narrative essay.

3. Interviews with J. Lawrence Duncan, Nov. 19, 1977; Louis Martin, Oct. 3, 1977; Albert C. Loving, Dec. 3, 1977; Oscar Oden, April 1,

1978. Unfortunately the one book-length study of Hamtramck, Arthur Evans Wood, *Hamtramck: A Sociological Study of a Polish-American Community* (New Haven, 1955), has only scattered references to blacks. For black population statistics in Hamtramck, whose population was near-ly 5 percent black in 1920, and about 7 percent black in 1930 and 1940, see United States Bureau of the Census, *Fourteenth Census of the United States, Volume 3: Population* (Washington, 1922), 478; *Fifteenth Census of the United States, Volume 3: Population* (Washington, 1932), 1132; and *Sixteenth Census of the United States, Volume 2: Population* (Washington, 1943), 864.

4. On Diggs, see Thomas Ralph Solomon, "Participation of Negroes in Detroit Elections" (Ph.D. dissertation, University of Michigan, 1939), 22; and Charles C. Diggs, Jr., to authors, Feb. 15, 1978. On Tenerowicz, see Louis Martin, "The Negro in the Political Picture," *Opportunity* 21 (July 1943): 106; Foote, "Special Report on Negro Housing Situation in De-troit," 16.

5. Untitled USIA Document, Chronology section, 1–7, *passim;* Charles S. Johnson and associates, *To Stem This Tide* (Boston, 1943), 50–51; Weaver, *Negro Ghetto*, 92. On White originally being in opposition to the project, see *News*, March 8, 1942, and Robert A. Crump, ANP dispatch, Feb. [?] [1942], in ANP Archives.

6. *News*, March 8, 1942; Weaver, *Negro Ghetto*, 92.

7. Bette Smith Jenkins, "The Racial Policies of the Detroit Housing Commission and Their Administration" (M.A. thesis, Wayne State Uni-versity, 1950) 76 n.; untitled USIA Document, chronology section, 7; *Chronicle*, Feb. 7, 1942; *Tribune*, Feb. 7, 1942. On specific accusation that as head of his local Edgecomb had opposed mixed public housing, see *Chronicle*, May 29, 1943.

8. Johnson *et al.*, *To Stem This Tide*, 52, 53; Foote, "Special Report on Negro Housing Situation in Detroit," 6–7; various documents concerning this committee, February to April, 1942, in Wayne County AFL-CIO Archives, Box 17; *Tribune*, Jan. 24, 1942; *Chronicle*, Feb. 7, 1942; James J. McClendon "To Officers and Members of Detroit Branch NAACP," Dec. 13, 1942, Gloster Current Papers; Louis Martin, "The Truth About Sojourner Truth," *Crisis* 49 (April 1942): 113. Interview with Gloster Cur-rent, Aug. 5, 1977, was also illuminating on the formation of the Commit-tee.

9. *Tribune*, Jan. 31, 1942; *Chronicle*, Jan. 31, Feb. 7, March 7, 1942; Martin, "The Truth About Sojourner Truth," 113.

10. *Chronicle*, Feb. 7, 14, 1942; documents reproduced in Detroit Civil Rights Federation, "Sojourner Truth Defense Homes," copy in Wayne

County AFL-CIO Archives, Box 17; Untitled USIA Document, chronology section, 12.

11. Foote, "Special Report on Negro Housing Situation in Detroit," 8; Johnson, *et al.*, *To Stem This Tide*, 56, 57; Martin, "The Truth About Sojourner Truth," 113; *News*, Jan. 21, 23, 1942; *Chronicle*, Jan. 31, Feb. 7, 21, March 21, 1942; *Tribune*, Feb. 14, 21, 1942; *UAW*, Feb. 15, 1942; Edward J. Jeffries to Charles F. Palmer, coordinator of Defense Housing and Others, Jan. 29, 1942, copy in Detroit Civil Rights Federation, "Sojourner Truth Defense Homes," and other documents in Wayne County AFL Archives, Box 17.

12. Untitled USIA Document, 8–9; *News*, Feb. 4, 16, 19, March 8, 1942; *Free Press*, Feb. 20, 1942. For union members participating in the city hall picket lines, see Frank Winn, "Labor Tackles the Race Question," *Antioch Review* 3 (Fall 1943): 358.

13. Untitled USIA Document, 1, and chronology section, 10; quotation from Foote, "Special Report on Negro Housing Situation in Detroit," 9; *News*, Feb. 28, March 1, 2, 1942; *Free Press*, March 1, 1942; *Times*, March 1, 1942.

14. *Times*, March 2, 1942; *Free Press*, March 2,3, 12, 1942; *News*, March 3, 11, 1942; *Chronicle*, March 21, 1942.

15. See pro-black AFL statements in *Free Press*, March 3, 1942, and esp. *Detroit Labor News*, March 13, 20, April 10, 1942.

16. *News*, March 4, 1942; *Chronicle*, March 7, 21, 28, 1942.

17. Minutes of UAW International Executive Board, March 15–22, 1942, George Addes Papers, Box 2; *Chronicle*, March 21, 1942; *UAW*, April 1, 15, 1942; *News*, March 18, 1942.

18. *News*, April 13, 1942.

19. *Free Press*, April 30, 1942.

20. For discussion of this subject, see Weaver, *Negro Ghetto*, esp. 74, 141, 173.

21. *Tribune*, Feb. 13, 20, March 6, 1943; *Chronicle*, Feb. 20, March 6, 1943.

22. *Chronicle*, March 6, 13, 1943; *Tribune*, March 6, 1943; for Mazey's statement, see *Defender*, March 13, 1943.

23. Addes's comment on Edgecomb in *Chronicle* of Feb. 27, 1943, as quoted in Edgecomb to R. J. Thomas, March 9, 1943, in Walter P. Reuther Papers (in process—Box 1); *Tribune*, March 13, 20, 1943 (quotation from Addes on FPHA in March 20 issue); *Chronicle*, March 13, April 3, May 1, 1943. For Edgecomb's defense of his action, see Edgecomb to Walter Reuther, April 13, 1943, Walter P. Reuther Papers (in process—Box 1).

24. *Chronicle*, May 1, and May 8, 1943, for the April 22 and 29 hear-

ings respectively; *Ford Facts, Local 600 Edition,* May 1, 15, 1943; "Transcript of Open Hearing on Bi-Racial Occupancy Before the Detroit Housing Commission, April 29, 1943," copy in Appendix C in Jenkins, "The Racial Policies of the Detroit Housing Commission and Their Administration," 146–52; and "NAACP Statement on Biracial Housing for Detroit," submitted to Detroit Housing Commission April 22, 1943, in Association of Catholic Trade Unionists Archives, Box 29. For Mazey's recollections of his stand and the criticism he suffered for it, see Michael D. Whitty, "Emil Mazey: Radical as Liberal" (Ph.D. dissertation, Syracuse University, 1968), 129.

25. "Transcript of Open Hearings on Bi-Racial Occupancy Before the Detroit Housing Commission, April 29, 1943," 146–47; *Tribune,* May 1, 1943; *Chronicle,* May 1, 8, 1943; *Free Press,* May 1, 7, 1943; *News,* May 1, 7, 1943; Jeffries quoted in Louis Martin, "Detroit—Still Dynamite," *Crisis* 51 (Jan. 1944): 8.

26. Walter White, *A Man Called White* (New York, 1948), 216–17.

27. White to Philip Murray, April 12, 1941, and White to William H. Hastie, May 9, 1941, both in NAACP Ford Strike File.

28. White to Russell Jeliffe, April 30, 1941; White to Grant Reynolds, April 30, 1941; White to Sidney Williams, April 30, 1941; Rowena Jeliffe to White, May 8, 1941; Williams to White, May 2, 1941; Charles Quick to White, May 4, 1941, all in NAACP Ford Strike File.

29. White to A. J. Muste, April 15, 1941, and White to Ira Jayne, April 15, 1941, both in NAACP Ford Strike File.

30. White to Murray, April 12, 24, July 7, 1941; Edward Levinson to White, April 24, 1941; White to Levinson, April 29, 1941; Murray to White, May 5, 1941; James B. Carey to White, July 25, 1941, all in NAACP Ford Strike File.

31. White to Hastie, May 9, 1941, NAACP Ford Strike File; White, telegram to R. J. Thomas, May 23, 1941, NAACP Ford Strike File; White to Thomas, Nov. 21, 1941, NAACP Labor 1941 File.

32. *Chronicle,* July 4, 1942; NAACP Board minutes, July 16, 1942, NAACP-NYC.

33. "Report of the Secretary, March Meeting of the Board," March 4, 1942, NAACP-NYC.

34. For accounts of the proceedings, see esp. *Free Press,* June 4, 5, 1943; Irving Howe and B. J. Widick, *The UAW and Walter Reuther* (New York, 1949), 221.

35. *Chronicle,* June 12, 1942; UAW International Executive Board minutes, April 10–21, 1943, in UAW Executive Board minutes, Box 2; Thomas's speech reported in *Free Press,* June 7, 1943.

36. Foote, "Special Report on Negro Housing Situation in Detroit";

Report of Rensis Likert to Office of Facts and Figures, April 14, 1942, quoted in *PM*, June 27, 1943; "The Social Dynamics of Detroit," Dec. 3, 1942, Report prepared for Bureau of Intelligence, Office of War Information, NA RG 44, Box 1814; *Wage Earner*, June 11, 1943.

37. "Detroit Is Dynamite," *Life* 13 (Aug. 17, 1942), 15. Authorship of this article was ascertained in interview with Louis Martin, Oct. 17, 1977. For Jeffries's reaction, Martin interview and *Free Press*, Aug. 17, 1942.

38. There are two book-length accounts of the riot: Alfred McClung Lee and Norman D. Humphrey, *Race Riot* (New York, 1943), and Robert Shogan and Tom Craig, *The Detroit Race Riot: A Study in Violence* (Philadelphia, 1964). The most succinct and the most scholarly—and most satisfactory—account is Harvard Sitkoff, "The Detroit Race Riot of 1943," *Michigan History* 53 (Fall 1969): 183–206.

39. "Minutes of Meeting of Citizens Committee and Other Civic and Labor Groups," June 21, 1943, Civil Rights Congress of Michigan Archives, Box 70; *Chronicle*, June 26, 1943; Thomas quote in *Free Press*, June 22, 1943. For Mason being elected vice-president of Wayne County CIO Council, see *ibid.*, Jan. 7, 1943.

40. UAW press release, June 22, 1943, in UAW War Policy Division, Box 6; *News*, June 23, 1943; *Free Press*, June 23, 24, 1943.

41. *Chronicle*, July 3, 1943; *Free Press*, June 29, 30, 1943.

42. *Free Press*, June 26, 29, 1943; *Chronicle*, July 3, 1943; Shogan and Craig, *The Detroit Race Riot*, 104–5; Lee and Humphrey, *Race Riot*, 51, 54, 108. Our evaluation of the work of the Mayor's Committee is based especially on Lethia W. Clore to Malcolm Ross, Sept. 28, 1943, FEPC Reel 75 (giving assessments by Geraldine Bledsoe and Louis Martin), and on Gloster Current, "What's Wrong with Detroit" [Jan. 1945], Detroit NAACP Branch Archives, Box 2. For the tepid do-gooder views of the committee's chairman, see William J. Norton, "The Detroit Riots—and After," *Survey Graphic* 32 (Aug. 1943): 317–18.

43. *Free Press*, June 29, 1943; Martin, "Detroit—Still Dynamite," 8; Jeffries quote in Lee and Humphrey, *Race Riot*, 55. For example of black demands regarding police brutality and other issues, see Detroit Branch NAACP, "Statements and Recommendations to the Mayor's Committee, Submitted June 29, 1943," Detroit Branch NAACP Archives, Box 1.

44. *Tribune*, July 3, 1943.

45. *Chronicle*, June 26, 1943; *Free Press*, June 25, 1943; NAACP Branch Executive Board minutes, June 26, 1943, Gloster Current Papers; "Report of Thurgood Marshall, Special Counsel of the National Association for the Advancement of Colored People, Concerning Activities of Detroit Police During the Riots June 21 and 22, 1943," July 26, 1943, Detroit

Branch NAACP Archives, Box 1 (also cited by Sitkoff as Thurgood Marshall, "Race Riot—Detroit, 1943," June 26, 1943, Record Group 42, Box 75, Folio 1, Michigan Historical Commission Archives); Walter White, "What Caused the Detroit Riots?" [Aug. 1943], NA RG 179, Box 1017.

46. *Chronicle*, July 31, Aug. 7, 14, 21, 1943. For Walter White, see *PM*, July 29, 1943.

47. Lee and Humphrey, *Race Riot*, 68.

48. *Chronicle*, July 31, 1943, and UAW press release, July 27, 1943, in UAW War Policy Division, Box 9; Weaver, *Negro Labor: A National Problem* (New York, 1946), 234.

49. For discussion of black role in Detroit politics during 1930's, see Ralph J. Bunche, *The Political Status of the Negro in the Age of FDR*, ed. Dewey W. Grantham (Chicago, 1973), 586–91.

50. For statistics on shift in Negro voting in Detroit during 1930's, see Edward H. Litchfield, "A Case Study of Negro Political Behavior in Detroit," *Public Opinion Quarterly* 5 (June 1941): 271.

51. Louis E. Martin, "The Big Stick in Detroit," *Crisis* 44 (Dec. 1937): 364, 378; *Tribune*, Sept. 18, Oct. 2, 9, 23, 30, Nov. 6, 1937; *West Side Conveyor*, September and October 1937, *passim*, esp. Sept. 14, 1937. In general on election, see also *UAW*, Sept. 11 to Oct. 30, 1937, *passim*; *Free Press*, Sept. 30 to Nov. 3, 1937, *passim*; *News*, Oct. 16 to Nov. 3, 1937, *passim*.

52. *Tribune*, April 29, 1939; *Chronicle*, April 22, June 10, July 2, 29, Sept. 2, 9, 30, Oct. 7, 1939; NAACP Detroit Branch Annual Report printed in *Tribune*, Nov. 8, 1939; *Kansas City Call*, Nov. 24, 1939.

53. *News*, Oct. 3, 6, 12, Nov. 1, 1939; *Chronicle*, Oct. 28, 1939.

54. *Chronicle*, Nov. 4, 1939.

55. On the Association and its modus operandi, see David L. Lewis, "History of Negro Employment in Detroit Area Plants of Ford Motor Company, 1914–1941" (paper submitted in partial fulfillment of the requirements of History 344, University of Michigan, 1954), 39; Bunche, *Political Status of the Negro in the Age of FDR*, 587–88; and undated press release, "Ford Agents Set Up an Organization to Coerce Negro Workers" [1939], UAW Public Relations Department Archives—Ford Motor Company, Box 2. On political maneuverings, see *Tribune*, Nov. 4, 1939, and esp. Lewis, "History of Negro Employment in . . . Ford Motor Company . . ." 39.

56. *News*, Oct. 25, 28, Nov. 1, 6, 8, 1939; *UAW, West Side Conveyor Edition*, Nov. 1, 1941, and *Ford Facts*, Oct. 24, 1941 (recalling that UAW had supported Jeffries in 1939); *Chronicle*, Nov. 11, 1939; *Tribune*, Nov. 11, 1939.

57. *Kansas City Call*, Nov. 24, 1939.

58. *Free Press*, esp. Oct. 26, 27, Nov. 5, 1941; *UAW, West Side Conveyor Edition*, Nov. 1, 15, 1941.

59. Martin, "Detroit—Still Dynamite," 8–9; *Chronicle* editorial, Aug. 7, 1943.

60. *Chronicle*, Sept. 18 (containing quotation from *PM*), Oct. 2, Sept. 25, 1943. Biographical information on Edwards and his role in *ibid.*, Sept. 18, July 3, 1943, and *UAW*, Oct. 1, 1943.

61. This reconstruction of events is based on information in *Chronicle*, Aug. 7, Oct. 30, 1943, and in Martin, "Detroit—Still Dynamite," 9.

62. *UAW*, Oct. 1, 1943; *Tribune*, Oct. 2, 1943.

63. *Chronicle*, Oct. 2, 1943.

64. For good discussion of the primary (including quotation), see Martin, "Detroit—Still Dynamite," 9. See also minutes of Detroit Branch Executive Board, Oct. 11, 1943, Current Papers; *Chronicle*, Oct. 2, 9, 1943; *News*, Oct. 6, 1943.

65. *Free Press*, Nov. 1, 1943; *News*, Oct. 21, 1943; *Free Press*, Oct. 13, 1943; *News*, Oct. 21, 1943; *Free Press*, Oct. 15, 16, 1943; Martin, "Detroit—Still Dynamite," 9.

66. *Chronicle*, Oct. 30, 1943; Horace White's column in *ibid.*, Oct. 23, 1943; Fitzgerald's charges in *Free Press*, Oct. 26, 1943; Martin, "Detroit—Still Dynamite," 10; "Radio Speech by Dr. James J. McClendon for Broadcast, Sunday, October 31, 1943," NAACP Detroit Branch Archives, Box 1; *News*, Nov. 3, 1943.

67. Martin, "Detroit—Still Dynamite," 10.

68. See especially good discussion in Henry Lee Moon, *The Balance of Power: The Negro Vote* (Garden City, N.Y., 1948), 149–56.

69. James Q. Wilson, *Negro Politics: The Search for Leadership* (Glencoe, Ill., 1960), 28–31.


CHAPTER V

1. *Chronicle*, Sept. 25, 1943; Louis Martin, "Detroit—Still Dynamite," *Crisis* 51 (Jan. 1944): 25.

2. See *Chronicle*, Sept. 18, Oct. 9, 1943; *Free Press*, Oct. 10, 1942; and *Wage Earner*, Oct. 15, 1943, for varied figures on which our estimate is based.

3. *Chronicle*, Aug. 14, 1943; *Tribune*, Aug. 14, 1943.

4. *UAW 1943 Convention Proceedings*, 414–22; *UAW*, Oct. 15, 1943.

5. *Tribune*, July 11, Aug. 15, 1942; *Chronicle*, July 25, 1942; *Defender*, Aug. 1, 8, 1942.

6. *Chronicle*, Sept. 4, 18 (respectively containing the two quotations), Sept. 25, Oct. 2, 1943; *Wage Earner*, Oct. 15, 1943; *Tribune*, Oct. 16, 1943.

7. *Chronicle*, Sept. 18, 25, Oct. 2, 1943; *Wage Earner*, Oct. 15, 1943.

8. *UAW 1943 Convention Proceedings*, 282–83, 370–88; *News*, Oct. 10, 1943; *Free Press*, Oct. 10, 1943; *Tribune*, Oct. 23, Nov. 6, 1943 (esp. for explanations offered by Sheffield and Hardin); *Wage Earner*, Oct. 8, 15, 22, 29, 1943; *UAW*, Oct. 15, 1943; Jack Skeels, transcript of Oral History interview with Nat Ganley, April 16, 1960, Reuther Library; Herbert Hill, transcript of Oral History interview with Shelton Tappes, Feb. 10, 1968, Reuther Library; Clayton W. Fountain, *Union Guy* (New York, 1949), 165–66.

9. George L. P. Weaver, "Pitfalls that Beset Negro Trade Unionists," *Opportunity* 22 (Jan. 1944): 13; Hill, transcript of Oral History interview with Tappes.

10. *Chronicle*, Sept. 16, 23, 1944; *Tribune*, Sept. 16, 1944; Horace Cayton's column, *Courier*, Sept. 23, 1944; *Defender*, Sept. 23, 1944.

11. George F. Addes, "Fundamental Unity—The UAW-CIO in Action," *Congress View* (published by NNC), 3 (Jan.–Feb. 1946), 1–2 (copy in UAW Archives, Ford Dept., Box 6). On numbers of international representatives, see *Chronicle*, Dec. 9, 1944, and George Crockett column in *Chronicle*, March 24, 1945, reprinted in *Detroit Would Be Twenty Years Ahead with George Crockett as Councilman* [Detroit, 1965]; also interviews with Horace Sheffield, March 15, 1978, and with Oscar Noble, March 16, 1978. On number of blacks in union, see Ray Marshall, *The Negro and Organized Labor* (New York, 1965), 52.

12. *News*, June 11, 1943; Hill, transcript of Oral History interview with Tappes.

13. On Hardin's dismissal and controversy over it, see *Tribune*, Oct. 28, Nov. 18, 1944; *Chronicle*, Oct. 29, Dec. 16, 1944; *Wage Earner*, Dec. 15, 1944.

14. On formation of Committee, see *Chronicle*, Oct. 14, 21, Dec. 23, 1944, *UAW, West Side Conveyor Edition*, Nov. 1, 1944. On the fact that no other union had a comparable set up, see Walter Reuther, "The Negro Worker's Future," *Opportunity* 23 (Oct.–Dec. 1945); 206. On Crockett, see his column in *Chronicle*, June 16, Sept. 8, 1945, reprinted in *Detroit Would Be Twenty Years Ahead with George Crockett as Councilman*, and R. J. Thomas, *Automobile Unionism (1944): Report of R. J. Thomas, Submitted . . . to 9th Convention of UAW . . .* (Detroit, 1944), 64. For work of Crockett's committee, see also *First Annual Summary of Activities, International UAW-CIO Fair Practices Committee* ([Detroit], 1946), and

"Report of International UAW-CIO Fair Practices Committee, First Quarter, 1945" [March 1945], both in Norman Matthews Collection, Box 1.

15. On formation of this Department, see Crockett column, *Chronicle*, May 11, 1946, reprinted in *Detroit Would Be Twenty Years Ahead with George Crockett as Councilman*, and "How the Fair Practices and Anti-Discrimination Department Was Established" [1947], Matthews Collection, Box 1. For some idea of the activities of the Department, see materials in Matthews Collection, Box 1, folders labelled "FEPC," esp. *UAW-CIO Fair Practices Sheet*, 1947–49, *passim*, and Clarence Mitchell, "Education UAW Style," *Crisis* 56 (March 1949): 73. On Oliver as recording secretary of Local 400, see *UAW, Ford Facts Edition*, May 15, 1942, and Oral History interview with William H. Oliver, May 5, 1963, Reuther Library.

16. Anthony Luchek to Joseph Keenan, July 14, 1943, NA RG 179, Box 1017; Robert C. Weaver, *Negro Labor: A National Problem* (New York, 1946), 289, 291, 292; Fleming to Will Maslow, July 17, 1943, FEPC Reel 6.

17. Lloyd H. Bailer, "The Automobile Unions and Negro Labor," *Political Science Quarterly* 59 (Dec. 1944): 570; *Free Press*, Oct. 30, 1943; *Chronicle*, Feb. 5, April 29, 1944. For excellent first-hand account of continuing problems over upgrading blacks at Hudson, see William H. Friedland, "Attitude Change Toward Negroes by White Shop-Level Leaders of the United Automobile Workers Union" (M. A. thesis, Wayne State University, 1956), 29–33.

18. Edward Swan to William McKnight, Oct. 14, 1944, FEPC Reel 51; L. W. Clore to McKnight, Nov. 11, 18, 1944, FEPC Reel 51; *Chronicle*, April 11, 18, 25, 1944.

19. See comments of Oscar Noble, Horace Sheffield, and Victor Reuther in *Chronicle*, March 11, March 18, Nov. 4, 1944, respectively.

20. For contemporary discussions of this, see Gloster Current, "How Will the Negro Hold His Job," July 13, 1943, Detroit Branch NAACP Archives, Box 1; Crockett's column in *Chronicle*, Nov. 17, 1945, reprinted in *Detroit Would Be Twenty Years Ahead with George Crockett as Councilman;* and Walter Reuther and William H. Oliver, to UAW-CIO International Executive Board Fair Practices Committee, Dec. 10, 1946, Matthews Collection, Box 1.

21. For activities of Crockett and Oliver, see esp. Crockett to Arnold Aronson, Oct. 1, 1945, Matthews Collection; the following in UAW Archives, Ford Dept., Box 6: Crockett to Richard T. Leonard, Feb. 7, 1946, UAW press release, Feb. 16, 1946, and Crockett to James B. Carey, March 15, 1946; *Chronicle*, March 3, 10, 31, 1945, clippings in Reuther

Library vertical file; Addes, "Fundamental Unity," 2. For text of model anti-discrimination clause approved by International Executive Board in January 1945, see *Free Press*, Jan. 29, 1945. For response of companies to this model clause, see Reuther's statement to U.S. Civil Rights Commission cited in note 30 below.

22. See esp. "Digest of Cases Considered by the International UAW-CIO Fair Practices Committee, First Quarter, 1945" [April 1945], Matthews Collection, Box 1; untitled document regarding St. Louis, Oct. 25, 1945, *ibid.;* several memoranda, Reuther and Oliver to UAW-CIO International Executive Board Fair Practices Committee, all dated Dec. 10, 1946, regarding specific cases during 1945–1946, *ibid.*

23. B. J. Widick, *Detroit: City of Race and Class Violence* (Chicago, 1972), 125–27, for firm stand in face of hate strikes. For situation in southern UAW Locals in Atlanta and Marietta and in Memphis, and the International's efforts to end dual seniority lists, segregated locker rooms, and even outright exclusion from the union, see *e.g.*, Atlanta *Journal*, March 14, 1956; Philadelphia *Tribune*, Feb. 20, 1960; Jack Stieber, *Governing the UAW* (New York, 1962), 11, 124–25; and "Digest of Cases Considered by the International UAW-CIO Fair Practices Committee, First Quarter, 1945." For the border city of St. Louis, where such discrimination was not eliminated until 1949–50, see untitled document regarding St. Louis, Oct. 25, 1945, Matthews Collection, Box 1; Reuther and Oliver to International Executive Board Fair Practices Committee, "In the Matter of Local 25," Dec. 10, 1946, *ibid.:* and Paul D. Brunn, "Black Workers and Social Movements of the 1930's in St. Louis" (Ph.D. dissertation, Washington University, 1975), 618–20.

24. Friedland, "Attitude Change Toward Negroes by White Shop-Level Leaders of the United Automobile Workers Union," 17–18, has data showing improvement in position of blacks in semi-skilled jobs, 1940–50. For agitation over opportunities in the highly skilled trades, see *e.g.*, *Chronicle*, April 9, 1955.

25. "The Social Dynamics of Detroit," Dec. 3, 1941, Report Prepared for Bureau of Intelligence, Office of War Information, NA RG 44, Box 1814; George L. P. Weaver, "Pitfalls That Beset Negro Trade Unionists," 13.

26. Walter Reuther, "The Negro Worker's Future," *Opportunity* 23 (Oct.–Dec., 1945): 206; Addes, "Fundamental Unity," 2.

27. *PM*, June 25, 1943; NUL press release, July 20, 1942, NUL Archives, Series VI, Box 15; Monroe Sweetland, "The CIO and the Negro American," *Opportunity* 20 (Oct. 1942): 294; Lester Granger, "Barriers to Negro War Employment," *Annals of the American Academy of Political*

*and Social Science* 233 (Sept. 1942): 72; Granger, "Negroes and War Production," *Survey Graphic* 31 (Nov. 1942): 544.

28. R. J. Thomas to All Local Unions, June 26, 1943; UAW Archives, Ford Department, Box 10; Walter White, *A Man Called White* (New York, 1948), 216–17.

29. *Chronicle*, Nov. 21, 1942; *Daily Proceedings to the Fifth Constitutional Convention of the Congress of Industrial Organizations,* November 8, 9, 10, 11, 12, 13, 1942 [no imprint, 1942], 183–84.

30. *UAW-CIO Fair Practices Sheet,* June–July 1947, copy in UAW Archives, Research and Engineering Department, Box 13; *Chronicle*, March 13, 1954, clipping, Reuther Library vertical file; Reuther's testimony in *Hearings Before the United States Commission on Civil Rights, Held in Detroit, Michigan, December 14, 15, 1960* (Washington, 1961), 40–44, 52–59.

31. *Crisis* 56 (Feb. 1949), 55; White quoted in Louis Martin article headlined, "Walter Reuther: UAW Chief Leads World's Biggest, Most Democratic Union," *Defender*, April 16, 1949.

32. Article by Sheffield in *Chronicle*, March 18, 1944; interview with Louis Martin, Oct. 3, 1977; John C. Dancy, *Sand Against the Wind* (Detroit, 1966), 204.

33. Statistics in documents submitted to Civil Rights Commission by Horace Sheffield, Robert Battle, and Douglas Brothers regarding Ford; by UAW Chrysler Department Director Norman Matthews; and by Hubert Gillespie, assistant director of UAW GM Department, in *Hearings Before the United States Commission on Civil Rights, Held in Detroit, Michigan, December 14, 15, 1960,* 56, 63–65.

34. *E.g., Chronicle*, Aug. 15, Oct. 24, 1959.

35. *Wage Earner*, March 29, 1946; *Daily Worker*, Feb. 18, 1955 (clipping in Nat Ganley Collection, Box 11); Stieber, *Governing the UAW*, 41–42.

36. Stieber, *Governing the UAW*, 52–54; Marshall, *The Negro and Organized Labor,* 68–70; Dick Brunder, "The Negro Bids for Union Power," *Nation* 190 (March 5, 1960), p. 209. For TULC being given credit for 1962 success, see *Negro American Labor Council Quarterly Newsletter,* June 1962.

37. For discussion of recent developments, see August Meier and Elliott Rudwick, *From Plantation to Ghetto,* 3rd ed. (New York, 1976), 331–33; William B. Gould, *Black Workers in White Unions* (Ithaca, N.Y., 1977), 371–95; Stieber, *Governing the UAW*, 59, 85, 99; James A. Geschwender, *Class, Race and Worker Insurgency: The League of Revolutionary Black Workers* (New York, 1977).

# Bibliographical Essay

The account set forth in this volume has been pieced together from a number of sources: chiefly, the archives of black and labor organizations and federal agencies; the Negro weekly newspapers and the Detroit daily press; and interviews with surviving participants in the events we have described. In addition, a number of published sources and unpublished dissertations provided helpful information.

Among the archival collections of black organizations, the NAACP papers at the Library of Congress were the most useful. These were supplemented with the Executive Board minutes and the secretary's monthly reports to the Board which are on file at the NAACP national headquarters in New York City. Although the relationship of blacks to organized labor was not a central concern of the NAACP, the unusually complete nature of its surviving records enables the scholar to reconstruct in detail the involvement of its national office with the AFL and CIO and especially the UAW. The surviving papers of the Detroit Branch NAACP, at the Walter P. Reuther Library, Wayne State University, contain only a few relevant items; more helpful are the papers of its first executive secretary, Gloster Current, consisting of branch minutes, 1942–1944, also at the Reuther Library. (Mr. Current kindly supplied us a personal copy of these minutes, together with detailed and helpful annotations explicating more fully the relevant references in them.)

The papers of both the National Urban League, Library of Congress, and the Detroit Urban League, in the Michigan Historical Collections, Bentley Library, University of Michigan, are woefully incomplete, yet do include some highly pertinent and illuminating data. The National Negro Congress Archives at the Arthur A. Schomburg Collection, Countee Cullen Branch, New York Public Library, are also incomplete; yet they too, along with materials in the Schomburg Collection's vertical file and related materials in the Archives of the Civil Rights Congress of Michigan, at the Reuther Library, contain helpful information and documents. (Unfortunately the Charles A. Hill collection of papers at the Reuther Library did not have materials relevant to our purposes.) A few useful items were also found in the Associated Negro Press Archives at the Chicago Historical Society.

Among the archives of labor organizations the most important, of course, were those of the United Automobile Workers and its relevant locals at the Reuther Library. All of these were surprisingly disappointing for our purposes. Not only are the records of the International incomplete, but those of important locals like Rouge Local 600 and Packard Local 190 proved virtually useless for us. The most helpful portions of the UAW records proved to be those of the War Policy Division, the Ford Department, Midland Steel Local 410, Dodge Local 3, and the minutes of the International Executive Board (which must be supplemented with Board minutes in the George Addes Papers in the Reuther Library). More valuable were scattered materials in the collections of certain UAW leaders, all at the Reuther Library: the Homer Martin Papers, the R. J. Thomas Papers, the Walter Reuther Papers, the Norman Matthews Papers (though again not useful for his period with the Packard Local), and the John Zaremba Papers (which were exceedingly illuminating on the Chrysler Strike of 1939). The Reuther Library has a set of the published proceedings of the UAW Conventions (except those of the convention of the Homer Martin faction in 1939, which were consulted through the courtesy of the UAW-AFL's successor, the Allied Industrial Workers). It also has a set of the printed annual presidential reports of R. J. Thomas, 1939–1944, and of the UAW constitutions as frequently amended. In addition, the Reuther Library has an excellent and highly useful clipping collection, both in its vertical file and in the Joe Brown scrapbooks. Mention should also be made of a few related collections at the Reuther Library, all of which provided a few good documents: those of the Association of Catholic Trade Unionists, the Wayne County AFL, the Detroit Civil Rights Federation, the Communist union leader Nat Ganley, and Donald C. Marsh collection (which has materials relating to the Detroit Metropolitan FEPC Council). Unfortunately the papers of the Council's chairman, Edward McFarland, at the Reuther Library, provided nothing of value. Some information on matters of interest to us were also found in the Notebooks of a one-time Director of Education in the UAW, Richard Deverall, located at Catholic University Library (copies of relevant materials supplied courtesy of Nelson Lichtenstein).

Other labor organizational material that proved useful in the preparation of this book included the AFL Council minutes and a portion of William Green's files in the AFL Archives at the AFL-CIO headquarters in Washington, the papers of the AFL leader John P. Frey at the Library of Congress, and the published annual AFL convention proceedings. For the CIO in the 1930's, we consulted the CIO Archives and the John Brophy Papers, both at Catholic University, each of which had occasional useful items. On the other hand, neither the Katherine P. Elickson Papers (consisting of the minutes of the early Committee for Industrial Organization, copy at the Reuther Library), nor the printed minutes of the CIO Executive Board, revealed an interest in the problem of black workers and interracial unionism. Somewhat more useful were the scattered references to racial matters in the CIO Convention Proceedings, 1939–1941.

The Burton Historical Collection Room at the Detroit Public Library also provided certain important materials—particularly a file of the black weekly, the Detroit *Tribune*, and a copy of the mimeographed report by the Mayor's Inter-racial Committee, "The Negro in Detroit" (Detroit, 1926). On the other hand the Archives of the Ford Motor Company at Dearborn, Michigan, never seem to have had much of relevance to Ford's interests in the black community or black workers (the principal exception being the autobiographical manuscript, "The Reminiscences of Mr. Willis F. Ward," typescript, May 1955). Indeed the best of the few items that were there have actually been removed from the files—evidently after they were cited by scholars in a manner deemed detrimental to the reputation of Ford or the company. Neither the official three-volume history of the company by Allan Nevins and Frank Ernest Hill nor the polemical anti-Ford biographies offered more than incidental bits of information that we could utilize.

Newspaper sources proved to be an essential source of information. The two Detroit black weeklies—the *Tribune* and the Michigan *Chronicle*—were especially valuable, even though their extant files are not complete. In addition the leading Negro weeklies with a national circulation—the Chicago *Defender*, Pittsburgh *Courier*, Baltimore *Afro-American*, Norfolk *Journal and Guide*, had important data not available elsewhere, as did on occasion the Philadelphia *Tribune* and the Cleveland *Call and Post*. Both

*Opportunity*, organ of the National Urban League, and *Crisis*, organ of the National Association for the Advancement of Colored People, had several highly useful articles.

The UAW's own newspaper, the *United Automobile Worker*, carried a number of significant items. This was even more true of its special editions for various locals, as well as the earlier independent papers published by certain locals, notably *Ford Facts* and the *West Side Conveyor*. The *Detroit Labor News*, organ of the Wayne County AFL; the journal published by the Association of Catholic Trade Unionists originally called the *Michigan Labor Leader*, and later the *Wage Earner;* and the organ of the old Auto Workers Union, the *Auto Workers News;* the Communist newspaper, the *Daily Worker;* and the Lovestoneite Publication, *Workers Age,* all carried nuggets of significant relevant information. The Pontiac, Michigan, *Daily Press,* carried information on Walter Hardin's radical activities in that city during the early 1930's. We also consulted the files of the *AFL Weekly News* and the *CIO News;* the latter, like the minutes of the CIO itself, proved surprisingly disappointing.

The Dearborn *Independent* was crucial for elucidating Henry Ford's racial views. The two Detroit dailies, the *News* and the *Free Press;* the Washington *Post;* and the two New York papers, the *Times* and *PM,* were all invaluable for our discussion of the major dramatic crises discussed in this book. Certain magazines of national circulation—the *Nation, Fortune, Life, Survey Graphic,* and the *Christian Century*—also carried a rare helpful article. These are cited in appropriate places, but special mention should be made of Horace A. White, "Who Owns the Negro Churches?", *Christian Century* 55 (Feb. 9, 1938), and the article authored anonymously by Louis Martin and Ted Poston, "Detroit Is Dynamite," *Life* 13 (Aug. 17, 1942).

Various Record Groups in the National Archives were essential to our understanding of developments during the World War II period. Easily the most complete and useful of these were the FEPC Archives (RG 228), of which the important sections are available on microfilm. The bulk of the papers in the War Production Board (RG 179), and the War Manpower Commission (RG 211) were destroyed, but a few items pertaining to the work of Robert Weaver and his staff do survive in these two record groups, as well as in the records of the WMC Region 5 in the Federal Record Center in Chicago. Published reports of both the FEPC and the WMC also provided some understanding of how these two agencies operated. Helpful reports by government investigators during the war are to be found in Record Group 44, Office of Government Reports, Record Group

208, Office of War Information, and Record Group 212, Committee for Congested Production Areas. Although it did not prove possible to find documentation in the National Archives for the War Department's and War Labor Board's intervention in the 1943 Packard hate strike, or in the Frank Knox Papers (Library of Congress) for the Navy secretary's role in settling the Hudson wildcat walkout of 1942, useful information concerning these key labor disputes is to be found in the Records of the Labor Department's Federal Mediation and Conciliation Service (RG 280), and of the Department of the Navy (RG 80). (All that was available in the War Labor Board Records, RG 202, were a few items supplied courtesy of Nelson Lichtenstein of the Ohio Historical Society and Joseph Howerton of the National Archives, none of which offered any insight into how R. J. Thomas was able to secure the WLB's help.) A final type of federal government source, statements of both contemporary and former UAW leaders in the published hearings of the House Un-American Activities Committee, 1938, 1939, and 1952, and of the Civil Rights Commission, 1960, provided valuable documentation for certain key points.

This book owes a great deal to interviews with participants in the events we have described. These fall into two categories: our own interviews, and transcripts of the Oral History interviews with UAW leaders on file at the Reuther Library. Easily the best of the latter from our point of view were the series of interviews conducted by then NAACP labor secretary, Herbert Hill, with Shelton Tappes in 1967 and 1968; interviews with others, most notably those conducted by Jack Skeels, offered some illumination of various points, as our citations indicate. Our own interviews, chiefly with black unionists, civic leaders, and war manpower officials, proved exceedingly valuable for our knowledge of a number of crucial topics, ranging from the background of the early UAW black organizers like Walter Hardin, to the nature of the interaction among federal agencies and union officials during the War period. These interviews were conducted both in personal conferences during trips to Detroit, New York, and Washington, and in briefer, but numerous, telephone conversations. Several key individuals were interviewed as many as half a dozen times.

The following persons generously shared their knowledge and recollections with us: Alexander J. Allen, Christopher C. Alston, Geraldine Bledsoe, Mrs. Joseph Billups, William Bowman, Erwin Baur, John Conyers, Sr., Gloster Current, J. Lawrence Duncan, Frank Evans, G. James Fleming, Richard T. Frankensteen, Truman K. Gibson, Jr., Mrs. Fred Hoare, Marcellus Ivory, Paul Kirk, James Landfair, Miriam Lee, Jay Lovestone, Alvin C. Loving, Hodges Mason, James J. McClendon, Louis E. Martin,

Oscar Noble, Oscar Oden, Phil E. Raymond, Leonard Schiller, Horace Sheffield, C. LeBron Simmons, Theodore Smith, George E. Strong, Shelton Tappes, Robert C. Weaver, and Roy Wilkins.

In addition we also had helpful interviews with several individuals in the field of labor and UAW history: Lloyd H. Bailer, Walter Beardslee, Ray Boryczka, David Brody, Peter Friedlander, Walter Galenson, Roger Keeran, David Montgomery, James Prickett, and B. J. Widick.

We are greatly indebted to certain unpublished monographs. Preeminent among them is Lloyd H. Bailer, "Negro Labor in the Automobile Industry" (Ph.D. dissertation, University of Michigan, 1943), which should be supplemented with the additional materials that appeared in other forms, especially in Bailer, "The Negro Automobile Worker," chapter X in Paul H. Norgren, "Negro Labor and Its Problems" (a research memorandum prepared for the Carnegie-Myrdal Study of the Negro in America, 1940), copy in Schomburg Collection of New York Public Library. Bailer's intimate personal knowledge of the Detroit scene around 1940 makes his work virtually a primary source. Also very valuable—especially because of its use of interviews with individuals now deceased, and of materials subsequently removed from the Ford Company Archives—is an unpublished term paper by David L. Lewis, "History of Negro Employment in Detroit Area Plants of Ford Motor Company, 1914–1941" (paper submitted in partial fulfillment of the requirements of History 344, University of Michigan, 1954), copy at Reuther Library. Two unpublished papers presented at the April 1977 convention of the Organization of American Historians, both of which were very helpful to us, are Ray Boryczka, "Militancy and Factionalism in the United Auto Workers Union, 1937–1941" (since published in *The Maryland Historian* 8 [Fall 1977]), and Peter Friedlander, "The Social Basis of Politics in a UAW Local: Midland Steel, 1933–1941."

Also useful were the following unpublished dissertations and masters theses: George D. Blackwood, "The United Automobile Workers of America, 1935–1951" (Ph.D. dissertation, University of Chicago, 1951); Paul Dennis Brunn, "Black Workers and Social Movements of the 1930's in St. Louis" (Ph.D. dissertation, Washington University, 1975); Glenn E. Carlson, "The Negro in the Industries of Detroit" (Ph.D. dissertation, University of Michigan, 1929); William E. Chalmers, "Labor in the Automobile Industry: A Study of Personnel Policies, Workers' Attitudes and Attempts at Unionism" (Ph.D. dissertation, University of Wisconsin, 1932); Henry Faigin, "The Industrial Workers of the World in Detroit and Michigan from the Period of Beginnings Through the World War" (M.A. thesis, Wayne University, 1937); George James Fleming, "The Administration of Fair Employment Practice Programs" (Ph.D. dissertation, University of Pennsylvania, 1948); William H. Friedland, "Attitude Change Toward Negroes by White Shop-Level Leaders of the United Automobile Workers Union" (M.A. thesis, Wayne State University, 1956); Bette Smith Jenkins, "The Racial Policies of the Detroit Housing Commission and Their Administration" (M.A. thesis, Wayne State University, 1950); Ronald Johnstone, "Militant and Conservative Community Leadership Among Negro Clergymen" (Ph.D. dissertation, University of Michigan, 1963); Roger R. Keeran, "Communists and Auto Workers: The Struggle for a Union, 1919–1941" (Ph.D. dissertation, University of Wisconsin, 1974); Irwin Klibaner, "The Origins of the United Automobile Workers" (M.A. thesis, University of Wisconsin, 1959); Gilbert W. Moore, "Poverty, Class Consciousness and Race Conflict in the UAW-CIO, 1937–1955" (Ph.D. dissertation, Princeton University, 1978); Sister M. Camilla Mullay, "John Brophy, Militant Labor Leader and Reformer: The CIO Years" (Ph.D. dissertation, Catholic University, 1966); Amber Cooley Neumann, "Twenty- Five Years of Negro Activity in Detroit, 1910–1935" (M.A. thesis, University of Detroit, 1935); Joyce Peterson, "A Social History of Automobile Workers Before Unionization, 1900–1933" (Ph.D. dissertation, University of Wisconsin, 1976); James R. Prickett, "Communists and the Communist Party Issue in the American Labor Movement, 1920–1950" (Ph.D. dissertation, University of California at Los Angeles, 1975); Delacy Wendell Sanford, Jr., "Congressional Investigation of Black Communism, 1919–1967" (Ph.D. dissertation, State University of New York at Stony Brook, 1973); Jack Skeels, "The Development of Political Stability Within the United Auto Workers Union" (Ph.D. dissertation, University of Wisconsin, 1957); Thomas Ralph Solomon, "Participation of Negroes in Detroit Elections" (Ph.D. dissertation, University of Michigan, 1939); Richard Thomas, "From Peasant to Proletarian: The Formation and Organization of the Black Industrial Working Class in Detroit, 1915–1945" (Ph.D. dissertation, University of Michigan, 1976); Michael D. Whitty, "Emil Mazey: Radical as Liberal: The Evolution of Labor Radicalism in the UAW" (Ph.D. dissertation, Syracuse University, 1968).

Finally we consulted a range of published books and articles in both labor and black history, of which the following proved useful either for general background, or for specific information on one or more points.

A. *Books and articles on the history of the UAW and other aspects of organized labor.* Alex Baskin, "The Ford Hunger March—1932," *Labor History* 13 (Summer 1972); Philip Borosky, *Brother Bill McKie: Building the Union at Ford* (New York, 1953); David Brody, "The Emergence of Mass-Production Unionism," in John Braeman, Robert H. Bremner, and

Everett Walters, eds., *Change and Continuity in Twentieth-Century America* (Columbus, 1964); Brody, "The Expansion of the American Labor Movement: Institutional Sources of Stimulus and Restraint," in Stephen E. Ambrose, ed., *Institutions in Modern America: Innovation in Structure and Process* (Baltimore, 1967); Brody, "Labor and the Great Depression; The Interpretive Prospects," *Labor History* 13 (Spring 1972); John Brophy, *A Miner's Life* (Madison, Wisc., 1964); Robert T. Dunn, *Labor and Automobiles* (New York, 1929); Sidney Fine, *Sit-Down: The General Motors Strike of 1936–1937* (Ann Arbor, 1969); Fine, "The Origins of the United Automobile Workers, 1933–1935," *Journal of Economic History* 18 (Sept. 1958); Clayton W. Fountain, *Union Guy* (New York, 1949); Walter Galenson, *The CIO Challenge to the AFL: A History of the American Labor Movement, 1935–1941* (Cambridge, Mass., 1960); Irving Howe and B. J. Widick, *The UAW and Walter Reuther* (New York, 1949); Roger R. Keeran, "The Communists and UAW Factionalism," *Michigan History* 60 (Summer 1976); Arthur Kornhauser, Harold L. Sheppard, and Albert J. Mayer, *When Labor Votes: A Study of Auto Workers* (New York, 1956); James O. Morris, *Conflict Within the AFL: A Study of Craft Versus Industrial Unionism, 1901–1938* (Ithaca, N.Y., 1958); Wyndham Mortimer, *Organize! My Life as a Union Man* (Boston, 1971); James R. Prickett, "Communists and the Automobile Industry in Detroit Before 1935," *Michigan History* 57 (Fall 1973); Victor G. Reuther, *The Brothers Reuther and the Story of the UAW* (Boston, 1976); Jack Skeels, "The Background of UAW Factionalism," *Labor History* 2 (Spring, 1961); Jack Stieber, *Governing the UAW* (New York, 1962).

B. *Articles and Books on Negro Labor and on blacks and the labor movement.* Lloyd H. Bailer, "The Automobile Unions and Negro Labor," *Political Science Quarterly* 59 (Dec. 1944); Bailer, "The Negro Automobile Worker," *Journal of Political Economy* 51 (Oct. 1943); Horace Cayton and George S. Mitchell, *Black Workers and the New Unions* (Chapel Hill, 1939); Donald T. Critchlow, "Communist Unions and Racism: A Comparative Study of the Responses of United Electrical Radio and Machine Workers and the National Maritime Union to the Black Question During World War II," *Labor History* 17 (Spring 1976); Philip Foner, *Organized Labor and the Black Worker, 1619–1973* (New York, 1974); James A. Geschwender, *Class, Race and Worker Insurgency: The League of Revolutionary Black Workers* (New York, 1977); William B. Gould, *Black Workers in White Unions* (Ithaca, N.Y., 1977); Lester Granger, "Barriers to Negro War Employment," *Annals of the American Academy of Political and Social Science* 223 (Sept. 1942); Granger, "Negroes and War Production," *Survey Graphic* 31 (Nov. 1942); Herbert Hill, "Labor Unions and the Negro," *Commentary* 28 (Dec. 1959); Hill "Racism Within Organized Labor: A Report of Five Years of the AFL-CIO, 1955–1960," *Journal of Negro Education* 30 (Spring 1961); Julius Jacobson, ed., *The Negro and the American Labor Movement* (New York, 1968); William Kornhauser, "The Negro Union Official: A Study of Sponsorship and Control," *American Journal of Sociology* 57 (March 1952); John C. Leggett, *Class, Race and Labor: Working-Class Consciousness in Detroit* (New York, 1968); Ray Marshall, *The Negro and Organized Labor* (New York, 1965); Herbert R. Northrup, *Organized Labor and the Negro* (New York, 1944); Northrup *et al., Negro Employment in Basic Industry: A Study of Racial Policies in Six Industries* (Philadelphia 1970); Ira De A. Reid, *Negro Membership in American Labor Unions* (New York [1930]); Sterling D. Spero and Abram L. Harris, *The Black Worker* (New York 1931); Robert C. Weaver, "Detroit and Negro Skill," *Phylon* 4 (Second quarter 1943); Weaver, "The Employment of the Negro in War Industries," *Journal of Negro Education* 12 (Summer 1943); Weaver, *Negro Labor: A National Problem* (New York, 1946); Weaver, "Recent Events in Negro Union Relationships," *Journal of Political Economy* 52 (Sept. 1944); Weaver, "With the Negro's Help," *Atlantic Monthly* 169 (May 1942); B. J. Widick, "Black Workers: Double Discontents," in Widick and Eli Ginzberg, eds., *Auto Work and its Discontents* (Baltimore, 1976); Frank Winn, "Labor Tackles the Race Question," *Antioch Review* 3 (Fall 1943); Raymond Wolters, *Negroes and the Great Depression: The Problem of Economic Recovery* (Westport, Conn., 1970), part II.

C. *Articles and Books on Black organizations, leaders, and protest, including the struggle for FEPC.* Ralph J. Bunche, *The Political Status of the Negro in the Age of FDR,* edited with an introduction by Dewey W. Grantham (Chicago, 1973); John C. Dancy, *Sand Against the Wind* (Detroit, 1966); Herbert Garfinkel, *When Negroes March: The March on Washington Movement in the Organizational Politics for FEPC* (Glencoe, Ill., 1959); Louis Kesselman, *The Social Politics of FEPC: A Study in Reform Pressure Movements* (Chapel Hill, 1948); B. Joyce Ross, *J. E. Spingarn and the Rise of the NAACP, 1911–1939* (New York, 1972); Louis Ruchames, *Race, Jobs, ad Politics: The Story of FEPC* (New York, 1953); Richard Thomas, "The Detroit Urban League, 1916–1923," *Michigan History* 60 (Winter 1976); Nancy J. Weiss, *The National Urban League, 1910–1940* (New York, 1974); Walter White, *A Man Called White,* (New

York, 1948); Lawrence S. Wittner, "The National Negro Congress: A Reassessment," *American Quarterly* 22 (Winter 1970); Wolters, *Negroes and the Great Depression*, part III.

D. *Other works concerning blacks and Detroit.* (These are in addition to items concerning Detroit cited in the preceding lists.) George Edmund Haynes, *Negro New-Comers in Detroit, Michigan: A Challenge to Christian Statesmanship* (New York, 1918); Charles S. Johnson and associates, *To Stem This Tide: A Survey of Racial Tension Areas in the United States* (Boston, 1943); David M. Katzman, *Before the Ghetto: Black Detroit in the Nineteenth Century* (Urbana, 1973); Alfred McClung Lee and Norman D. Humphrey, *Race Riot* (New York 1943); David A. Levine, *Internal Combustion: The Races in Detroit, 1915–1926* (Westport, Conn., 1976); Edward H. Litchfield, "A Case Study of Negro Political Behavior in Detroit," *Public Opinion Quarterly* 5 (June 1941); John Ragland, "The Negro in Detroit," *Southern Workman* 52 (Nov. 1923); Robert Shogan and Tom Craig, *The Detroit Race Riot: A Study in Violence* (Philadelphia, 1964); Harvard Sitkoff, "The Detroit Race Riot of 1943," *Michigan History* 53 (Fall 1969); Arthur Turner and Earl R. Moses, *Colored Detroit: A Brief History of Detroit's Colored Population* (Detroit, 1924); Lester Velie, "Housing: Detroit's Time Bomb," *Collier's* (Nov. 23, 1946); Robert C. Weaver, *The Negro Ghetto* (New York, 1948); B. J. Widick, *Detroit: City of Race and Class Violence* (Chicago, 1972); Arthur Evans Wood, *Hamtramck: A Sociological Study of a Polish-American Community* (New Haven, 1955).

# Index